Cisco Network
Design Handbook

D1596057

Cisco Network Design Handbook

Michael Salvagno

M&T Books
An imprint of IDG Books Worldwide, Inc.
An International Data Group Company
Foster City, CA ■ Chicago, IL ■ Indianapolis, IN ■ New York, NY

Cisco Network Design Handbook

Published by
M&T Books
An imprint of IDG Books Worldwide, Inc.
919 E. Hillsdale Blvd., Suite 400
Foster City, CA 94404
www.idgbooks.com (IDG Books Worldwide
Web site)

ISBN: 0-7645-4696-1

Printed in the United States of America

10 9 8 7 6 5 4 3 2 1

1O/SY/QU/QQ/FC

Distributed in the United States by IDG Books Worldwide, Inc.

Distributed by CDG Books Canada Inc. for Canada; by Transworld Publishers Limited in the United Kingdom; by IDG Norge Books for Norway; by IDG Sweden Books for Sweden; by IDG Books Australia Publishing Corporation Pty. Ltd. for Australia and New Zealand; by TransQuest Publishers Pte Ltd. for Singapore, Malaysia, Thailand, Indonesia, and Hong Kong; by Gotop Information Inc. for Taiwan; by ICG Muse, Inc. for Japan; by Intersoft for South Africa; by Eyrolles for France; by International Thomson Publishing for Germany, Austria, and Switzerland; by Distribuidora Cuspide for Argentina; by LR International for Brazil; by Galileo Libros for Chile; by Ediciones ZETA S.C.R. Ltda. for Peru; by WS Computer Publishing Corporation, Inc., for the Philippines; by Contemporanea de Ediciones for Venezuela; by Express Computer Distributors for the Caribbean and West Indies; by Micronesia Media Distributor, Inc. for Micronesia; by Chips Computadoras S.A. de C.V. for Mexico; by Editorial Norma de Panama S.A. for Panama; by American Bookshops for Finland.

For general information on IDG Books Worldwide's books in the U.S., please call our Consumer Customer Service department at 800-762-2974. For reseller information, including discounts and premium sales, please call our Reseller Customer Service department at 800-434-3422.

For information on where to purchase IDG Books Worldwide's books outside the U.S., please contact our International Sales department at 317-596-5530 or fax 317-572-4002.

For consumer information on foreign language translations, please contact our Customer Service department at 800-434-3422, fax 317-572-4002, or e-mail rights@idgbooks.com.

For information on licensing foreign or domestic rights, please phone +1-650-653-7098.

For sales inquiries and special prices for bulk quantities, please contact our Order Services department at 800-434-3422 or write to the address above.

For information on using IDG Books Worldwide's books in the classroom or for ordering examination copies, please contact our Educational Sales department at 800-434-2086 or fax 317-572-4005.

For press review copies, author interviews, or other publicity information, please contact our Public Relations department at 650-653-7000 or fax 650-653-7500.

For authorization to photocopy items for corporate, personal, or educational use, please contact Copyright Clearance Center, 222 Rosewood Drive, Danvers, MA 01923, or fax 978-750-4470.

Library of Congress Cataloging-in-Publication Data

Salvagno, Michael, 1957-
    Cisco network design handbook / Michael Salvagno.
        p. cm.
    Includes index.
    ISBN 0-7645-4696-1 (alk. paper)
    1. Computer networks--Handbooks, manuals, etc.
I. Title
TK5105.5 S23 2000
004.6--dc21   00-027806

is a registered trademark or trademark under exclusive license to IDG Books Worldwide, Inc. from International Data Group, Inc. in the United States and/or other countries.

is a registered trademark of IDG Books Worldwide, Inc.,

ABOUT IDG BOOKS WORLDWIDE

Welcome to the world of IDG Books Worldwide.

IDG Books Worldwide, Inc., is a subsidiary of International Data Group, the world's largest publisher of computer-related information and the leading global provider of information services on information technology. IDG was founded more than 30 years ago by Patrick J. McGovern and now employs more than 9,000 people worldwide. IDG publishes more than 290 computer publications in over 75 countries. More than 90 million people read one or more IDG publications each month.

Launched in 1990, IDG Books Worldwide is today the #1 publisher of best-selling computer books in the United States. We are proud to have received eight awards from the Computer Press Association in recognition of editorial excellence and three from Computer Currents' First Annual Readers' Choice Awards. Our best-selling ...For Dummies® series has more than 50 million copies in print with translations in 31 languages. IDG Books Worldwide, through a joint venture with IDG's Hi-Tech Beijing, became the first U.S. publisher to publish a computer book in the People's Republic of China. In record time, IDG Books Worldwide has become the first choice for millions of readers around the world who want to learn how to better manage their businesses.

Our mission is simple: Every one of our books is designed to bring extra value and skill-building instructions to the reader. Our books are written by experts who understand and care about our readers. The knowledge base of our editorial staff comes from years of experience in publishing, education, and journalism — experience we use to produce books to carry us into the new millennium. In short, we care about books, so we attract the best people. We devote special attention to details such as audience, interior design, use of icons, and illustrations. And because we use an efficient process of authoring, editing, and desktop publishing our books electronically, we can spend more time ensuring superior content and less time on the technicalities of making books.

You can count on our commitment to deliver high-quality books at competitive prices on topics you want to read about. At IDG Books Worldwide, we continue in the IDG tradition of delivering quality for more than 30 years. You'll find no better book on a subject than one from IDG Books Worldwide.

John Kilcullen
Chairman and CEO
IDG Books Worldwide, Inc.

Eighth Annual
Computer Press
Awards 1992

WINNER

Ninth Annual
Computer Press
Awards 1993

WINNER

Tenth Annual
Computer Press
Awards 1994

WINNER

Eleventh Annual
Computer Press
Awards 1995

IDG is the world's leading IT media, research and exposition company. Founded in 1964, IDG had 1997 revenues of $2.05 billion and has more than 9,000 employees worldwide. IDG offers the widest range of media options that reach IT buyers in 75 countries representing 95% of worldwide IT spending. IDG's diverse product and services portfolio spans six key areas including print publishing, online publishing, expositions and conferences, market research, education and training, and global marketing services. More than 90 million people read one or more of IDG's 290 magazines and newspapers, including IDG's leading global brands — Computerworld, PC World, Network World, Macworld and the Channel World family of publications. IDG Books Worldwide is one of the fastest-growing computer book publishers in the world, with more than 700 titles in 36 languages. The "...For Dummies®" series alone has more than 50 million copies in print. IDG offers online users the largest network of technology-specific Web sites around the world through IDG.net (http://www.idg.net), which comprises more than 225 targeted Web sites in 55 countries worldwide. International Data Corporation (IDC) is the world's largest provider of information technology data, analysis and consulting, with research centers in over 41 countries and more than 400 research analysts worldwide. IDG World Expo is a leading producer of more than 168 globally branded conferences and expositions in 35 countries including E3 (Electronic Entertainment Expo), Macworld Expo, ComNet, Windows World Expo, ICE (Internet Commerce Expo), Agenda, DEMO, and Spotlight. IDG's training subsidiary, ExecuTrain, is the world's largest computer training company, with more than 230 locations worldwide and 785 training courses. IDG Marketing Services helps industry-leading IT companies build international brand recognition by developing global integrated marketing programs via IDG's print, online and exposition products worldwide. Further information about the company can be found at www.idg.com. 1/26/00

Credits

Acquisitions Editor
Jim Sumser

Project Editor
Kurt Stephan

Technical Editor
André Paree-Huff

Copy Editor
Julie M. Smith

Project Coordinators
Linda Marousek
Louigene A. Santos

Illustrators
Shelley Norris
Karl Brandt

Graphics and Production Specialists
Robert Bilhmayer
Jude Levinson
Michael Lewis
Ramses Ramirez
Dina F Quan
Victor Pérez-Varela

Book Designer
Kurt Krames

Proofreading and Indexing
York Production Services

Cover Illustrator
Lawrence S. Huck

About the Author

Michael Salvagno has worked in the IT industry since 1983. Since 1988, he has provided networking support, configuration, design and implementation services on a wide variety of projects. His clients range from networking services companies to health care organizations, Big 5 consulting firms, and manufacturing and insurance companies in the Northeast Ohio area. He is currently working with corporations in the Northeast Ohio area providing strategic directions for their enterprise networks.

Salvagno holds several industry certifications along with the Cisco CCNA and CCDA.

When he's not writing or working on network projects, Salvagno raises alpacas on his small farm in Ohio with his wife Karen, a professional alpaca breeder. Salvagno can be reached at `salvagno@apk.net`.

To my lovely wife, Karen

Preface

Cisco network products account for approximately 75 percent of the Internet backbone. Along with that, corporations all over the globe look to Cisco to provide high quality hardware and software solutions for changing technology needs. Cisco products can be deployed to almost any internetworking environment. The knowledge of Cisco technologies is vital to understanding how enterprise networks function.

About this Book

Welcome to *Cisco Network Design Handbook*. This book provides network engineers, administrators, and information technology professionals with a handy desktop reference containing Cisco-specific network design information. This book includes practical information about Cisco hardware, Cisco software, and Cisco network management solutions. *Cisco Network Design Handbook* is a one-of-a-kind tool for Cisco networking design issues. Other Cisco network design titles are more theoretical in nature, or more detailed in technical knowledge. *Cisco Network Design Handbook* provides quick access to important Cisco-specific information that network professionals need in their daily work.

Is This Book for You?

Are you responsible for the operation, design, maintenance, or implementation of a Cisco-related network? This book will help you understand Cisco-specific product line offerings and technical information. It's a handy reference tool that will help you learn the technology that is driving today's enterprise networks. If you are a network professional who is faced daily with the sometimes overwhelming tasks of maintaining and designing a Cisco network, then this book is for you.

How This Book is Organized

This book is organized into four parts as follows.

Part I: Choosing Your Network Topology and Technology

Chapter 1 covers some of the more common network topology models. After reading this chapter, you will be able to decide which design is best for your network project, and have the knowledge and understanding as to why that certain topology is best for your network design. Chapter 2 describes popular network technologies, followed by information about how the technology actually works within an internetwork. Upon completion of this chapter, you will have a better understanding of the major network technologies and how one or more of these will fit into your network design.

Part II: Choosing Your Network Protocols

With the different and sometimes confusing array of network routing protocols and their uses, it's a challenge to understand, plan, test, and implement the correct protocol for your Cisco network. Chapter 3 covers some of the more popular routing protocols in use today. In Chapter 4 the unique operations of proprietary protocol suites are covered. TCP/IP, which is not proprietary system, is also covered in Chapter 4. TCP/IP is universally used and widely accepted in almost any internetworking environment. Often, when Cisco needs a solution to an interoperability issue, it will attempt to provide a solution with a Cisco-specific protocol, technology, or implementation. Chapter 5 covers Cisco-specific protocols and some other important switching and bridging protocols.

Part III: Choosing Your Network Components

Network hardware components comprise the infrastructure of your network design. Putting them all together into a functioning, productive, and optimized structure can be challenging. Chapter 6, Network Hardware, covers the main network hardware components that are necessary to complete your network design. Chapter 7 delves into the software features and applications that you can use to develop, maintain, secure, and optimize your network design such as the Cisco Internetwork Operating System (Cisco IOS), network optimization methods, and Cisco-specific product offerings.

Part IV: Managing Your Network Design

IP addressing mechanisms such as VLSM and NAT can give you the tools to configure your network and provide IP addressing and routing capabilities that would be hard to come by with straight classful IP addressing. Network security is fast becoming a major concern as more and more businesses move their corporate data and communication systems to infrastructures that they can sometimes not control. In Chapter 8, we talk about network addressing and security, two very important topics when designing a network. Designing and implementing an overall security policy is not an easy task, but well worth the effort. In Chapter 9 we discuss the design proposal, testing, and management of your network. The network design proposal can be the most important part of your network project. Testing is an ongoing process that starts prior to the network design and continues on after the implementation is complete. The network management section covers infrastructure management and maintenance, network processes, and personnel.

Appendix

This book concludes with an appendix that provides a network design checklist taken from each of the main sections of *Cisco Network Design Handbook*. You may use this appendix as a high-level design guide for your internetworking project.

Acknowledgments

First and foremost, I acknowledge the Lord Jesus Christ for his amazing guidance and providence, allowing me to do the things that I dream about but thought impossible. Next, my wife Karen who understands what encouragement means, and put her needs aside so that I could write. Without her patience and support, the book would not have been completed.

Thanks also to acquisition editor Jim Sumser, whose professionalism and encouragement allowed me to write the way I wanted and still complete the manuscript, and project editor Kurt Stephan, who knew what I needed before I asked and was very instrumental in enabling me to meet deadlines. Technical editor André Paree-Huff provided great feedback about the technical information in the chapters, and copy editor Julie Smith did a great job editing the manuscript. Additional thanks to the graphic artists, who changed my scribbles into artwork, and to all the other people at IDG Books that made contributions to this handbook. Thank you also to my friends, family, and extended family, some who knew I was writing this book, and some who did not. Your consistent caring and friendship provide a fabric for a life that's worth living.

Contents at a Glance

Contents

Part II: Choosing Your Network Protocols **67**

xxii   Contents

Part I

Choosing Your Network Topology and Technology

Chapter 1

Network Topologies

One of the first steps in creating good network design is to choose your network topology, or network map. How will you start your design? Is it a small LAN with a few workstations? Is it a campus LAN or a massive enterprise implementation? Is scalability important? How about network management? What about cost? Certainly, cost is always an issue in a network design project.

In most situations, you'll find yourself with a network already in existence. There will certainly be opportunities to develop a network from scratch, but more than likely you'll end up inheriting an existing network. This network will probably have been created with a long line of additions and upgrades that somehow work together.

This chapter will cover some of the more common network topology models. No one topology is right for every network environment, but based on the material in this chapter, you should be able to decide which design is best for your network project. Along with your new decision-making ability, you'll have the knowledge and understanding as to why a certain topology is best. This gives you the ability to discuss and present the issues to clients, employers, and coworkers.

Each of the network topologies discussed can be integral parts of another topology design. Redundant and secure topologies should be part of every network design. For the purposes of discussion, each topology is presented in a separate section of the chapter. The network topologies are discussed in this order:

- Flat network topology
- Hierarchical network topology
- Mesh network topology

- Redundant network topology
- Campus/LAN network topology
- Enterprise/WAN network topology
- Secure network topology

Flat Network Topology

A flat network topology design is generally used for very small networks. Each network device, such as a hub, bridge, switch, or router is used for a general rather than specific purpose. In flat networks, modular units or discrete functions are usually non-existent. Most network components in a flat network design are used for simple broadcasting and providing limited switching capabilities. The flat network design is based on a common broadcast domain. Each of the network components is brought together within a common layer. More often that not, the flat network design is relegated to earlier and simpler network designs without complex switching requirements.

Description

In a flat network topology, network components usually communicate in a looping fashion. If routers are used, each router will send routing updates throughout the internetwork. Since the internetwork is usually small, routing updates will occur quickly. Convergence is not often an issue since updates and changes in a flat network are minimal. Communication through routing loops requires a limited number of routers or switches to route traffic or send routing updates.

Flat network designs are not generally created in a modular fashion. Flat networks provide a consistent and easy-to-manage network environment, but they provide limited modularity to reduce cost.

Also, scalability is not usually an important design factor for flat network designs. If you need a network that will grow and scale well, a flat network topology is limited in its ability to scale to enterprise-wide infrastructures and is usually not a good design option. Routing protocol convergence is generally fast and efficient as long as the flat internetwork is small and compact. Figure 1-1 shows a sample flat network topology.

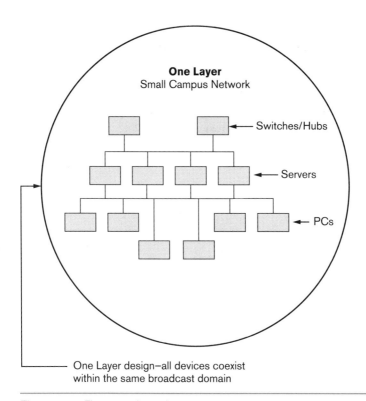

Figure 1-1 *Flat network topology*

Summary

A flat network topology design is generally used for very small networks. More often than not, the flat network design is relegated to older and simpler network designs without complex switching requirements. Flat networks provide a consistent and easy-to-manage network environment, but they provide limited modularity in order to reduce cost. If you need a network that will grow and scale well, a flat network topology is limited in its ability to scale to enterprise-wide infrastructures and is usually not a good design option.

Advantages

The following list summarizes the advantages of the flat network design model:

- Lower cost — A flat network topology is lower in initial cost due to the smaller size of the network and lower equipment costs. Special routing and switching components are not used to a wide extent in a flat network topology design.

- Reliability — Flat networks are reliable due to the simplistic design and general static nature of the topology.

- Easy to design — Flat networks do not generally incorporate modularity; therefore, the design is easy to create and implement. Flat networks aren't usually concerned with scalability either, which contributes to the ease of design.

- Easy to implement — Implementation is generally easier due to the lack of specialized switching equipment and configuration anomalies.

Disadvantages

The following list summarizes the disadvantages of the flat network design model:

- Not modular — Changes to the environment will usually affect all internetworking devices.

- Bandwidth domain — In a flat network design, most if not all devices are usually in the same bandwidth domain. This can cause a problem if applications require specific bandwidth resources.

- Broadcast domain — All systems are in the same broadcast domain and can cause broadcast congestion.

Hierarchical Network Topology

Hierarchical network typologies are created in layers to allow specific functions and features to be implemented in each of the layers. Each component is carefully placed in a hierarchical design for maximum efficiency and specific purpose. Routers, switches, and hubs all play a specific role in routing and distributing data and packet information. In a hierarchical design, each layer of the hierarchy has a purpose and works together with the other layers of the hierarchy to bring order and maximum performance in the internetwork. Most Cisco networks today are built on the hierarchical design philosophy, at least in part. With changing technologies and complex corporate network environments, a true-layered hierarchical design may be uncommon, but certainly worth the effort to attain.

Description

A hierarchical network design incorporates three key layers for internetworking component communication, and Cisco adheres to the three-layer design philosophy for its hierarchical networks. The three hierarchical layers are the core layer, the distribution layer, and the access layer. The core layer provides the backbone, or high-speed switching component, to the network. In a pure hierarchical design, this core layer will provide only the specialized task of switching data. The distribution layer is the demarcation point between the core layer and the end-user access layer. The distribution layer components provide packet manipulation, filtering, addressing, policy enforcement, and other data-manipulation tasks. The access layer provides end-user access to the network. But, prioritization and bandwidth switching can also be configured at the access layer to optimize use of network resources.

Modularity is important in a network that will need to grow and evolve with business needs and new technology implementations. Networks today are increasingly complex and have evolved as rapidly as the technology. With modularity, hierarchically designed networks can limit the effect of each component change to the immediate area of the change only. This means that the entire network won't be affected as it would be in a flat network design. Routers, switches, and other internetworking devices can be added to complement the design when needed. Hierarchical network designs are created to be scalable.

Scalability will allow new components and applications to be integrated into the existing network design with limited reconstruction or design. One of the key advantages to hierarchical topologies of any network size is the ability to scale to new business requirements while using the existing technology investment that's already in place. Because of the complexity and size of the network design, routing protocols used in a hierarchical network must have quick convergence and low processor utilization for routing updates. Most newer routing protocols have been designed with hierarchical topologies in mind and require fewer resources to maintain a current network routing table or map.

Figure 1-2 shows a hierarchical network topology.

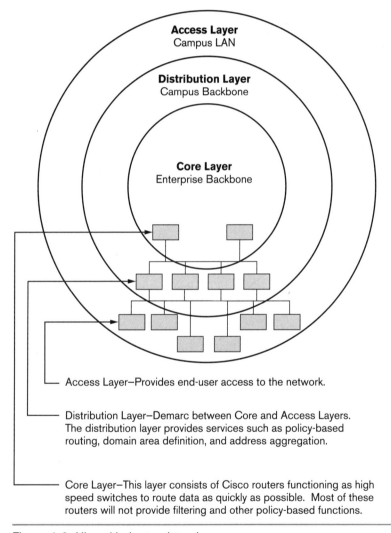

Figure 1-2 *Hierarchical network topology*

Summary

Hierarchical network typologies are created in layers to allow specific functions and features to be implemented in each of the layers. Most networks today are built on the hierarchical design philosophy, or at least part of the hierarchical design. A hierarchical network design incorporates three key layers for internetworking component communication. Cisco adheres to the three-layer design philosophy for designing hierarchical networks. The three hierarchical layers are the core layer, the distribution layer, and the access layer. The core layer provides the backbone, or high-speed switching component, to the network. In a pure hierarchical design, this core layer will provide only the specialized task of switching data. The distribution layer is the demarcation point between the core layer and the end-user access layer. The distribution layer components provide packet manipulation, filtering, addressing, policy enforcement, and other data manipulation tasks. The access layer provides end-user access to the network. One of the key advantages to hierarchical topologies of any network size is the ability to scale to new business requirements while using the existing technology investment that is already in placc.

Advantages

The following list summarizes the advantages of the hierarchical network design model:

- Scalable — The modular aspect of a hierarchical-designed network enables routers, switches, and other internetworking devices to be added to complement the design when needed.

- High availability — Redundancy, alternate paths, optimization, tuning, filtering, and other network processes contribute to the overall high availability in hierarchical networks.

- Low delay — With routers delineating broadcast domains, and multiple paths for switching and routing, traffic moves quickly with very little delay.

- Fault isolation — Using a hierarchical design can facilitate changes and improve fault isolation. A modular design will promote quick problem resolution through logical problem-solving and component isolation.

- Modular — The modular design of hierarchical networks allows each component to perform a specific purpose in the internetwork, thereby increasing performance and allowing easier and more organized network management.

- Cost efficient — Certain bandwidth utilization reductions can be realized with optimization and tuning of switching and routing paths in a hierarchical network.

- Network management — With an efficient and well-designed network in place, the management of the components will be more automated and easier to deploy. This can result in cost reductions for staff and training.

Disadvantages

With the redundancy that is often integrated into a hierarchical network topology and specialized switching equipment, the initial cost of a hierarchical network is significantly higher than a flat network design. With the higher investment in a hierarchical design, it's important to choose routing protocols, components, and processes carefully.

Mesh Network Topology

Mesh network topologies are constructed with many different interconnections between network nodes. Fully meshed and partially meshed are the two types of mesh network topologies.

Description

A fully meshed network is typically the backbone of the enterprise network. Fully meshed networks provide excellent redundancy and reliability. Mission-critical services and applications are frequently running on fully meshed network topologies. Partially meshed networks are much like fully meshed networks except that each network node or switch does not necessarily have an immediate connection to each other network node or switch.

Fully Meshed Networks

In a fully meshed network, each network node or switch will have a path to every other network node or switch. Typically, the nodes are located at the core level or backbone level of the network. Fully meshed network topologies are generally not a cost-effective solution. Although you can (for the most part) assure that certain service-level agreements are met with a fully meshed design, you can't guarantee that server or application failures will be redundant with just a fully meshed backbone. A fully meshed design would be best for a specific WAN application that could not operate in a lower or reduced bandwidth scenario. Fully meshed designs are expensive to implement due to circuit cost. Figure 1-3 shows a fully meshed network topology between WAN switches.

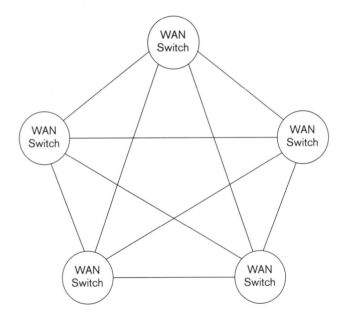

Each network node has a path to every other
network node or switch (full redundancy).

Figure 1-3 *Fully meshed network topology*

Partially Meshed Networks

Partially meshed networks can still provide redundancy through alternate paths. Usually in this design, if a network connection fails, the network will remain operational with reduced bandwidth and service levels. Partially meshed network topologies are more likely to be implemented in an enterprise network. In a partially meshed network design, if a circuit or component fails, the data is routed through an alternate path. The alternate path may not be able to provide the bandwidth required for all network services, but will generally maintain connectivity and allow mission critical applications to continue processing. Of course, circuit failures and component failures do occur on occasion, so partially meshed network designs need to be planned carefully to assure that if outages do occur, either the effect is minimal or an alternate or redundant configuration is available. Figure 1-4 shows a partially meshed network topology.

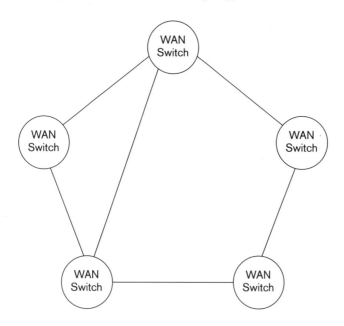

Network nodes are partially meshed.

Figure 1-4 *Partially meshed network topology*

Summary

Meshed network topologies are constructed with many different interconnections between network nodes. Fully meshed and partially meshed are the two types of mesh network topologies. Fully meshed networks provide excellent redundancy and reliability. A fully meshed design would be best for a specific application that could not operate in a lower or reduced bandwidth scenario. Partially meshed networks are much like fully meshed networks except that each network node or switch does not necessarily have an immediate connection to each other network node or switch. Partially meshed network designs need to be planned carefully to assure that if outages do occur, either the effect is minimal or an alternate or redundant configuration is available.

Advantages

The main advantage of the meshed network topology is the redundancy that is provided by having multiple links connecting each network site. Especially with the fully meshed configuration, network availability is enhanced with redundant paths.

Disadvantages

Meshed network topologies can be expensive due to high circuit costs. If a fully meshed design is constructed, the redundancy and full network availability may not be worth the extra cost. Data circuit costs, implementation costs, and support costs may be higher than the cost of the service degradation that a fully meshed design was implemented to prevent.

Redundant Network Topology

Redundant network topologies should be incorporated into all network designs. Because businesses run critical applications and services, every one of their networks needs some type of redundant topology to ensure bandwidth is available to deliver required network services. When early network provider companies first designed networks, they made redundancy a key element in their marketing strategy for new and existing clients.

Description

Transmission media, routers, servers, and workstations are several areas where you can incorporate redundancy into network design.

Redundancy at the core or backbone layer is of extreme importance. Some type of data circuit or media will connect each of your routers or WAN switches. Most of the time, the transmission media (especially in very large networks) is supported by a third-party vendor, such as a telco carrier or network service provider. When provisioning transmission media, it is very important to know and understand the routes that the data links travel. Often, circuit vendors will provide a route through their "network cloud," but you won't have a clear understanding of what path your data is traveling to reach its destination.

Caution

Be sure you are aware of "single points of failure" in the data circuits that you provision for your network. Even using multiple network providers won't guarantee that your network redundancy is intact.

Even having a map provided by your network provider won't guarantee that the circuits are redundant. Often when network outages occur (such as a fiber cut or other failure), backup circuit paths are put into service, used as the primary path, and not returned to backup status once the primary path has been repaired. It's possible that your redundant network design (at the core media level) was based on the primary path on the network providers' network. Once the primary network path is unavailable, your network may not be redundant at the most-basic level. Stay in contact with your network service provider representative and be sure that you have the most current network map available.

As an alternative to using multiple data circuits or multiple network providers, you can select two media types to provide redundancy. Satellite and data circuits are good combinations for redundancy since the satellite link won't travel over the same geographic area as the data circuits. Again, be cautious. Some satellite links eventually do connect to data circuits before they reach your network. In serious network outage situations, redundancy may fail on both network paths. If you are connecting to areas outside of the United States, you'll have to rely on your international support team to get network redundancy information, as the international carriers will be reluctant to give out circuit path information. To create an even stronger redundancy into your network design, and depending on the size and critical nature of your network, you may want to consider have multiple vendors, multiple circuits, and multiple technologies. Often, cost considerations prohibit multiple technologies, but you'll need to weigh the cost of an outage versus the cost of the technology that may prevent the outage.

Once you have created a redundant network design for your backbone or core layer, you'll need to take a look at your routers. Cisco routers can provide load balancing and multiple path routing depending on the protocols being used in your internetwork.

Another area of concern is the workstation and server level of your network. More than likely, the workstation will be not designed for redundancy, since a failure at that level will only affect that particular workstation. So, limited or intermittent failures won't generally affect any other network users or services. However, as we all know, full data backups are important, especially at the workstation and server level where users keep their most sensitive data.

At the server level, a redundant hardware design is also critical. Use a mirrored disk or system to provide the minimum redundancy needed. Sometimes, a software solution for mirroring data can lead to disastrous results when hardware fails. Servers should be designed to withstand disk outages and power failures. Redundant Array of Inexpensive Disks (RAID) technology will allow disk mirroring and disk striping. RAID disk striping is used to write data across several physical disks. If one disk fails, the network operating system will request a new disk be inserted and then re-create lost data that is based on parity information from the remaining disks. There are different RAID standards for network operating systems as well as applications. Check with your application vendor for more specific information on how the application works with RAID technology.

Figure 1-5 shows a redundant network topology.

Summary

Redundant network topologies are incorporated into all network designs. With businesses running critical applications and services, every network will need some type of redundant topology to ensure that services and bandwidth are available to deliver required network services. Transmission media, routers, servers, and workstations are several areas of the network design where you can incorporate redundancy.

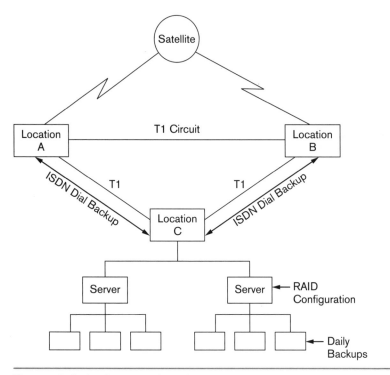

Figure 1-5 *Redundant network topology*

Advantages

The following list summarizes the advantages of the redundant network design model:

- Provides high network availability
- Secures data transactions from hardware failures
- Allows easier and more cost-effective network management of redundant nodes

Disadvantages

Redundancy should be approached with caution and should be developed as a strategy that will provide service-level enhancements and cost savings. Redundancy should not be designed into a network for the sake of redundancy. If the cost of an outage or data loss is less than the cost of the redundant technology to prevent it, you should carefully consider whether the redundant technology is worth installing.

Campus/LAN Network Topology

Campus and LAN network topologies have typically been limited in size and complexity due to the smaller amount of network nodes and network services. Current technologies such as ATM and switched LANs are increasing network complexity while providing end users increased bandwidth for multimedia and other resource-intensive applications.

Description

LAN networks have moved out of the traditional one-server, multi-user environment in one building to multiple-building campus environments that require more specific technology that is not necessary broadcast based. The progression of network complexity at the LAN level can be broken down into three general areas. First, the more traditional LANs, such as ring, bus, and star topologies, started the LAN environments years ago when networking personal computers began to appear in most businesses. When user requirements for bandwidth exceeded the traditional limits, the next major LAN technology involved switched LANs. Switched LANs, or campus LANs, also came about as corporations moved out of the one-room LAN to multiple buildings and areas. Finally, VLANs were introduced. VLANs allow like-users across a campus environment to share a common broadcast domain.

Traditional LANs

Traditional LANs are those LAN environments that allow workgroup access to network services. Most of these LANs were implemented years ago when Novell created NetWare for multiple users to share data. Later, Microsoft developed Windows NT Server as an alternative for file, print, and application services on a LAN. Small businesses can use these traditional LAN topologies to share data within an office, building, or smaller internetworking environments. Ring, bus, and star LAN network topologies are typical traditional LAN designs.

Ring The ring network topology describes Token Ring as well as FDDI designs. Ring networks provide media access methods that do not create a collision-based network. Each station on the ring transmits data at the required time and processes packets according to a token-passing methodology. Token Ring networks are traditional IBM technology networks. Token Ring networks connect all the user stations to the ring. FDDI ring networks are higher speed but use the same token-passing methodology that allows only one user to transmit data on the ring at any one time.

Bus A bus topology network is traditionally Ethernet. A bus network connects all stations together on the same cable media. Each station taps into the bus (or wire) to send and receive data on the network. Like the Token Ring environments, each station processes each and every data packet that is sent across the media wire. However, unlike Token Ring, the bus networks use a media access method called Carrier Sense Multiple Access/Collision Detection (CSMA/CD). In a CSMA/CD network, each station listens to the media for traffic that is being transmitted. When a station wants to send data, it will wait until there is no traffic being transmitted on the network before sending data. If it happens to send data at the same time as another station, both stations will back off and wait a specified period of time before transmitting again.

Star Star topology networks depend on a central switching component to deliver network services to each end station. Each end station is connected to the central switching component independent of any other end station. If one end station fails, there will be no effect on the other end stations. However, in the star topology configuration, if the central switching component fails, all stations attached will also lose communication to the network.

Campus LANs – Switched LANs

Campus LAN environments have exploded over the past several years due to the demand for networked PCs and instant business communication. Most of the move to switched internetwork LANs is a result of the demand for higher bandwidth to the desktop. More and more users require high-speed access to Internet and other business applications. The traditional 80/20 rule of network design, where 80 percent of the traffic remains within a local network segment, has been challenged by the consolidation of data and services within corporate intranets.

Generally, switched internetworks are more highly managed and efficient as compared to its predecessor, the shared bandwidth network. Switches are able to handle increased data speed and more traffic, and can provide dedicated bandwidth to specific users based on business need. Switches can also prioritize traffic and provide increased performance throughout the internetwork. Many switches today have OSI layer 3 routing capabilities built into them. Layer 3 Switching will be discussed in Chapter 6.

Asynchronous Transfer Mode (ATM) can provide LAN as well as WAN capabilities, and therefore presents itself as a unique technology alternative for the campus/LAN environment. Some network designers are choosing ATM for its bandwidth-on-demand capabilities as well as its ability to support multimedia to the desktop.

Figure 1-6 shows a campus/LAN network topology.

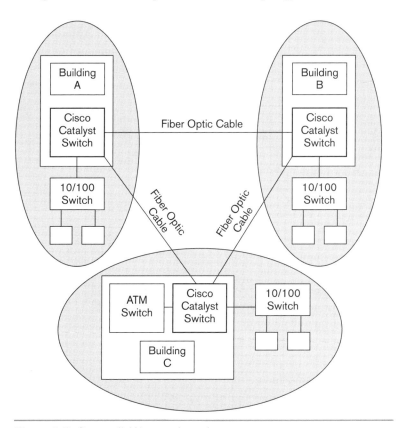

Figure 1-6 *Campus/LAN network topology*

VLANs

VLANs have been introduced into campus/LAN design scenarios due to the ease of administration and flexibility when personnel are reassigned or move frequently. With VLANs, an end-user's unique network services are available in any geographical location regardless of physical location. VLANs allow businesses to link departments and project staff onto the same virtual segment. A VLAN management interface is available for network personnel to configure VLANs. VLANs are basically a way for broadcast traffic to be limited to a certain domain of users. Often, groups of users are connected through a VLAN for projects and temporary assignments. For this reason, VLANs need to be flexible and scalable. Routers are not required to implement a VLAN infrastructure. Only cross-segment traffic would require a router for networking and addressing functions.

From port-based traffic to policy-based traffic, VLANs can be configured in a number of ways. Some of the more popular VLAN configurations are port-based, protocol-based, and policy-based designs.

Port-based VLANs The port that the user has a physical connection to defines port-based VLANs. Implementation of this type of VLAN is probably the easiest of all types of VLAN implementations. An example of a VLAN configuration would be VLAN-X running on Switch A ports 1,3,5,7 and Switch B ports 1,3,5,7. VLAN-Y would be configured as running on Switch A ports 2,4,6,8 and Switch B ports 2,4,6,8. This type of configuration provides very high security due to the static nature of the VLAN assignment. Manual intervention will be required to move a user to another VLAN. Port-based VLANs are not as flexible as other VLAN implementations and are more useful with smaller and more permanent switching environments. You can also assign ports to multiple VLANs.

Protocol-based VLANs Protocol-based VLANs are based on protocol type. User groups can be defined by network personnel based on whether the protocol is IP, IPX, or the like. Protocol-based VLANs don't relate well to real-world scenarios where end systems are running multiple protocols and multiple applications. Of course, protocol-based VLANS do allow end-user systems to be members of multiple VLAN networks. Protocol-based VLANs also allow protocol segmentation and isolation that in several situations can provide better throughput and also limit broadcast traffic.

Policy-based VLANs Policy management is by far the most powerful type of VLAN implementation. Switches that operate on policy-based VLANs can determine VLAN membership based on certain policies such as configuration detail, security, and performance. Policy-based VLANs are more flexible and business-friendly. Software applications often change or are upgraded, and the associated VLAN switches can dynamically determine the most appropriate VLAN for the application. Policy-based VLAN switches check data frames to determine the most efficient VLAN membership based on policy filters.

Summary

Campus and LAN network topologies have typically been limited in size and complexity due to the smaller amount of network nodes and network services. Traditional LANs are those LAN environments that allow workgroup access to network services and include bus, star, and ring LAN implementations. Current technologies such as ATM and switched LANs are increasing network complexity while providing end-users increased bandwidth for multimedia and other resource intensive applications. VLANs allow businesses to link departments and project staff onto the same virtual segment. A VLAN management interface is available for network personnel to configure VLANs.

Advantages

The following list summarizes the advantages of campus/LAN network topologies:

- Switched internetworks can provide dedicated bandwidth to the desktop.
- More efficient use of network resources at the LAN level.
- Reduced cost due to easier physical implementation.

Disadvantages

One of the main disadvantages to campus/LAN topologies is the possibility that newer technologies are implemented too early and do not take full advantage of the network components that are already in place. Frequently, interoperability issues arise, and equipment, processes, and applications are discarded in favor of a new technology that promises to cure all network issues and problems.

Enterprise/WAN Network Topology

With multiple network technologies and applications that run through them, enterprise networks are as varied as the businesses they serve and the network personnel that run them.

Description

Enterprise networks grow and evolve as company services and locations change and expand. Early enterprise networks were handled by service providers, such as GE, Tymnet, and others. Early timesharing mainframe services are much like the Internet Service Providers (ISPs) of today. Since the cost of data transmission and equipment was high, most companies accessed their data from massive mainframe computers at remote locations. As time progressed and information services grew more and more important to companies and their businesses, each company began to develop its own computer system infrastructure. The enterprise networks of today are the end result of the business growth and the heavy reliance on information processing and flow. Enterprise networks can take on many different designs depending on the business need. It's important to remember that enterprise networks should be built to serve the applications that are needed to support the business, not the other way around. "If you build it, they will come" is not a good enterprise network design philosophy.

Enterprise Networks

Three main types of enterprise class network topologies are popular today. Remote access networks, Intranet/Internet, and WAN topologies all work together to provide needed business services and communication capabilities. In this section, each topology will be discussed separately.

Remote Access Networks Remote access is a growing area of network design. With telecommuters and increased business travel, what was once a luxury has become a necessity to conduct business. Traditional access methods such as dialup are used, as well as ISDN and cable access to corporate networks. ISDN is a high-speed dial-up access method using digital phone lines. The one main advantage is the ability for home users and telecommuters to have high-speed access to the Internet and corporate WANs. Digital Subscriber Line (DSL) uses existing telephone lines to provide multimedia service to end subscribers.

Intranet/Internet Intranet web servers are becoming the standard for internal business communications. Online learning, employee orientation Web sites, and time tracking are just a few of the many applications that are available through corporate intranets.

Internet access is everywhere. Companies over the past years have moved from a wait-and-see attitude about the Internet to allowing access to desktops all across organizational levels. Of course, tracking and security is of extreme importance when implementing an Internet solution for your company or client. To reduce the possibility of lost time due to Internet web site surfing, a standard policy of tracking Web access should be implemented. Be sure that all employees are aware of the conditions of Internet usage when on company time.

Internet servers that are used to transact e-commerce solutions are becoming as important to the business as the storefront. Online sales will continue to increase and be more and more of a profit center for all types of businesses and industries.

WAN WAN implementations take on many shapes and sizes. Depending on the application, client, and business, WAN implementations can be as varied as the businesses that implement them. WANs combine intranet services, Internet access, remote access, and mainframe applications to allow corporations to communicate with distributors, clients, and suppliers. Technologies that are commonly implemented in WAN infrastructures include Asynchronous Transfer Mode (ATM) and Frame Relay. ATM is a newer technology that provides a technology solution for voice, data, and video, and has still not gained widespread acceptance. Frame Relay is a packet-switching technology that takes advantage of the increased reliability and stability in transmission media. WAN technologies are discussed in Chapter 2.

Figure 1-7 shows an Enterprise/WAN network topology that incorporates remote access, Internet, intranet, and WAN services.

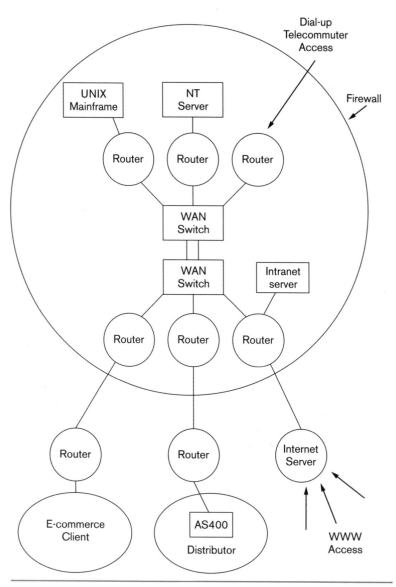

Figure 1-7 *Enterprise/WAN network topology*

VPNs

Virtual Private Networks (VPNs) are becoming more popular as a network design alternative due to the widespread availability of the Internet and the associated cost savings. VPNs can connect business suppliers and distributors through a third-party proprietary network. VPNs save money in a variety of ways. Businesses that use VPNs don't require a support staff for the backbone infrastructure. Equipment cost savings, as well as keeping up on the latest technology for backbone speed and service offerings, contribute to the popularity of VPN technology.

Early timesharing companies such as Tymnet and GE were the first to offer VPN services. Although not thought of as VPNs, early service providers built networks on X.25 technology, and corporations would link offices and locations through a proprietary infrastructure.

Of course, one of the drawbacks to a VPN is the control of the network infrastructure. Service providers control backbone connections and service availability. Another concern with VPNs is the possible lack of security. Data encryption is one security feature that will allow businesses to process secure transactions within VPNs at a low cost.

The Internet is the ultimate VPN. Using tunneling and encryption, companies can conduct business without providing network infrastructure components.

Figure 1-8 shows a Virtual Private Network topology.

Summary

No two enterprise networks are alike. With multiple network technologies and applications that run through them, enterprise networks are as varied as the businesses and network personnel that run them. Three main types of enterprise class network topologies are popular today. Remote access networks, Intranet/Internet, and WAN topologies all work together to provide needed business services and communication capabilities. Virtual Private Networks (VPNs) are becoming more popular as a network design alternative due to the widespread availability of the Internet and the associated cost savings. VPNs can connect business suppliers and distributors through a third-party proprietary network. The Internet is the ultimate VPN. Using tunneling and encryption, companies can conduct business without providing network infrastructure components.

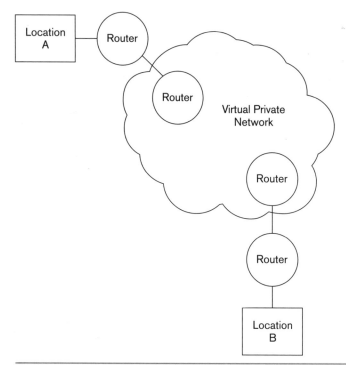

Figure 1-8 *VPN topology*

Advantages

The advantages to having an Enterprise/WAN network topology are not as important as the fact that they are becoming an absolute necessity to conduct business. Intranets, extranets, Internet, and VPNs are all ways that businesses use enterprise-wide infrastructure solutions to remain competitive.

Disadvantages

A disadvantage to Enterprise/WAN network topologies is the staffing and support that is needed to implement and maintain the network. The outsourcing of staff and support functions continues to be discussed with wide-ranging views. Outsourcing limits your control over your network, but allows non-technical businesses to concentrate on core business strategies rather than spending business resources on information technology management.

Secure Network Topology

Security is one of the most important considerations in a network design, especially as businesses move sensitive data to intranet servers for internal employee use. With the relatively new use of Internet technology and access, security will play a more active role in choosing technologies and methods for employee productivity, customer support, and online business transactions.

Description

Policy and standardization, implementation, and audit are three main areas to consider when designing a secure network topology.

Policy and Standardization

When designing a secure network topology, putting policies and standards in place is not only a good idea for security, but also a best practice for network management. Policies and standards will allow network users the freedom to use network services and to perform company business in a secure environment.

There are other issues when implementing network policies and standards. The culture, or the way of doing business for a particular company, will many times influence secure topology design. When an executive cannot access important sales data because of a user account lockout due to an excessive number of failed logins, certain security policies must be in place so that the executive can still conduct business. Remote access has become an increasingly important issue for many businesses. With more extensive networks and telecommuters, secure topologies must allow access to sensitive data at any time and from any place.

There are several key areas of network policies and standardization that need to be addressed when designing a secure network. Software features such as data encryption and authentication are important, as well as hardware solutions such as firewalls. It is also important to remember physical security when implementing secure networks. Is your physical network hardware in a place where no one can access it? Are there limits to the number of people who have access to the computer room, wiring closets, and servers? Is access to those rooms and wiring closets audited?

Implementation

Implementation of a secure network topology will be the next step once the standards, policies, and procedures are in place. Be sure that these policies are communicated as appropriate. Company executives or your clients should be aware of the security policies and the reasons for them. Be sure that you get agreement from key personnel before any security policies are in place. As much as you want a secure network, personnel must have access to critical business data. Once you've designed a solution to provide consistent and reliable service, the next step is to set policies and procedures in place to assure a secure networking environment.

Firewalls are a common implementation of network security. Firewalls, of course, provide limited access to data. Cisco has hardware and software firewall solutions. Firewalls and the technology to limit user access are key components to a secure network topology. Firewalls will be discussed further in Chapter 8.

Mainframe systems, network servers, and business-critical workstations need to have a security system of some type implemented. It may not be necessary to have an audit log for each and every workstation, or even every network server. You'll need to identify the risk to the business if the network resource is compromised. It is a good idea to keep the security mechanisms low-key for most of the end-user population. End-users, except for key management, do not need to know what level of security is implemented on the network. You may want to check with the corporate legal department before monitoring or accessing specific user data. Be sure that employees have been notified that the data that they are working with is company property and can be seized or accessed as necessary for business purposes. Let the legal department take the necessary steps to communicate certain security policies, or at least be sure that your implementation does coincide with your company's business practices and culture.

Audit and Review

Once your security policies and procedures have been decided and are in place, it will be critical to review and audit your network security. Often, you will have a security officer take responsibility for specifically auditing your network policies, or you will have an external agency audit your network.

Caution

There is a difference between being paranoid and being aware. Often, security threats are internal to the company. Creating a review process for internal security should be taken on with both caution and an awareness that your critical network systems can be compromised by internal employees.

Certainly, you should be aware of the latest news on hacker activity and threats to your network systems. Stay current on new technologies as well as the latest software patches, security holes, and enhancements to your implemented systems.

Figure 1-9 shows a secure network topology.

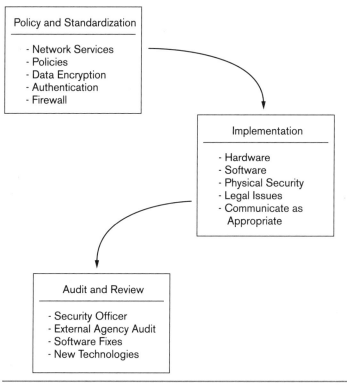

Figure 1-9 *Secure network topology*

Summary

Security is one of the most important considerations in a network design, especially as businesses move sensitive data to intranet servers for internal employee use. Policy and standardization, implementation, and audit are three main areas to consider when designing a secure network topology. Policies and standards will allow network users the freedom to use network services and to perform company business in a secure environment. Implementation of a secure network topology will be the next step once the standards, policies, and procedures are in place. Once your security policies and procedures have been decided and are in place, it will be critical to review and audit your network security.

Advantages

The main advantage to a secure network topology is the fact that business can be conducted electronically and much quicker than in non-secure environments. If a network topology has no security, then it has really no effective means to conduct important business. Secure network topologies that are implemented over the next few years will be able to take advantage of the Internet market and all the possibilities that it has to offer.

Disadvantages

The main disadvantage to a secure network topology is the cost associated with the implementation and support. You'll have to make tradeoffs in regards to security versus the effect that is has on day-to-day business. In creating secure network topologies and processes, the effect should be seamless and enhance, if possible, rather than hinder, business processes and productivity.

Key Points

The network topologies discussed in this chapter all work together to provide reliable network services. Depending on the applications and services that you'll provide to your end-user community, you can choose to implement portions of each network topology type. Secure network topologies are increasingly important as more and more businesses put proprietary information on departmental servers and corporate intranets. Here is a summary of the network topologies that were discussed:

- Flat Network Topology—A flat network topology design is generally used for very small networks. More often that not, the flat network design is relegated to earlier and simpler network designs without complex switching requirements. Flat networks provide a consistent and easy-to-manage network environment, but they provide limited modularity to reduce cost. If you need a network that will grow and scale well, a flat network topology is limited in its ability to scale to enterprise-wide infrastructures and is usually not a good design option.

- Hierarchical Network Topology—Hierarchical network typologies are created in layers to allow specific functions and features to be implemented in each of the layers. Most networks today are built on the hierarchical design philosophy, or at least part of the hierarchical design. A hierarchical network design incorporates three key layers for internetworking component communication. Cisco adheres to the three-layer design philosophy for designing hierarchical networks. The three hierarchical layers are the core layer, the distribution layer, and the access layer. The core layer provides the backbone, or high-speed switching component, to the network. In a pure hierarchical design, this core layer will provide only the specialized task of switching data. The distribution layer is the demarcation point between the core layer and the end-user access layer. The distribution layer components provide packet manipulation, filtering, addressing, policy enforcement, and other data manipulation tasks. The access layer provides end-user access to the network. One of the key advantages to hierarchical topologies of any network size is the ability to scale to new business requirements while using the existing technology investment that is already in place.

- Mesh Network Topology—Mesh network topologies are constructed with many different interconnections between network nodes. Fully meshed and partially meshed are the two types of mesh network topologies. Fully meshed networks provide excellent redundancy and reliability. A fully meshed design would be best for a specific application that could not operate in a lower or reduced bandwidth scenario. Partially meshed networks are much like fully meshed networks except that each network node or switch does not necessarily have an immediate connection to each other network node or switch. Partially meshed network designs need to be planned carefully to assure that if outages do occur, either the effect is minimal or an alternate or redundant data path is available.

- Redundant Network Topology—Redundant network topologies are incorporated into all network designs. With businesses running critical applications and services, every network will need some type of redundant topology to ensure services and bandwidth are available to deliver required network services. Transmission media, routers, servers, and workstations are several areas of the network design where you can incorporate redundancy.

- Campus/LAN Network Topology—Campus and LAN network topologies have typically been limited in size and complexity due to the smaller amount of network nodes and network services. Traditional LANs are those LAN environments that allow workgroup access to network services and include bus, star, and ring LAN implementations. Current technologies such as ATM and switched LANs are increasing network complexity while providing end-users increased bandwidth for multimedia and other resource-intensive applications. VLANs allow businesses to link departments and project staff onto the same virtual segment.

- Enterprise/WAN Network Topology—With multiple network technologies and applications that run through them, enterprise networks are as varied as the businesses and network personnel that run them. Three main types of enterprise class network topologies are popular today. Remote access networks, Intranet/Internet, and WAN topologies all work together to provide needed business services and communication capabilities. Virtual Private Networks (VPNs) are becoming more popular as a network design alternative due to the widespread availability of the Internet and the associated cost savings. VPNs can connect business suppliers and distributors through a third-party proprietary network. The Internet is the ultimate VPN. Using tunneling and encryption, companies can conduct business without providing network infrastructure components.

- Secure Network Topology—Security is one of the most important considerations in a network design, especially as businesses move sensitive data to intranet servers for internal employee use. Policy and standardization, implementation, and audit are three main areas to consider when designing a secure network topology. Policies and standards will allow network users the freedom to use network services and to perform company business in a secure environment. Implementation of a secure network topology will be the next step once the standards, policies, and procedures are in place. Once your security policies and procedures have been decided and are in place, it will be critical to review and audit your network security at regular intervals.

Chapter 2

Network Technologies

From the beginning of network technology, change has been constant. Ethernet speeds have moved into the gigabit arena, and high-speed digital technology has reached home users at the local loop. Depending on your unique internetwork scenario, there is a technology suited to meet your needs. In this chapter, you'll find some of the common network technologies available today. For reference, they are listed in alphabetical order:

- ATM (Asynchronous Transfer Mode)
- DSL (Digital Subscriber Line)
- Ethernet/802.3
- FDDI (Fiber Distributed Data Interface)
- Frame Relay
- Gigabit Ethernet
- ISDN (Integrated Services Digital Network)
- PPP (Point-to-Point Protocol)
- SMDS (Switched Multimegabit Data Service)
- Token Ring/802.5

Each section in this chapter describes a particular network technology, followed by information about how the technology actually works within an internetwork. In addition, the advantages and disadvantages of each technology are summarized. At the end of this chapter, you will have a better understanding of the major network technologies and how one or more of these will fit into your network design.

ATM (Asynchronous Transfer Mode)

Asynchronous Transfer Mode (ATM) can operate at the campus/LAN network topology level and scale to the enterprise level. ATM's transfer method is cell relay and operates reliably at very high speeds.

Description

ATM is an international standard for cell relay. ATM is capable of high-speed data transfer of voice, video, and data in fixed 53-byte cells.

ATM is one of the fastest growing WAN technologies today. The rapid increase in Internet traffic, along with voice applications and real-time video demands, have pushed the bandwidth demands.

One of the reasons for the popularity of ATM is the possibility that with one technology in a fully integrated ATM network an end-user can send voice, data, and video applications to another end-user, desktop-to-desktop.

An ATM network is comprised of two main components:

- ATM switch — Accepts incoming cells, reads cell header information, updates the cell header information, and switches the cell to its destination. The ATM switch supports two primary interfaces. The User to Network Interface (UNI) connects ATM end systems to an ATM switch. The Network Node Interface (NNI) connects two ATM switches.

- ATM endpoints — Receives ATM data; equipped with ATM network adapter hardware and ATM protocol-specific configuration.

ATM technology has a standard to emulate traditional, or legacy, LAN environments called LANE (Local Area Network Emulation). LANE allows Novell, Microsoft, and AppleTalk environments to function as if they are in a traditional LAN environment while running in an ATM environment.

Another ATM technology is MPOA (Multiprotocol over ATM). MPOA provides a process and the technology to combine routing and switching functions in a diverse protocol environment.

Caution

ATM is not the best solution for all network designs that are looking for single technology solutions. ATM can be expensive, with hardware upgrades at the workstation level.

How ATM Works

An ATM switch receives a cell on a known Virtual Channel Identifier (VCI) or Virtual Path Identifier (VPI). The ATM switch looks up the VCI or VPI value in a translation table. The cell is then retransmitted to the appropriate outgoing link.

ATM is comprised of the ATM Physical Layer and the ATM Adaption Layers.

- The ATM Physical Layer is subdivided into two parts:
  - Physical Medium Dependent Sublayer (PMD), which is responsible for synchronizing transmission and reception, and for specifying physical media
  - Transmission Convergence Sublayer (TC), which is responsible for maintaining ATM cell boundaries, error control, payload capacity for cells, and adapting cells to physical implementation
- ATM Adaption Layers
  - AAL1 — Handles circuit emulation applications such as voice and video conferencing
  - AAL3/4 — Supports connection-oriented and connectionless data
  - AAL5 — The primary ATM adaption layer that supports both connection-oriented and connectionless data.

LANE (LAN Emulation) is the method to allow legacy applications and LAN systems to function in an ATM environment. LANE has four main components.

- LANE Client (LEC) — End system; handles data transfer
- LANE Server (LES) — Server; handles address resolution
- LANE Configuration Server (LECS) — Assigns LECs to LANE services
- Broadcast and Unknown Server (BUS) — Sends and receives broadcast and multicast data

Figure 2-1 depicts the internetworking components of an ATM internetwork.

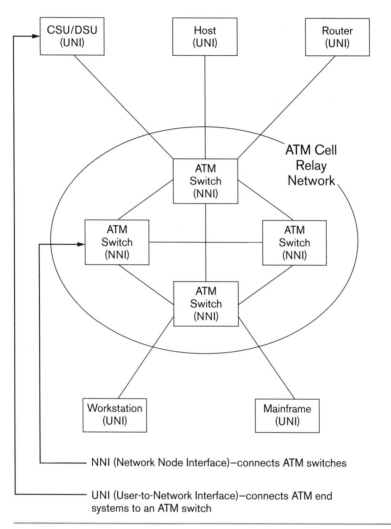

NNI (Network Node Interface)–connects ATM switches

UNI (User-to-Network Interface)–connects ATM end systems to an ATM switch

Figure 2-1 *ATM internetworking components*

Summary

ATM is a newer technology that has still not gained widespread acceptance. Although it's a one-technology solution for voice, data, and video, it does have disadvantages as far as complexity and higher implementation costs.

Advantages

The following list summarizes the advantages of ATM:

- One-technology solution for voice, data, and video to the desktop
- Compatible with most existing physical media
- LANE compatible with IP, Novell, AppleTalk, and Microsoft networks
- Incremental implementation available
- International standard

Disadvantages

The following list summarizes the disadvantages of ATM:

- Complex technology to implement; fewer skilled engineers
- High cost relative to other solutions
- High overhead for data transmission over LAN media

DSL (Digital Subscriber Line)

Digital Subscriber Line is a WAN access technology that is providing end subscribers with speeds of up to 6Mbps.

Description

DSL is a promising new access technology that uses existing telephone lines to provide multimedia service to end subscribers. The local loop from the end subscriber (such as residential phone service) to the telephone companies' CO (Central Offices) has been one of the last areas of technology advancement in the POTS (Plain Old Telephone Service) network.

One of the key advantages to DSL is the ability to use existing telephone lines to provide high bandwidth to end subscribers. The most prominent technology in the DSL family is ADSL (Asymmetric Digital Subscriber Line).

ADSL is an asymmetric technology much like cable modem; the service from the network service provider's side has more bandwidth available than from the end subscriber to the CO. If ADSL technology is widely accepted and implemented, end-users such as telecommuters and home offices will benefit from increased speeds and application services such as video and multimedia.

How ADSL Works

ADSL works by using existing copper facilities on the existing telephone network. An ADSL circuit from the end subscriber has three separate channels:

- High-speed — Downstream only from CO to end subscriber (1.5–6Mpbs service). The data rate for the downstream data will vary widely based on the length of the circuit between the end subscriber and the CO, the ADSL modem that is being used, and the physical facility conditions at the CO.

- Medium speed — Duplex channel data both directions (16–640Kbps service). These medium-speed channels can be multiplexed into several different channels and services.

- Voice speed — Regular telephone service (64Kbps). Although the voice speed channel is within the ADSL circuit, the service is separated by a filtering mechanism that allows telephone service to remain operational even if the ADSL service fails.

Figure 2-2 shows a sample ADSL internetwork.

Summary

DSL (Digital Subscriber Line) is a promising new access technology that uses existing telephone lines to provide multimedia service to end subscribers.

Advantages

The following list summarizes the advantages of DSL:

- Uses existing telephone network
- Ideal technology for Internet access to home users
- Can provide multimedia to home users as applications are developed

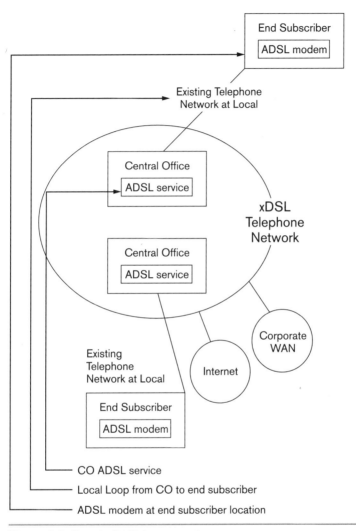

Figure 2-2 *Sample ADSL internetwork*

Disadvantages

The following list summarizes the disadvantages of DSL:

- DSL is a promising new technology but is not yet available in all areas of the world.

- The data rate for the downstream data will vary widely based on the length of the circuit between the end subscriber and the CO.

Ethernet/802.3

The Ethernet access technology operates at the campus/LAN network topology level and can operate at speeds from 10Mbps to 100Mbps. Gigabit Ethernet, described later in this chapter, operates at speeds of up to 1,000Mbps.

Description

Ethernet is a simple and widely implemented technology for internetworking transmission over campus and LAN networks. Ethernet is the most popular technology for small to medium-sized companies.

Most computer manufacturers and systems are compatible with Ethernet. This makes Ethernet the most widely recommended and implemented access technology.

Ethernet was developed with an open systems specification in mind. It was the intention of early Ethernet developers to create an access technology that could be implemented in any internetworking scenario. Multiple vendors worked together to create the Ethernet standard.

Ethernet is very closely linked to the IEEE 802.3 standard. There are a few differences, however. Ethernet has only one physical layer implementation. IEEE 802.3 has several 802.3 physical connections and names. Today, IEEE standards are synonymous with Ethernet and are used in the same context.

How Ethernet Works

Each station in an Ethernet network is connected to shared media. Each station will listen to the network medium to be sure that there is no transmission occurring. When the link is clear, the data is sent. If the data is sent and a collision occurs, the Ethernet station will transmit a jam signal to indicate to all stations on the network that a collision has occurred. The station will wait for a "backoff interval" and then retransmit the data.

The MAC (Medium Access Control) component of each Ethernet station interface on the network is responsible for controlling media access.

Media access in an Ethernet environment is based on CSMA/CD (Carrier Sense Multiple Access/Collision Detection) technology. CSMA/CD works as shown in Figure 2-3.

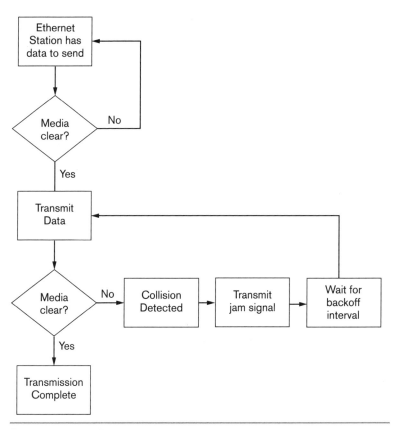

Figure 2-3 *How Ethernet works*

Summary

Ethernet is a simple and widely implemented technology for internetworking transmission over campus and LAN networks. Ethernet is the most popular technology for smaller networks.

Advantages

The following list summarizes the advantages of Ethernet:

- Proven technology
- Widely implemented
- Scalable with newer high-speed implementations
- Easy to configure
- Limited staff training

Disadvantages

The following list summarizes the disadvantages of Ethernet:

- Not recommended for WAN implementations
- Broadcast technology; every Ethernet station processes traffic

FDDI (Fiber Distributed Data Interface)

Fiber Distributed Data Interface operates at the campus/LAN/ network topology level and is an access technology that passes data traffic at speeds of up to 100Mbps.

Description

FDDI was developed in the mid-1980s and seen as a replacement technology for Token Ring and Ethernet networks. Although FDDI technology has not overtaken Ethernet and Token Ring, the FDDI standard has a place in high-speed LAN communications. The ISO (International Standards Organization) has developed an international FDDI standard that is compatible with the existing ANSI standard.

The FDDI specification is for a token-passing dual-ring LAN implementation using fiber optic 100Mbps media. FDDI can support up to 1,000 stations and, as an alternative, can be implemented over copper wire that uses electrical transmission rather than fiber. The copper implementation is called CDDI (Copper Distributed Data Interface).

Caution

Fiber optics transmission media is very delicate. Be sure that fiber strands are terminated correctly. It's advisable for a licensed electrician to terminate fiber ends.

How FDDI Works

FDDI works by using counter-rotating rings. Traffic on each ring moves in opposite directions. The primary ring is used for transferring data, and the secondary ring is used for fault tolerance.

The two types of stations on an FDDI ring are SAS (Single Attached Stations) and DAS (Dual Attached Stations. SASs are attached to the FDDI ring through an FDDI concentrator. If an SAS fails, the unit will stop communicating without interruption to the ring. DASs are attached to the FDDI ring through two ports for fault tolerance. If the primary ring fails, the DAS can connect to the ring through the secondary ring. If the DAS fails, the ring will loop at the DAS connection and provide services back to the other stations.

FDDI uses a token-passing methodology much like Token Ring to initiate data transfer over the ring. A station will have the right to pass data when a token is generated in the network and the station has possession of the token. This token-passing methodology allows the FDDI network to pass data without collision and media contention problems.

Figure 2-4 shows the FDDI ring data transfer process.

Figure 2-5 shows the token-passing methodology as it works on a Token Ring-based FDDI network.

FDDI Summary

FDDI was developed in the mid-1980s as a replacement technology for Token Ring and Ethernet networks. The FDDI specification is for a token-passing dual-ring LAN implementation using fiber optic 100Mbps media.

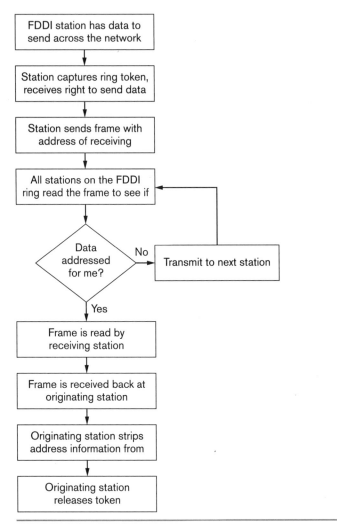

Figure 2-4 *How FDDI works*

Advantages

The following list summarizes the advantages of FDDI:

- International standard
- Excellent for campus networks, wide-range ability
- Fault-tolerant design with dual ring
- Immune to electrical interference

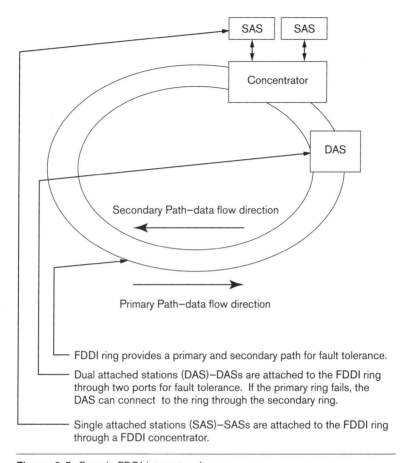

Figure 2-5 *Sample FDDI internetwork*

Disadvantages

The overall cost of an FDDI implementation can be higher than Token Ring or Ethernet implementations.

Frame Relay

Frame Relay is a WAN packet switching network technology that operates efficiently with reliable high-speed digital data lines.

Description

Frame Relay is a packet-switching technology developed for WANs. Packet-switched networks based on Frame Relay enable bandwidth sharing and variable length packets that allow efficient use of available resources. Frame Relay is based on virtual circuit transmission of data.

Frame Relay has been seen as a more efficient replacement for X.25 networks. Frame Relay operates over newer and more reliable high-speed data circuits.

There are two main types of devices in a Frame Relay network. The DCE (Data Circuit Terminating Equipment) provides clocking and switching service for the Frame Relay network. The DTE (Data Terminal Equipment) types are end-user network devices such as network hosts, PCs, bridges, or routers.

Virtual circuits on a Frame Relay network are identified by DLCIs (Data Link Connection Identifiers). DLCIs are significant only at a local level, not enterprisewide. Frame Relay networks use two types of virtual circuits. SVCs (Switched Virtual Circuits) are used when only sporadic data transfer occurs and requires call setup and termination for each separate data transmission. PVCs (Permanent Virtual Circuits) are used for consistent data transfers between DTE devices.

How Frame Relay Works

Frame Relay uses both SVCs and PVCs as transmission methods. VCs (Virtual Circuits) are defined by Frame Relay software and act as transmission lines through the network. Most early Frame Relay implementations were based on PVCs, but SVCs have gained prominence as the cost benefits have been realized and SVC-type applications are in place.

Frame Relay transmission of data is simple and efficient as compared to X.25 network transmission and overhead. When Frame Relay transmits data, a header is added to the data packets and the data is sent.

An important part of the Frame Relay header is the DLCI (Data Link Connection Identifier). A DLCI is a local virtual circuit identifier that corresponds to a particular logical circuit in the Frame Relay network.

Tip

When ordering Frame Relay service from your network provider, be sure to specifically ask for redundancy in your data circuit paths. Look for common points of failure. Even having multiple network providers will not assure redundancy.

The DLCI is user-defined. A corporation that has a Frame Relay network will more than likely have vendor-supplied switches, and the network personnel will configure the DLCIs as appropriate for their internetwork. DLCIs are not like IP addresses. DLCIs are local in their significance and do not need to be unique across the domestic or global Internet. An example of a unique address, of course, would be an Internet IP address. Another example of a unique address would be an X.25 address.

The DLCI is the identifier contained in each frame of data. DLCI information is read by switches and routers in order to route traffic to the appropriate destination.

Unlike the extensive error checking and overhead of X.25, Figure 2-6 shows Frame Relay data transmission simplified and defined in three steps.

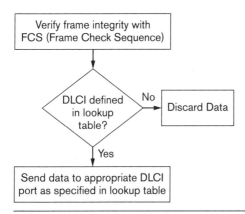

Figure 2-6 *Frame Relay simplified*

Figure 2-7 shows a sample Frame Relay internetwork.

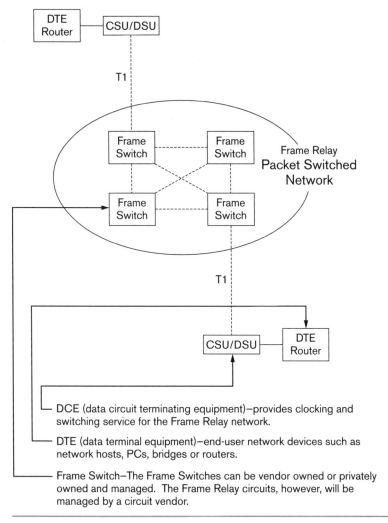

Figure 2-7 *Sample Frame Relay internetwork*

Frame Relay Summary

Frame Relay is a packet switching technology that takes advantage of increased reliability and stability in transmission media. Frame Relay is a common replacement for slower X.25 networks.

Advantages

The following list summarizes the advantages of Frame Relay:

- Efficient use of bandwidth
- Flexible bandwidth support
- Low latency
- Excellent solution for high-speed data circuits
- Proven technology

Disadvantages

Although today most circuits are reliable digital circuits, when Frame Relay was first deployed, the main disadvantage was the cost of the technology and the cost of digital circuits to carry the information without error checking. Today that disadvantage has disappeared, and Frame Relay remains one of the most popular WAN technologies.

Gigabit Ethernet

Gigabit Ethernet breaks that 100Mbps speed barrier by offering gigabit data transfer rates over campus/LAN/ networks.

Description

Gigabit Ethernet is a high-speed LAN technology that was developed to replace traditional Ethernet implementations. Gigabit Ethernet has the ability to provide 1Gbps of bandwidth on LANs and campus-style internetworks.

How Gigabit Ethernet Works

Gigabit Ethernet is compatible with existing Ethernet implementations, just at a higher speed. Both technologies use CSMA/CD (Carrier Sense Multiple Access/Collision Detection) as the primary access method to transmit data over the transmission media.

Gigabit Ethernet uses the same 802.3 frame format as traditional Ethernet, so the implementation from one Ethernet technology to another may be easier. Gigabit Ethernet can be connected to low-speed Ethernet network devices by using switching devices to provide line-speed change adaptability.

Why upgrade to Gigabit Ethernet? Is higher speed really necessary? This technology is all about speed. Here are a few things to consider and some of the advantages of Gigabit Ethernet over other technologies.

Full compatibility with traditional Ethernet—Management objects (MIB type) remain the same, data format remains the same, and access method of CSMA/CD changes only slightly.

Cost of ownership—One of the important factors with this new technology is the fact that network personnel are familiar with Ethernet technology. Training cost will be minimal, if even necessary. The cost per port of Gigabit Ethernet is lowering as time goes on. Since the technology is new, of course the cost is higher.

One of the reasons for upgrading to Gigabit Ethernet is the increased bandwidth. With additional bandwidth, new applications and services, such as video and data warehousing services, can be provided within a corporate environment.

The 100/1000Mbps GigaSwitch will replace two 100Mbps Switches as the core switching components in the internetwork. Figure 2-8 shows the proposed initial use for Gigabit technology within a traditional Ethernet 10/100 internetwork.

Summary

Gigabit Ethernet is a high-speed LAN technology that is being developed to replace traditional Ethernet implementations. Gigabit Ethernet has the ability to provide 1Gbps of bandwidth on LANs and campus-style internetworks.

Advantages

The following list summarizes the advantages of Gigabit Ethernet:

- Easy migration path from traditional Ethernet implementations
- Supports new applications (RSVP, VLAN)
- No need to train staff on new technology

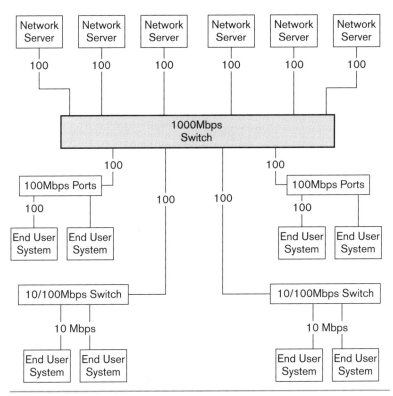

Figure 2-8 *Sample Gigabit internetwork*

Disadvantages

The following list summarizes the disadvantages of Gigabit Ethernet:

- New technology; price per port is high at this time.
- Most networks are not in condition to update to gigabit speed on the LAN infrastructure yet.

ISDN (Integrated Services Digital Network)

Integrated Services Digital Network is both a campus/LAN network topology and an Enterprise WAN access technology that provides very quick connection and reliable data transfer.

Description

ISDN is an access technology method to transfer data over the existing digital telephone network. ISDN is offered by local telephone companies in certain areas of the country based on expected demand and use. ISDN is used by telecommuters for high-speed access from home or travel and also for leased-line backup on corporate networks.

There are several unique components to an ISDN network:

- Terminal Adapters (TAs)—Adapter boards or stand-alone components to provide compatibility between TE2 devices and the ISDN network

- Terminal Equipment Type 1 (TE1)—ISDN-compatible devices

- Terminal Equipment Type 2 (TE2)—Pre-ISDN devices; not compatible without TA adapter or TA component

- Network Termination Type 1 (NT1)—Connects user devices to ISDN network

- Network Termination Type 2 (NT2)—PBX-type connector to ISDN network

Reference Points define interfaces between the above components:

- R—Interface between TE2 and TA
- S—Interface between TE1 and NT2
- T—Interface between NT1 and NT2
- U—Interface between NT1 and ISDN network

ISDN is offered in two basic service types:

- BRI (Basic Rate Interface) - Two B channels at 64Kbps and one D channel at 16Kbps = 144Kbps

- PRI (Primary Rate Interface) - Twenty-three B channels at 64Kbps and one D channel at 64Kbps = 1.544Mbps

How ISDN Works

Figure 2-9 shows a simplified call sequence process over an ISDN network.

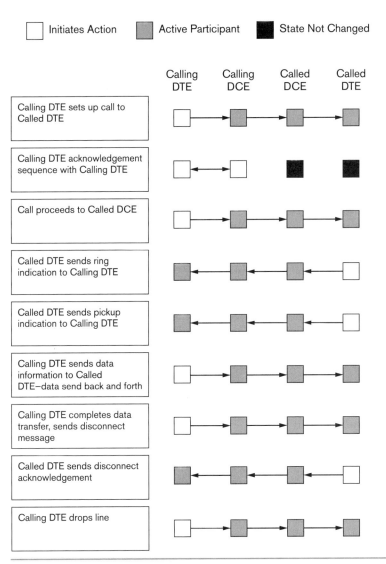

Figure 2-9 *A simplified call sequence on an ISDN network*

Figure 2-10 shows the typical ISDN network components.

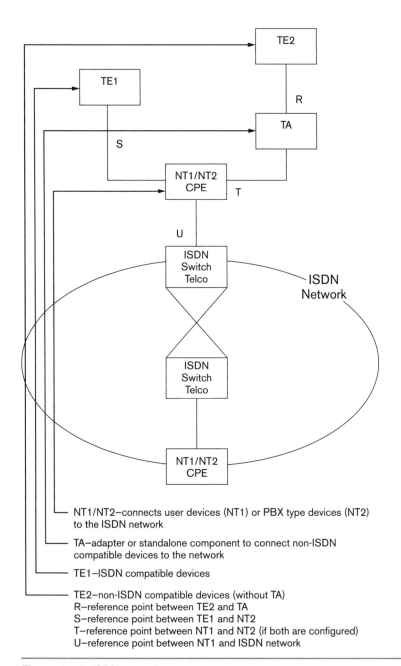

Figure 2-10 *ISDN network components*

Summary

ISDN is a high-speed dial-up access method using digital phone lines. The one main advantage is the ability for home users and telecommuters to have high-speed access to the Internet and corporate WANs.

Advantages

The following list summarizes the advantages of ISDN:

- Reasonable price for high-speed network access for telecommuters
- Improved Internet access speed
- Ability to provide voice, data, and video

Disadvantages

One main disadvantage of ISDN is that although it is not a new technology, it is still not implemented in all areas of the world, or all areas of the United States.

PPP (Point-to-Point Protocol)

Point-to-Point Protocol is a WAN access technology that passes serial line data traffic reliably.

Description

PPP is a method to transfer data over point-to-point serial communication links in a multi-vendor network. PPP was developed by the Internet Engineering Task Force (IETF) as an alternative to SLIP (Serial Link Interface Protocol). PPP provides authentication services and address assignment, and enables multiple protocols to run over one serial link.

There are three main components to PPP:

- HDLC (High Data Link Control) protocol — Used to encapsulate datagrams.

- LCP (Link Control Protocol)—Used for connection establishment, configuration, and testing. There are three types of LCP frames that work together during a communications process. Link establishment frames are used for establishment and configuration of a link. Link termination frames are used for link termination. Finally, link maintenance frames are used for troubleshooting and management functions.
- NCP (Network Control Protocol)—Used to create and configure other layer protocols. NCP provides compatibility to multiple protocols including AppleTalk, DECnet, IP, and IPX.

How PPP Works

There are several steps that PPP takes to establish a connection over a serial communications link:

1. PPP sends LCP frames to configure the serial line.
2. Link is established.
3. Authentication via PAP (Password Authentication Protocol) or CHAP (Challenge Handshake Authentication Protocol) takes place.
4. PPP sends NCP frames to configure the network layer protocols.
5. Network layer protocol packets are sent over the serial link.
6. Serial line remains open for data packet transfer.
7. LCP or NCP closes the serial link when the operation is complete.

Figure 2-11 shows a sample PPP frame.

Summary

PPP is a method to transfer data over point-to-point serial communication links in a multi-vendor network. PPP has gained widespread acceptance due to its ability to work in a variety of protocol and internetworking environments.

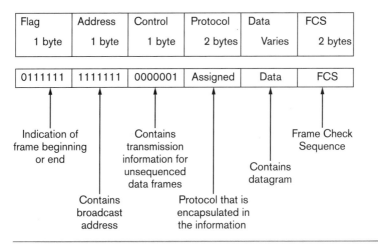

Figure 2-11 *Sample PPP frame*

Advantages

The following list summarizes the advantages of PPP:

- Industry standard for point-to-point communications over serial links
- Compatible with heterogeneous networks through NCP
- Automatic configuration
- Data compression
- Authentication via PAP or CHAP

Disadvantages

Due to the advantages that PPP has as compared to SLIP, the apparent disadvantages of PPP are difficult to come by.

SMDS (Switched Multimegabit Data Service)

Switched Multimegabit Data Service is an Enterprise WAN network technology that operates packet-switching services.

Description

SMDS is a packet-switching network technology developed for high-speed WAN environments. SMDS is available over fiber- and copper-based facilities.

The high-speed abilities of SMDS enable DS3 speeds over Public Data Networks. SMDS operates at the physical and data link layer of the OSI reference model. SMDS is a connectionless packet-switching technology that requires addressing in each packet of information across the internetwork. Bellcore, the SMDS standards organization, allocates a unique 64-bit network address for each addressable SMDS network component. There are several important components to SMDS networks:

- CPE (Customer Premises Equipment)
- Terminal equipment — Computers and dumb terminals.
- Intermediate nodes — Routers, modems, and multiplexers. The SMDS carrier will own some intermediate nodes.
- Carrier equipment — WAN switches that perform high-speed switching.
- SNI (Subscriber Network Interface) — Demarcation between customer's equipment and the carrier network.

SIP (the SMDS Interface Protocol) is the media access method to the SMDS network. SIP is based on the DQDB (Distributed Queue Dual Bus) protocol. DQDB is an open standard for connecting MANs (Metropolitan Area Networks). Routers, multiplexers, and modems use DQDB as the media access method to SMDS network services.

The SIP protocol is the main protocol implementation in SMDS. The SIP protocol has three layers. Layer 1 defines the physical media connectivity; Layer 2 and Layer 3 define the data link layer functionality.

How SMDS Works

SMDS connectivity functions by way of a unique network address. Bellcore, the organization responsible for addressing on SMDS networks, assigns addresses as shown in Figure 2-12.

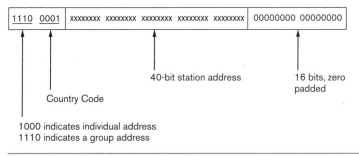

Figure 2-12 *SMDS addressing*

Since SMDS is a connectionless protocol, network addressing is accomplished by inserting the SMDS node address in the destination field of the SMDS frame.

SMDS data transfer is accomplished through the SIP protocol. The SIP protocol's three levels provide functionality as follows:

- SIP Level 3 — (OSI Layer 2) expands frames with SMDS source and destination addresses including 64-bit addresses.

- SIP Level 2 — (OSI Layer 2) takes frames from SIP Level 3 and adds header and trailer. The frames are packaged into 44-byte sections and are transmitted to the destination address. The 44-byte sections are called PDUs (Protocol Data Units).

- SIP Level 1 — (OSI Layer 1) specifies physical connections and provides timing for transmission media.

Figure 2-13 shows a sample SMDS internetwork.

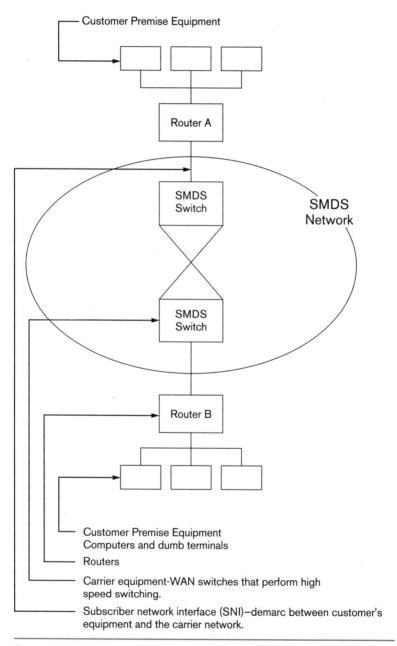

Figure 2-13 *Sample SMDS internetwork*

Summary

SMDS is a high-speed technology that can offer up to DS3 speeds in WAN environments. Frame Relay is another high-speed WAN technology that has gained in popularity over SMDS.

Advantages

The following list summarizes the advantages of SMDS:

- Easy administration for network personnel as network grows
- High-speed data transfer

Disadvantages

The following list summarizes the disadvantages of SMDS:

- Expensive as compared to other WAN technologies
- Not implemented in a wide-scale; fewer skilled engineers

Token Ring/802.5

Token Ring is a campus/LAN access technology that passes data traffic over IBM LAN networks.

Description

Token Ring was developed by IBM as its proprietary LAN access technology. The IEEE 802.5 specification for token passing is compatible with IBM's Token Ring implementation, and, in general, Token Ring and 802.5 are synonymous.

Token Ring networks use token-passing to transmit data over the LAN. The token is actually a frame bit that is changed when a station has data to send over the wire. If a station has possession of the token, or the frame bit has changed to indicate possession of the token, then data can be sent. Only when the transmission is complete and the station has released the token is the network available for transmission by another station. This method eliminates collisions and media contention.

Token Ring networks have a method to prioritize token possession sequences. The method, called access priority, is a process where certain stations on the network have priority and privileges to access the network more frequently.

When a station fails on a Token Ring network, or if the communication to a station has been lost, the remaining stations will attempt to reconfigure a new network topology. When a station detects a failure, it sends a beacon frame to its nearest neighbor. The new network topology is detected, and, usually, data transfer can proceed to all stations except the failed station. Most new network implementations are based on Ethernet as opposed to Token Ring technology. Ethernet currently has the advantage of reliability and ease of use.

How Token Ring Works

Figure 2-14 shows the typical token-passing methodology on a Token Ring network.

Summary

Token Ring was developed by IBM as its proprietary LAN access technology. The IEEE 802.5 specification for token passing is compatible with IBM's Token Ring implementation.

Advantages

Token Ring is a popular LAN access technology; there are many skilled network personnel available for support.

Disadvantages

The following list summarizes the disadvantages of Token Ring:

- Costlier to implement and scale than Ethernet
- Not as reliable as Ethernet

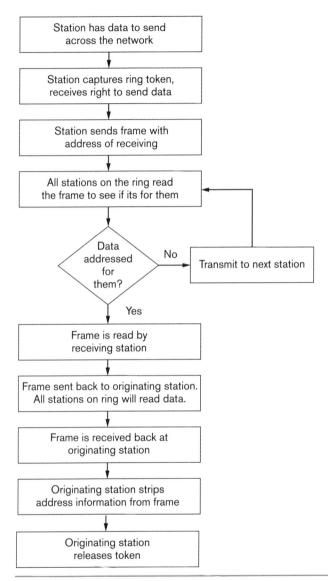

Figure 2-14 *Token-passing methodology as it works on a Token Ring network*

Key Points

Each network technology or access method has its advantages and disadvantages. Many options are available. You'll need to consider the overall cost of implementation, including long-term support, ability to be upgraded, compatibility with the existing infrastructure, and how your client or company is structured. Geography, politics, and budget will steer you or your client to the technology that is best suited for your needs. Here's a summary of the technologies that were presented in this chapter.

- ATM is a newer technology that has still not gained widespread acceptance. Although it's a one-technology solution for voice, data, and video, it does have disadvantages as far as complexity and higher implementation costs.

- DSL is a promising new access technology that uses existing telephone lines to provide multimedia service to end subscribers.

- Ethernet is a simple and widely implemented technology for internetworking transmission over campus and LAN networks. Ethernet is the most popular technology for smaller networks.

- FDDI was developed in the mid-1980s as a replacement technology for Token Ring and Ethernet networks. The FDDI specification is for a token-passing dual-ring LAN implementation using fiber optic 100Mbps media.

- Frame Relay is a packet-switching technology that takes advantage of increased reliability and stability in transmission media. Frame Relay is a common replacement for slower X.25 networks.

- Gigabit Ethernet is a high-speed LAN technology that is being developed to replace traditional Ethernet implementations. Gigabit Ethernet has the ability to provide 1Gbps of bandwidth on LANs and campus-style internetworks.

- ISDN is a high-speed dial-up access method using digital phone lines. Its one main advantage is the ability for home users and telecommuters to have high-speed access to the Internet and corporate WANs.

- PPP is a method to transfer data over point-to-point serial communication links in a multi-vendor network. PPP has gained widespread acceptance due to its ability to work in a variety of protocol and internetworking environments.

- SMDS is a high-speed technology that can offer up to DS3 speeds in WAN environments. Frame Relay is another high-speed WAN technology that has gained in popularity over SMDS.

- Token Ring was developed by IBM as its proprietary LAN access technology. The IEEE 802.5 specification for token passing is compatible with IBM's Token Ring implementation.

Part II

Choosing Your Network Protocols

Chapter 3

Routing Protocols

With the different and sometimes confusing array of network routing protocols and their uses, it's a challenge to understand, plan, test, and implement the correct protocol for your Cisco network.

This chapter will cover several of the more popular network routing protocols in use today. For reference, each protocol is listed in alphabetical order:

- BGP (Border Gateway Protocol)
- EIGRP (Enhanced Interior Gateway Routing Protocol)
- IGRP (Interior Gateway Routing Protocol)
- IS-IS (Intermediate System to Intermediate System) (OSI Protocol)
- NLSP (NetWare Link Services Protocol)
- OSPF (Open Shortest Path First)
- RIP v1 (Routing Information Protocol, version 1)
- RIP v2 (Routing Information Protocol, version 2)

Each section in this chapter describes a particular internetworking protocol, followed by information about how the protocol actually works within an internetwork. In addition, there's a summary of the advantages and disadvantages of each protocol.

At the end of this chapter, you will have a better understanding of the major network routing protocols in use today and, more importantly, how one or more of these will fit into your network design.

You can use this information to be able to discuss the advantages and features of each routing protocol with your peers, your boss, and your clients.

BGP (Border Gateway Protocol)

Border Gateway Protocol is a link-state exterior routing protocol that is in prominent use today on the Internet.

Description

BGP is a link-state protocol that was developed to replace the old exterior gateway protocol, Exterior Gateway Protocol (EGP). BGP is now the standard exterior gateway protocol in use on the Internet.

Caution

Don't confuse the Exterior Gateway Protocol (EGP), which is a routing protocol, with exterior gateway protocol types. BGP is an exterior routing protocol that is replacing EGP.

The main function of the BGP is to perform interdomain routing in an IP network, and it addresses the task of path determination.

BGP systems exchange network-reachability information with other BGP systems. This information exchange is used to create a network topology map of the connectivity between autonomous systems. In a BGP network, certain routers act as BGP speakers to learn about all the multiple paths on the internetwork. The best path is selected, and the IP routing table is forwarded to neighboring BGP routers.

There are three types of routing that BGP performs:

- Pass-through autonomous system routing is used between BGP peer routers. Traffic is passed between peer BGP routers over a non-BGP autonomous system. A BGP router receives traffic destined for a BGP peer network and must traverse a non-BGP autonomous system.

- Interautonomous system routing is the type of routing that occurs on the Internet. Peer routers use BGP to maintain a consistent topology map of the internetwork. BGP is used to select path determination and routing. Interautonomous routing is also called External BGP.

- Intra-autonomous system routing is used between BGP peer routers within the same autonomous system. BGP is used to maintain a consistent topology map of the internetwork as well as router selection and external connectivity to outside autonomous systems. Intra-autonomous routing is also called Internal BGP.

How BGP Works

BGP uses routing metrics to maintain the network topology routing tables. Each BGP router maintains a routing table that contains network path information. When a BGP router initializes in the internetwork, the entire routing table is exchanged with neighboring routers. After the initial exchange, the routing table is updated only when an update from a neighboring router is received.

BGP routers communicate through a series of message types. There are four main message types:

- Open Message — This initiates a BGP session between neighboring BGP routers. An open message is sent by each side of the communications link.

- Update Message — This provides routing updates to peer BGP systems. An update message is sent, and a consistent network topology map is defined.

- Notification Message — This is sent to peer routers when errors are detected on a BGP network.

- Keep-Alive Message — This message maintains sessions and notifies BGP peer routers of router status.

BGP works within an autonomous system to assure that all routing paths are reachable before advertising routes to an external autonomous system. Intra-autonomous routing is used between peer BGP routers to verify routes. This information is distributed to Interior Gateway Routing Protocols, such as OSPF (Open Shortest Path First), that are running with the autonomous system.

BGP selects an autonomous system path to announce to BGP routers. BGP has a path selection algorithm that selects a system path based on criteria in this order:

1. BGP administrative weight
2. Local preference
3. Local router source
4. Shortest autonomous system path
5. Lowest origin code
6. Lowest MED (Multi Exit Discriminator) metric
7. External paths over Internal paths

8. If only Internal paths, closest neighbor

9. Lowest IP address value for BGP Router ID

Figure 3-1 shows an example of BGP routing.

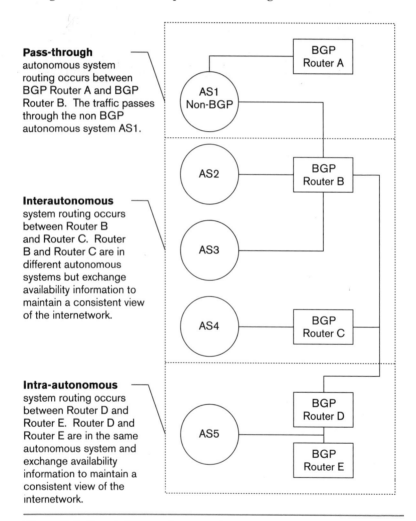

Pass-through autonomous system routing occurs between BGP Router A and BGP Router B. The traffic passes through the non BGP autonomous system AS1.

Interautonomous system routing occurs between Router B and Router C. Router B and Router C are in different autonomous systems but exchange availability information to maintain a consistent view of the internetwork.

Intra-autonomous system routing occurs between Router D and Router E. Router D and Router E are in the same autonomous system and exchange availability information to maintain a consistent view of the internetwork.

Figure 3-1 *Sample BGP routing examples*

Summary

BGP has replaced EGP (Exterior Gateway Protocol) as the exterior gateway routing protocol of choice on the Internet. BGP can be used to route between domains connecting an organization or to reliably connect to the Internet.

Advantages

The following list summarizes the advantages of BGP:

- Compatible with hierarchically designed networks
- Scalable
- Reliable
- Supports CIDR (classless interdomain routing)
- Multihome capability
- Supports route aggregation

Disadvantages

The following list summarizes the disadvantages of BGP:

- Complex routing protocol, not easy to configure or support
- High bandwidth links needed

EIGRP (Enhanced Interior Gateway Routing Protocol)

The Enhanced Interior Gateway Routing Protocol is a distance-vector interior gateway routing protocol that is used exclusively in Cisco networks.

Description

Enhanced IGRP was developed by Cisco Systems as a replacement for IGRP (Interior Gateway Routing Protocol). The main feature of EIGRP is enhanced convergence capabilities due to the DUAL (diffusing-update algorithm) routing algorithm that was selected for use with the EIGRP protocol. DUAL is a specification for routers to store neighboring information to allow quick routing updates and network convergence.

Tip

Enhanced IGRP has also been identified as a link-state routing protocol because of its enhanced routing algorithm.

There are several key concepts that make up an EIGRP configuration:

- Neighbor Table — Holds entries for adjacent neighborhood routers. The neighbor table also holds sequence and acknowledgement information.

- Topology Table — Contains all destinations advertised by neighboring routers. Also included is the advertised metric, which is the metric stored in each neighboring routing table. Topology table destination entries are in one of two states. When a router is not calculating a route, it is said to be in a passive state. When a router is in the process of calculating a route, it is in the active state.

- Feasible Successors — Routers that are downstream with respect to the destination. Feasible successor allow a router to avoid active state route calculation.

- Packet Formats — There are five types of packets in an EIGRP network. These include:

  - Hello/Ack — Multicast used for neighbor discovery
  - Updates — Conveys reachability information
  - Queries — Active state request
  - Replies — Sent in response to queries
  - Request — Gets specific neighbor information

- Route Tag — Routes are tagged with interior or exterior route information. Interior routes operate within an autonomous system. Exterior routes are static routes or routes that have been acquired from a routing protocol discovery process.

How EIGRP Works

There are four new components implemented as an improvement over IGRP:

- Neighbor Discovery — When a router becomes unreachable, routers within the internetwork must learn of the router state. Each router periodically sends out Hello packets to other routers and receives Hello packets as well. With this verification procedure, routers are assured that neighboring routers are functioning as part of the routing process.

■ The Reliable Transport Protocol — Used to guarantee data packet delivery to all EIGRP neighboring routers.

■ DUAL (diffusing update algorithm) — Used as the decision-maker for route computation. DUAL selects the most efficient loop-free route, which is then inserted into the routing table. A feasible successor is also determined and inserted into the routing table. The feasible successor is guaranteed to not be part of a routing loop and is a least-cost path alternative to be used for packet forwarding. If there is no feasible successor available, a new route is computed and a feasible successor is chosen. DUAL attempts to avoid this route computation by testing for a feasible successor whenever a topology change occurs.

■ Protocol Dependent Modules — Responsible for network layer protocol-specific requirements. EIGRP supports AppleTalk, IP, and NetWare protocols.

EIGRP is fully compatible with IGRP. An EIGRP implementation can be done incrementally, with no adverse effect on existing routes. IGRP routes are treated as external routes by EIGRP and are easily configured with the new EIGRP networks.

EIGRP is compatible and can redistribute routes for:

■ RIP (Routing Information Protocol)

■ IS-IS (Intermediate System to Intermediate System)

■ BGP (Border Gateway Protocol)

■ OSPF (Open Shortest Path First)

■ AppleTalk RTMP (AppleTalk Routing Table Maintenance Protocol)

■ Novell IPX RIP (Novell Internetwork Packet Exchange, Routing Information Protocol)

■ Novell IPX SAP (Novell Internetwork Packet Exchange, Service Advertisement Protocol)

Tip

Both IGRP and EIGRP are Cisco-specific interior routing protocols. Both are only compatible with Cisco routing environments.

Summary

EIGRP has significant advantages over its predecessor, IGRP. The main enhancement is the convergence efficiency due to the DUAL route selection method.

Advantages

The following list summarizes the advantages of EIGRP:

- Very quick convergence on large networks
- Less bandwidth-intensive than IGRP
- Scales well
- Max hop count of 224
- Supports VLSM (Variable Length Subnet Mask)
- Supports AppleTalk, IP, and Novell NetWare through Protocol Dependent Modules
- Fully compatible with IGRP

Disadvantages

One key disadvantage to EIGRP concerns compatibility with the Cisco IOS. If EIGRP is deployed in Cisco environments running Cisco IOS versions that were released prior to May 1996, certain routing problems can occur on low bandwidth networks. This shouldn't be a concern, however, since Cisco IOS versions released prior to May 1996 weren't Y2K-compliant and therefore weren't fully functional after 12-31-1999.

IGRP (Interior Gateway Routing Protocol)

Interior Gateway Routing Protocol is a Cisco-specific protocol that operates as a distance vector routing protocol.

Description

IGRP was developed by Cisco to enable routing in heterogeneous, autonomous systems. The original intent was to create stable routing, no routing loops, quick network convergence, and low routing overhead.

There are three types of routes advertised within an IGRP network:

- Interior — Routes between subnets in the network attached to an access server interface
- System — Routes to networks within an autonomous system
- Exterior — Routes to networks outside the autonomous system

IGRP uses a combination metric for routing based on several factors that can be manually configured by a network administrator. The routing metric for IGRP is a combination of:

- Bandwidth — Bandwidth of the lowest bandwidth segment in the path
- Delay — Sum of all the delays on outgoing interfaces
- Reliability — Reliability of the slowest link
- Load — Heaviest load on any link

To reduce the possible occurrence of routing loops, IGRP uses split horizon, poison reverse, hold-down intervals, and flush updates.

 Tip

Although EIGRP has been developed as a successor to IGRP, there are thousands of IGRP networks in use today. If the existing network does not have any routing problems to fix, IGRP is a good stable routing environment.

How IGRP works

There are several key components to the IGRP routing process that work to enhance the stability of the protocol.

- Timers — Four timers that set frequencies for routing update processes:
  - Update Timer — Specifies how the frequently routing updates should be sent. The IGRP default is 90 seconds.
  - Invalid Timer — Specifies routing wait time before declaring a route invalid if it has not received any routing update messages. IGRP default is three times the update period, or 270 seconds.
  - Hold-down Timer — Specifies the hold-down period. IGRP default is three times the update period +10 seconds, or 280 seconds.

- Flush Timer — How much time passes before a route should be flushed from the routing table. IGRP default is seven times the routing update period, or 630 seconds.

- Split Horizon — To provide extra stability, IGRP uses the split horizon mechanism to prevent routing loops. Split horizon prevents information about a specific route to be sent back to the direction from which it came.

- Poison Reverse Updates — Used to prevent large routing loops. Poison reverse sends explicit updates that indicate that a network or subnet is unreachable.

- Hold-downs — When a router goes down or becomes otherwise disconnected from the network, neighboring routers will stop receiving updates and will calculate new routes. These new routes will be sent to neighboring routers. These are triggered updates that filter through the internetwork. It is possible that a router may still be advertising the downed router as reachable. A hold-down, or the hold-down period, is usually set to be slightly longer than the full network convergence time.

Figure 3-2 shows an example of IGRP routes.

Summary

IGRP is a stable and widely used routing protocol in Cisco network environments. There are advantages to remaining with IGRP rather than a large-scale conversion to the more popular and efficient Enhanced IGRP (EIGRP).

Advantages

The following list summarizes the advantages of IGRP:

- Scalable
- Easy migration from RIP
- Uses multiple metrics for routing decisions
- Fully compatible with EIGRP
- Easy migration path to EIGRP

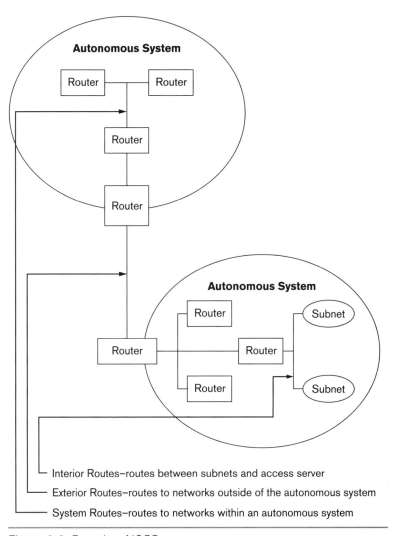

Figure 3-2 *Examples of IGRP routes*

Disadvantages

The following list summarizes the disadvantages of IGRP:

- No support for VLSM (Variable Length Subnet Mask)
- Uses more bandwidth than EIGRP
- Slower network convergence

IS-IS (Intermediate System to Intermediate System)/ OSI Protocol Suite

Intermediate System to Intermediate System is a link-state interior gateway routing protocol.

Description

The ISO (International Organization for Standardization) developed the OSI routing protocol suite to be used in conjunction with the OSI protocol suite.

In an OSI routing network, there are several concepts that are important and unique:

- End Systems — Non-routing network nodes.
- Intermediate Systems — Routers or routing-capable network components.
- Area — Group of contiguous networks and hosts.
- Domain — Collection of connected areas.
- Level 1 Routing — Understand the topology of their immediate area, including end systems and routers. Level 1 routers route all information to a Level 2 router in their area.
- Level 2 Routing — Understand the Level 2 topology. Only Level 2 routers can communicate with external routers outside of the routing domain.

The ISO included three main protocols in its suite, Intermediate System to Intermediate System (IS-IS), End System to End System (ES-IS), and Interdomain Routing Protocol (IDRP).

IS-IS (Intermediate System to Intermediate System) is a link-state, interior gateway routing protocol that builds a network topology by flooding the network with link-state information. IS-IS contains the Hello Protocol, which is used to identify Level 1 and Level 2 routers. The Flooding Protocol floods the network with link-state messages during topology updates.

ES-IS (End System to Intermediate System) is a protocol that works by defining how low-end systems communicate with routers. This path discovery works by a process called configuration.

IDRP (Interdomain Routing Protocol) is a protocol that distinguishes how routers communicate with the routers in different routing domains.

How IS-IS Works

Figure 3-3 shows how the OSI routing protocols work within an internetwork.

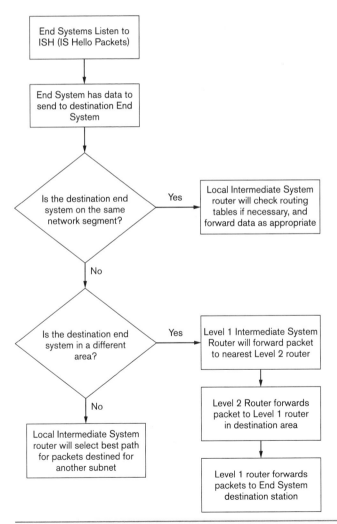

Figure 3-3 *How IS-IS and the OSI routing protocols work*

Figure 3-4 shows a sample OSI routing network.

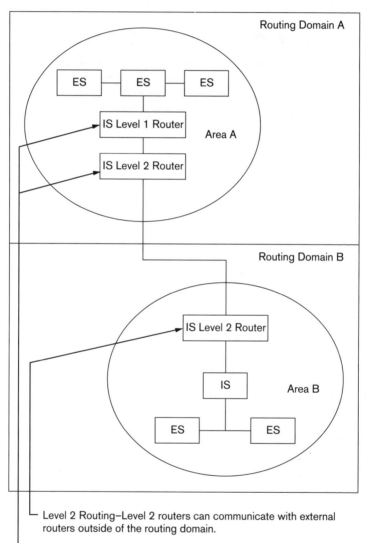

Figure 3-4 *Sample OSI Routing Network*

Summary

The ISO developed the OSI routing protocol suite to be used in conjunction with the OSI protocol suite. IS-IS is a link-state routing protocol.

Advantages

The following list summarizes the advantages of IS-IS:

- Very quick convergence on large networks
- Compatible with CNLP (Connectionless Network Layer Protocol)
- Supports authentication
- Scalable

Disadvantages

High use of router resources during topology updates is the one main disadvantage to IS-IS in enterprise WAN environments.

NLSP (NetWare Link Services Protocol)

Netware Link Services Protocol is a link-state routing protocol developed for Novell NetWare internetworks.

Description

NLSP was developed by Novell to overcome some limitations of IPX RIP (IPX Routing Information Protocol) and SAP (Service Advertisement Protocol). NLSP was developed to replace IPX RIP and has significant advantages over IPX RIP.

NLSP is able to reduce data packet size due to support of IPX header compression. NLSP also reduces routing update traffic by sending routing information only to NLSP routers.

Support for load balancing is another advantage that NLSP has over IPX RIP. NLSP is able to support 127 hops as opposed to 15 hops for RIP. Also, NLSP can be addressed in a hierarchical fashion. The hierarchical routing is organized by area, domain, and global internetwork components. Several key concepts concerning NSLP routing include:

- Area—Collection of connected networks all having the same area address
- Routing Domain—Collection of areas belonging to the same organization
- Global Internetwork—Collection of domains belonging to different organizations

NLSP routing incorporates routing levels to determine how routers communicate within the internetwork.

- Level 1 routing—Data transfer between routers within the same area. Level 1 routers communicate with only Level 1 and Level 2 routers.
- Level 2 routing—Routing between areas. A group of Level 2 routers will form a Routing Domain. Level 2 routers communicate with all Level 1 routers and other Level 2 routers, as well as with Level 3 routers.
- Level 3 routing—Routing between Routing Domains. Level 3 routers communicate with Level 2 routers and other Level 3 routers.

How NLSP Works

NLSP routers exchange Hello packets to determine neighbor reachability information (adjacency information). Adjacency information is stored in the adjacency database.

Each NLSP router will query the adjacency database to construct a link-state packet (LSP) that contains neighboring router information. Each of the routers on the internetwork contains an LSP. All LSPs are combined into one database, the link-state database.

To keep the link-state database current, all NLSP routers synchronize the LSPs throughout the internetwork whenever a topology change occurs. The two specific methods to assure that network convergence information and topology changes are correct are flooding and receipt confirmation.

- Flooding—When an NLSP router detects a topology change, the router creates a new LSP and sends it to its neighbor router. The receiver router will check to see if the LSP is new based on the sequence number. If the LSP is a newer update, the LSP is sent to all the neighboring routers, except to the one that it was sent from.

- Receipt confirmation—On a WAN, a router receives an updated LSP and sends an acknowledgement. On a LAN, the designated router (DR) sends out a complete sequence number packet (CSNP) containing all LSP sequence numbers. Routers can synchronize with the latest link-state database.

Migrating from IPX RIP to NLSP can be accomplished by upgrading one system at a time, as NLSP is backward-compatible with IPX RIP networks. Table 3-1 shows some general guidelines for migrating from RIP to NLSP based on network number volume.

Table 3-1 *Migration Guidelines for NLSP*

Number of Network Numbers	Routing Loops Present?	NLSP Migration Solution
<100	N/A	Single Routing Area
100–400	No	Single Routing Area
100–400	Yes	Single Routing Area
>400	No	Multiple Areas
>400	Yes	Multiple Areas

Caution

On a network with between 100–400 network numbers and routing loops present, it's important to upgrade in a hierarchical fashion. First upgrade the core routers and then the local area routers.

Figure 3-5 shows the NLSP routing process.

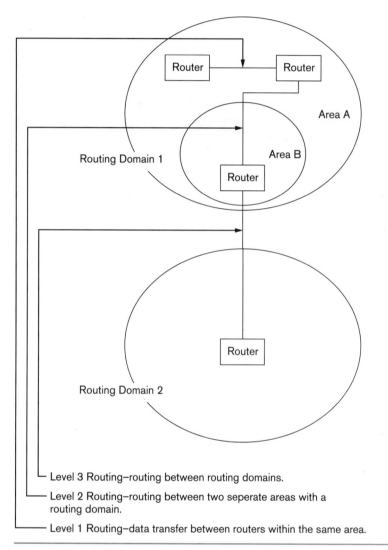

Figure 3-5 *NLSP Routing*

Summary

NLSP is a newer and improved routing protocol developed to replace IPX RIP. NSLP supports load balancing and only sends routing updates throughout the internetwork. NLSP is also backward-compatible with

IPX RIP routers. A migration plan and a possible network redesign may be in order to take advantage of NLSP features.

Advantages

The following list summarizes the advantages of NSLP:

- Improved routing over IPX RIP.
- More efficient than IPX RIP.
- Scalable.
- NSLP routers store full topology map, not just next hop information.
- Routing updates contain only update information, not full routing table.

Disadvantages

Networks will be migrating from IPX RIP and SAP. To take advantage of NLSP routing and addressing, a more hierarchical network design may be needed. Implementing a hierarchical-designed network can be expensive.

OSPF (Open Shortest Path First)

Open Shortest Path First is a link-state interior gateway routing protocol.

Description

OSPF is a link-state protocol that was originally developed to meet the needs of larger heterogeneous enterprise networks. OSPF was designed and is being presented as a replacement to the older and widely used routing protocol: RIP (Routing Information Protocol).

OSPF networks operate within an Autonomous System (AS), which is a collection of networks that share a common routing strategy.

OSPF networks are designed in entities called *areas*. Areas control the traffic and reduce memory and CPU utilization on the routers. Areas are a group of routers that route from the same topology database and maintain the same routing algorithms. Area 0 is the backbone area required in an OSPF network. Each of the other areas in the network is connected to the OSPF Area 0 routers with an Area Border Router (ABR). Stub areas are

OSPF areas that have internal routes but no external routes other than a default route.

There are four types of routers that can be present in an OSPF network:

- Area Border Routers (ABRs) can attach to several different areas in the network
- Internal Routers (IRs) have all interfaces connected to the same area.
- Autonomous System Border Routers (ASBRs) connect to more than one Autonomous System.
- Backbone Routers (BRs) have only interface to the network backbone.

OSPF propagates only updates to the internetwork, not full routing tables during a network update. First, a metric (cost of the transmission) is determined, then the LSA (Link-state Advertisements) report the status of all neighboring routers and the cost of sending the packets on that interface.

OSPF routers use the SPF (Shortest Path First) algorithm to calculate the shortest path to the destination. The SPF algorithm is frequently called the *Dijkstra* algorithm in recognition of the creator of the algorithm. The Dijkstra algorithm is a complex mathematical formula that determines the least cost path. These calculations on least cost populate the link-state database that is resident on each router in the internetwork.

Tip

The word "Open" in Open Shortest Path First is in reference to the open architecture of the routing protocol.

How OSPF Works

There are three important components to the OSPF protocol. The first, the Hello protocol, verifies router operation on the network. Next, the Exchange protocol synchronizes the routing table database. Finally, the Flooding protocol distributes link-state changes throughout the network.

Step 1: The Hello Protocol

The Hello protocol verifies that other routers on the internetwork are up and operational. It also processes the election of Designated Routers (DRs). An OSPF router will first use the Hello protocol to verify that all links are operational. Upon inspecting the internetwork, neighboring routers will be discovered. The OSPF router will send out Hello packets to neighboring routers and receive Hello packets in response. Hello packets are also used as keep-alive messages to maintain the neighbor relationship with other routers in the area. The Hello protocol will then elect a designated router (DR) and backup designated router. The DR is responsible for generating link-state advertisements (LSAs) for the entire internetwork. This will reduce the network traffic and size of the topology database.

Step 2: The Exchange Protocol

The Exchange protocol is used to synchronize the routing database for the internetwork. Once two routers have established communication, the Exchange protocol will synchronize the link-state database. Once this synchronization has occurred, the routers are *adjacent*.

Step 3: The Flooding Protocol

The Flooding protocol distributes the link-state database whenever a change occurs in the internetwork. A router that changes a link-state will send a flooding packet to inform the other routers of the change or changes. This flooding packet is sent (or flooded) out to all of the routers interfaces.

Figure 3-6 shows a sample OSPF internetwork.

Summary

OSPF is a link-state routing protocol that has gained wide acceptance as a replacement for RIP (Routing Information Protocol).

Advantages

The following list summarizes the advantages of OSPF:

- Is compatible with hierarchical designed networks
- Not bandwidth-intensive
- Quick convergence
- Sends multicast frames, not broadcast frames
- Open protocol, available for third-party implementations

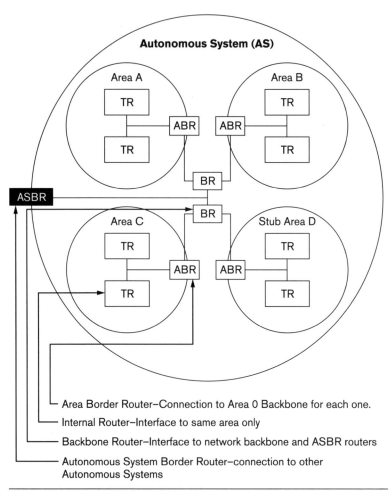

Area Border Router—Connection to Area 0 Backbone for each one.

Internal Router—Interface to same area only

Backbone Router—Interface to network backbone and ASBR routers

Autonomous System Border Router—connection to other Autonomous Systems

Figure 3-6 *Sample OSPF internetwork*

Disadvantages

The following list summarizes the disadvantages of OSPF:

- The design requirement that an OSPF network be configured into areas makes migration difficult.

- Not as scalable as other routing protocols. Constant updates within an OSPF network will require constant reconfigurations and evaluations.

RIP (Routing Information Protocol)

Routing Information Protocol is a distance-vector routing protocol that is the routing protocol that is responsible for early Internet connectivity.

Description

RIP is a distance-vector routing protocol used extensively on the Internet. RIP uses hop count as the routing metric for best path selection.

RIP sends UDP data packets to exchange routing updates when the network topology changes and at regular timed intervals. RIP routing tables are then updated with the best path selection.

There are several factors that provide routing stability on an RIP network:

- Hop count limit — RIP specifies a maximum hop count of 15. This feature is used to reduce the likelihood of routing loops.

- Hold-downs — Used to tell routers to hold down or wait to update any changes that might affect unreachable routers for a specific period of time. Hold-downs prevent regular routing updates from advertising unreachable routes.

- Split horizons — Used as a process to not send information about a route from the direction from which it came.

- Poison reverse updates — Used to stop larger routing loops in a RIP network. Poison reverse updates are updates that announce a network path as unreachable, rather than excluding it from network updates.

How RIP Works

A router configured with RIP will send out periodic updates to the internetwork every 30 seconds. In addition, anytime a topology change occurs, each RIP-enabled router sends out routing table updates.

An RIP router receiving an update will compare the information with its existing internal routing table. If the updated information has a smaller metric to a specific destination, the changes are reflected in the routing table. If a router becomes unreachable, it is not able to communicate the topology change. RIP uses a variety of timers to overcome this problem. There are three types of timers that are used in an RIP network:

- Update Timer — Interval for periodic routing updates. RIP routers send the entire routing table to its neighboring routers. Default is 30 seconds.

- Invalid Timer — If a specific route is not heard from within a specified amount of time (default is 180 seconds), the routers assume that the route is no longer available. An invalid timer message is sent to all neighboring routers with an update about the unreachable route.

- Flush Timer — If a route has not been heard from for 90 seconds (default value) after the Invalid timer has been sent, the router will inform its neighboring routers, and then the route is flushed from the router's routing table.

There are a few differences between RIP v1 and RIP v2. RIP v2 was developed to expand the amount of information carried in an RIP message. RIP v2 also contains additional security features such as authentication. RIP v2 is a distance-vector protocol that uses hop count as the routing metric.

RIP v2 has several key advantages over RIP v1:

- Authentication — RIP v1 has very limited security features. An authentication mechanism was incorporated into RIP v2.

- Classless interdomain routing — Allows routers to group routes together to reduce routing information.

- VLSM (variable length subject masking) — RIP v2 routers can specify a different length subnet mask for the same network number at different locations in the network.

The default Cisco IOS is configured to receive RIP v1 and RIP v2 packets, but only sends RIP v2 packets. You can configure Cisco routers to send and receive only RIP v2 packets. Table 3-2 shows the major differences between RIP version 1 and RIP version 2.

Table 3.2 *Differences Between RIP v1 and RIP v2 Protocols*

Version	RIP v1	RIP v2
Type	Distance vector	Distance vector
Use	Interior gateway	Interior gateway
Addressing	Classful	Classless
Metric	Hop count	Hop count
Hop count	15	15
Convergence time	Long	Long
Memory use	Low	Low
CPU use	Low	Low
Bandwidth use	High	High
Authentication method	No	Yes
Supports VLSM	No	Yes
Configuration	Easy	Easy
Design	Easy	Easy
Troubleshooting	Easy	Easy
Compatible with other RIP version	Yes	Yes

Caution

The Cisco IOS default setting is to receive both RIP v1 and RIP v2 information and to only send RIP v1 information. You must configure the router interface to send and receive RIP v1 or send and receive RIP v2 information.

Summary

RIP v1 is a proven and widely implemented protocol. Although it is easy to configure, there are major security concerns.

Advantages

The following list summarizes the advantages of RIPv1:

- Easy to configure
- Proven protocol, widely used on Internet
- Stable
- Compatible with a wide variety of internetworking systems

Disadvantages

The following list summarizes the disadvantages of OSPF:

- Slow convergence compared with other routing protocols
- Not efficient routing on variable bandwidth paths
- Max hop count of 15 limits practical use in large networks
- Creates high bandwidth usage with full routing updates
- No authentication method

RIP Version 2 Summary

RIP v2 has significant advantages over RIP v1. RIP v2 remains a distance-vector routing protocol that uses hop count as the routing metric, and adds support for VLSM, authentication, and classless interdomain routing.

Advantages

The following list summarizes the advantages of RIP v2:

- Support for VLSM
- Authentication mechanism added; not available with RIP v1
- Compatible with a wide variety of internetworking systems
- Easy to configure

Disadvantages

The following list summarizes the disadvantages of RIP v2:

- Uses hop count as only metric.
- Max hop count of 15 limits practical use in large networks.

Key Points

Network routing protocols have been developed for specific purposes. There are many routing protocols available. Some of the older technologies such as RIP have proven themselves in some ways and are lacking in others. Newer routing protocols such as OSPF and the Cisco proprietary IGRP protocols are widely implemented and gaining support in many internetworking scenarios. You'll need to consider cost to implement, application support, technical staff skills, budget, and corporate culture. Here's a summary of the routing protocols that were presented in this chapter.

- BGP has replaced EGP as the exterior gateway routing protocol of choice on the Internet. BGP can be used to route between domains connecting an organization or to reliably connect to the Internet.

- EIGRP has significant advantages over its predecessor, IGRP. The main enhancement is the convergence efficiency due to the DUAL route selection method.

- IGRP is a stable and widely used routing protocol in Cisco network environments. There are advantages to remaining with IGRP rather than a large-scale conversion to the more popular and efficient Enhanced IGRP (EIGRP).

- IS-IS is a link-state routing protocol that was developed by the ISO to be used in conjunction with the OSI protocol suite.

- NLSP is an improved routing protocol developed to replace IPX RIP. NSLP supports load balancing and only sends routing updates throughout the internetwork. NLSP is also backward-compatible with IPX RIP routers.

- OSPF is a link-state routing protocol that has gained wide acceptance as a replacement for RIP.

- RIP v1 is a proven and widely implemented protocol. Although it is easy to configure, there are major security concerns.

- RIP v2 has significant advantages over RIP v1. RIP v2 remains a distance-vector routing protocol that uses hop count as the routing metric, and it adds support for VLSM, authentication, and classless interdomain routing.

Chapter 4

Protocol Suites

Most protocol suites were developed to meet a specific internetworking need within a proprietary network environment. Although most protocol suites can integrate with standard protocols, they generally operate within the context of the proprietary environment. TCP/IP is one major exception — universally used and widely accepted in almost any internetworking environment.

This chapter covers several of the more popular protocol suites in use today. For reference, each protocol suite is listed in alphabetical order:

- AppleTalk — Apple Corporation
- DECnet — Digital Equipment Corporation
- IBM SNA — IBM System Network Architecture
- Novell IPX — Novell Internetworking Packet Exchange
- TCP/IP — Transmission Control Protocol/Internet Protocol

Each section in this chapter describes a particular protocol suite, followed by information about how the protocol suite actually works within an internetwork. In addition, the advantages and disadvantages of each protocol suite are summarized.

AppleTalk

The AppleTalk protocol suite includes routing and routed protocols, interior and exterior gateway protocols, and distance-vector routing protocols.

Description

Apple, Inc. developed AppleTalk to allow network users to share access to printers and files, specifically on Macintosh computers. AppleTalk network capability was built into each Macintosh PC. The early Apple computers were inherently networked and provided network capabilities without end-user configuration or intervention.

Sockets, Nodes, Networks, and Zones are key concepts in an AppleTalk network environment.

- Sockets are addressable locations that are unique in an AppleTalk network.

- Nodes can be a variety of connected devices, including PCs, routers, or printers, on a network.

- Networks consist of one logical connection with attached nodes.

- Zones are a logical group of nodes or networks that are configured by network personnel.

In an AppleTalk network, each node is assigned to a Network and a Zone. Logical connections on AppleTalk networks can be made up of multiple nodes, routers, or bridges. There are two types of Networks in an AppleTalk environment, and these are Nonextended Networks (NN) and Extended Networks (EN). NNs are physical network segments that have network numbers that range between 1 and 1024. One network number supports an NN network, and one Zone can be configured for each NN. ENs can have multiple network numbers that belong to one physical network segment. ENs have generally replaced NNs. ENs can have multiple AppleTalk Zones configured.

How AppleTalk Works

When a Macintosh PC or other Apple computer connected to an AppleTalk network powers up and is connected to the network, the computer chooses a network layer address and verifies that the address is not in use.

There are several key protocols that make up the operation of an AppleTalk network and the AppleTalk protocol suite:

- AppleTalk Address Resolution Protocol (AARP) has not yet been retired, contrary to most people's belief. AARP associates AppleTalk network addresses with hardware addresses of Macintosh computers.

- Data Delivery Protocol (DDP) is a network layer protocol that provides services between network sockets. DDP administers AppleTalk addresses, providing connectionless socket-to-socket delivery of AppleTalk packets.

- Routing Table Maintenance Protocol (RTMP) is a distance-vector interior native routing protocol that establishes and maintains AppleTalk routing tables. Routing tables contain entries for each reachable network. A router coming up into an AppleTalk network will generate an initial routing table that will include port information, AppleTalk network numbers, and node information. RTMP performs full routing updates every 10 seconds.

- AppleTalk Update-Based Routing Protocol (AURP) is both an interior and exterior routing protocol that allows AppleTalk networks to be connected through a TCP/IP network to create a WAN environment. AURP performs packet encapsulation to transport AppleTalk packets through a TCP/IP network.

Figure 4-1 describes common AppleTalk network components.

Summary

AppleTalk was developed by Apple, Inc. to allow network users to share access to printers and files, specifically on Macintosh computers. AppleTalk network capability was built into each Macintosh PC. The early Apple computers were inherently networked and provided network capabilities without end-user configuration or intervention.

Advantages

The one main advantage of AppleTalk is its ability to seamlessly integrate into existing Macintosh-based networks.

Disadvantages

The AppleTalk RTMP can cause congestion with its frequent routing updates.

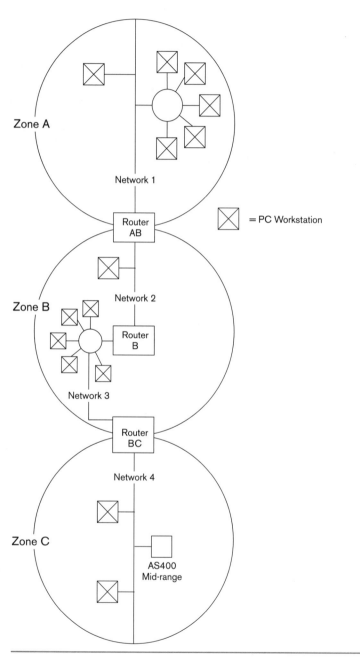

Figure 4-1 *AppleTalk network components*

DECnet (Digital Equipment Corporation)

DECnet is a suite of communication technologies developed by Digital Equipment Corporation. DECnet was developed to allow Digital mainframes to communicate with end systems.

Description

There are currently two main versions of DECnet in use today. DECnet Phase IV is the most widely implemented version and is based on Digital Network Architecture (DNA) Phase IV. The other more current release is DECnet Phase V, which is based on DNA Phase V.

How DECnet Works

Digital Network Architecture (DNA) is a network architecture that supports Digital proprietary as well as other standard protocols. The DECnet Routing Protocol (DRP) implements DECnet routing. DRP provides the functionality to find the best routing path in a DECnet network. The DRP routing metric is cost, which can be assigned by network personnel. Both hop count and bandwidth use can be included in the cost metric.

DRP uses a hierarchical method of routing within a Digital network environment. Level 1 routers communicate with end nodes and other Level 1 routers. Level 2 routers communicate with other Level 2 routers, which typically are in separate areas. Figure 4-2 shows the components of a DECnet hierarchical network.

Summary

DECnet is a suite of communication technologies developed by Digital Equipment Corporation. DECnet was developed to allow Digital mainframes to communicate with end systems.

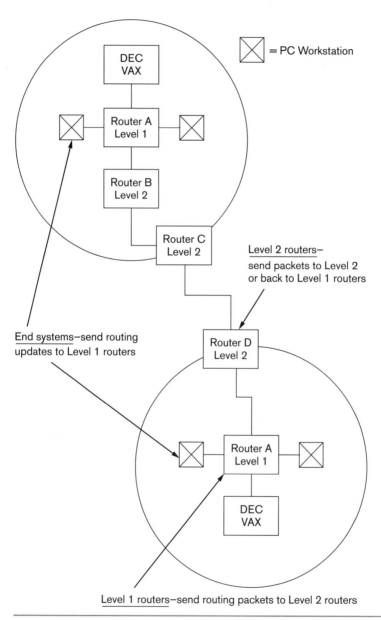

Figure 4-2 *DECnet hierarchical network*

Advantages

The following list summarizes the advantages of the DECnet protocol suite:

- Provides backward-compatibility for previous DECnet internetworks
- Proven technology, which has been in use for many years
- Works with standard protocols over LAN
- Fairly consistent with OSI model

Disadvantages

The disadvantage of the DECnet protocol suite is that it was developed specifically for Digital environments and its interoperability is limited by the proprietary architecture.

IBM SNA (System Network Architecture)

System Network Architecture (SNA) was developed by IBM to perform data communications functions within an IBM mainframe environment.

Description

SNA is a network model that maps very closely to the OSI reference model. There are several main components to the SNA network model:

- Data Link Control (DLC) defines protocols for hierarchical communication.
- Path Control performs network layer functions.
- Transmission Control provides end-to-end communication services.
- Data Flow Control determines sequencing and messaging.
- Presentation Services translate data formats.
- Transaction Services provide distributed processing or management application services.

The SNA environment is made up of three network addressable units. Logical Units (LU) provide end-user access on an SNA network. Physical Units (PU) are used to monitor and control network resources. They also cause action to occur within the network. Control Points (CP) manage SNA nodes and resources and determine which actions should be taken to provide needed network services.

How SNA Works

Two key parts of the SNA protocol suite are Synchronous Data Link Control (SDLC) and Advanced Peer-to-Peer Networking (APPN).

Synchronous Data Link Control

SDLC is an IBM protocol that manages synchronous, serially transmitted bit information over a data link. SDLC works between SNA devices using a CRC error checking and acknowledgement routine to reliably transmit data.

In an SNA network, there are two types of network nodes. A primary node is used to administer other secondary node stations. The primary node is responsible for session establishment to the secondary node. The primary node polls secondary nodes for data. Secondary nodes are used to transmit link information to primary nodes.

Within the primary-to-secondary node structure, there are several basic configurations that are used in an SDLC SNA network environment. In a point-to-point configuration, one primary node communicates with one secondary node. A multipoint configuration will allow one single primary node to communicate with a variety of secondary nodes. Loop configurations enable communication by connecting a primary node to the first and last secondary node. All of the other secondary nodes communicate through the loop to the primary node.

In most practical applications, SDLC works in half duplex mode, although it is capable of full duplex transmission. Primary nodes control the operation of all secondary nodes. Only a limited number of frames are sent per transmission, and all are controlled by the primary node, sometimes referred to as the master node.

The steps for transmitting over a point-to-multipoint link are:

1. Primary station A polls Secondary station B to send data.

2. Secondary B (a modem or CSU/DSU) will turn on Request To Send signal (RTS) to enable carrier on circuit.

3. Secondary B turns on Clear To Send (CTS) signal.

4. Secondary B transmits to Primary A.

5. Secondary B drops RTS signal.

6. Secondary D drops CTS signal.

7. Primary A polls next Secondary station to transmit, and the process is repeated through all multipoint circuits.

To assure reliable delivery of error-free data, SDLC uses a CRC byte. Correctly received frames are acknowledged by the receiving station. Acknowledgements are encoded in data packets so that acknowledgement packets are not sent back and forth from the receiving station.

Figure 4-3 shows a sample SDLC internetwork.

Advanced Peer-to-Peer Networking (APPN)

APPN is an enhancement to SNA that provides client/server LAN capabilities such as resource allocation and discovery. Network Node Control Points (CPs) are responsible to manage adjacent node communications.

There are three main types of nodes in an APPN network. Local Entry Networking (LEN) nodes participate in peer networking by using the services of an adjacent node. End Nodes access network services by using adjacent node access. Network Nodes connect to each other by single channels, called Transmission Groups (TGs). The Network Node Control Point (CP) manages resources of LEN nodes and End Nodes.

APPN resides in Cisco IOS software, licensed from IBM. APPN is used by applications to provide network data transport. A few of the features that Cisco APPN provides include:

- Priority queuing, custom queuing, or weighted fair queuing can be used with the SNA class of service to prioritize traffic and reserve bandwidth.

- SNMP management with CiscoWorks Blue management software.

Figure 4-4 shows APPN network components.

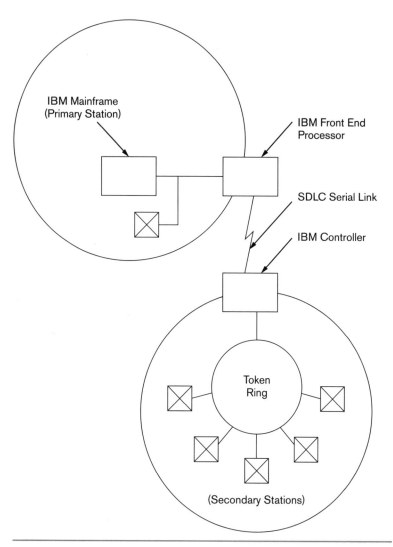

Figure 4-3 *SDLC internetwork*

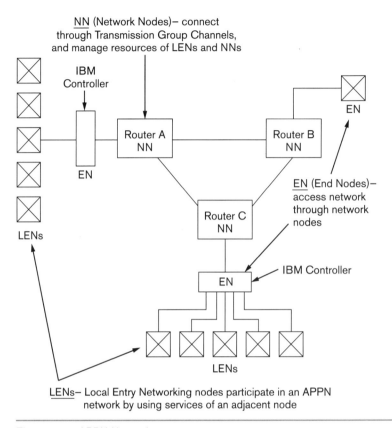

Figure 4-4 *APPN Network components*

Summary

System Network Architecture (SNA) was developed by IBM to perform data communications functions within an IBM mainframe environment. Two key parts of the SNA protocol suite are Synchronous Data Link Control (SDLC) and Advanced Peer-to-Peer Networking (APPN). SDLC is an IBM protocol that manages synchronous, serially transmitted bit information over a data link. APPN is an enhancement to SNA that provides client/server LAN capabilities such as resource allocation and discovery.

Advantages

The following list summarizes the advantages of the IBM protocol suite:

- SNA is a proven and widely used technology.
- SNA mainframes can be used as high-speed file servers.
- APPN supports native SNA routing.
- APPN supports peer-to-peer connection without VTAM involvement.
- SDLC is capable of point-to-point and multipoint configurations.

Disadvantages

One main disadvantage to using IBM SNA is that it is not optimized for WAN environments and data traffic switching.

NetWare IPX (Internetwork Packet Exchange)

NetWare IPX is a network protocol suite developed by Novell to route data packets though a Novell internetwork.

Description

The Novell NetWare protocol suite is comprised of IPX RIP, IPX Service Advertisement Protocol (IPX SAP), NetWare Core Protocol (NCP), and Sequenced Packet Exchange Protocol (SPX). Novell Link State Protocol (NLSP) is also part of the Novell protocol suite and is described in greater detail in Chapter 3. Here are the components of the Novell NetWare protocol suite and their specific uses:

- IPX RIP is a network layer service used for routing and addressing. IPX RIP sends routing updates every 60 seconds.
- IPX SAP is used by network components to advertise their services. Service advertisements are sent every 60 seconds. Routers use SAP to build a table of services and unique network addresses. NetWare client machines request services, and the router will reply with addressing information to fulfill network service requests.

- NCP is used by NetWare clients to access services on NetWare network servers. NCP manages access to file and print services.

- SPX is a connection-oriented protocol that is part of the IPX protocol stack. SPX is used to provide reliable delivery of data packets.

How NetWare IPX Works

Novell NetWare-configured network servers can (and do) act as network routers. These network routers are referred to on a Novell network as internal routers.

These are the steps that occur when a Novell client workstation attempts to send data across an IPX network:

- The client workstation attempts to send data; if the destination is one of its own segment, the destination will be easily found and the data sent.

- If the source and destination clients are on different network segments, the source station sends an IPX RIP packet to request the fastest route (shortest number of hops) to the destination.

- The router that is on the source segment with the least cost (shortest number of hops) will send its own addressing and routing information.

- The router will then receive the IPX packet and verify the Transport Control field of the packet. The Transport Control field has updated information on the number of hops that the packet has taken to get to its destination. On an IPX RIP router, if the Transport Control field has a value greater than 16, the packet will be discarded. If you are using NLSP, the router will discard any packet that has a Transport Control field value that is greater than the "Hop Count Limit" as configured by network personnel.

- If the router accepts the packet, the next check is to verify the type of service requested by looking at the IPX header packet type.

- The router checks the destination address of the IPX packet.

- If the router needs to forward the data to another router that is directly connected, the router will put its own node address in the source address field of the MAC header, increment the Transport Control field by a value of 1, and forward the packet.

■ If the destination is not on the same network segment, the router will look in its routing information table for the next hop router on the path to the destination node.

■ The router will then place the node address of the next router in the source address of the MAC header, increment the Transport Control field by a value of 1, and forward the packet to the next router.

Figure 4-5 describes the IPX routing process.

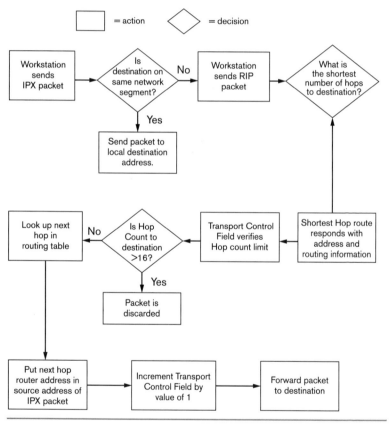

Figure 4-5 *The IPX routing process*

Summary

The NetWare IPX protocol suite that includes IPX RIP, IPX SAP, NCP, and SPX was developed by Novell to integrate internetworks based on the Novell Server 3.x platform. Novell 4.x environments also use IPX to request routing information to NDS servers.

Advantages

The following list summarizes the advantages of the Novell NetWare protocol suite:

- Compatible with Novell NDS
- NetWare servers act as internal routers.

Disadvantages

The following list summarizes the disadvantages of the Novell NetWare protocol suite:

- Not efficient in WAN environments with slow links
- Uses broadcast traffic for network management

TCP/IP (Transmission Control Protocol/Internet Protocol

The Transmission Control Protocol/Internet Protocol suite is the most widely used protocol in use on the Internet today. Millions of computer systems and end-users connect through unique network addresses.

Description

The TCP/IP suite is a collection of internetworking protocols. TCP/IP has the ability to interconnect with a variety of vendor applications, networking components, and platforms. The networking reference model for TCP/IP is slightly different than the seven-layer OSI model. The TCP/IP model is divided into four layers, which include the network layer, the Internet layer, the Transport layer and the Application layer.

How TCP/IP Works

The TCP/IP reference model can be divided into four distinct layers. The Network layer defines access to network media, the Internet layer defines routing functions, the Transport layer provides data delivery, and the Application layer provides application services.

Network Layer

The Network layer defines access to specific network media and roughly maps to the OSI physical and data link layers. The Network layer of the TCP/IP model works to transmit raw bits across the physical interface. Some of the functions of this layer are to convert the bits into frames to be sent across the network through the Internet layer. Data that is sent from the Internet layer will be converted from frames to bits for transmission across the physical media.

Internet Layer

The Internet layer defines frame format and performs routing functions. IP, ICMP, ARP, and RARP all function at the Internet layer, which maps the OSI Network layer. There are several important protocols that function at the Internet layer of the TCP/IP model, including Address Resolution Protocol (ARP), Internet Protocol (IP), Internet Control Message Protocol (ICMP), and Reverse Address Resolution Protocol (RARP).

Address Resolution Protocol (ARP) ARP allows IP address resolution to a physical network address (MAC address). ARP will broadcast to all attached devices on a LAN the corresponding IP address of the node that it wants to communicate with.

Internet Protocol (IP) IP is a connectionless protocol that provides packet delivery on a TCP/IP network. The IP addressing scheme allows various internetworking devices to be connected and to communicate throughout the world. Included in IP are all the various distance-vector and link-state routing protocols.

Internet Control Message Protocol (ICMP) ICMP performs error reporting, flow control, connectivity validation (the PING utility uses ICMP), and redirection services.

Reverse Address Resolution Protocol (RARP) RARP is used when a workstation boots up into the internetwork and it doesn't know its own IP address. RARP is commonly used with diskless workstations and will use broadcasting to determine an IP address based on a physical layer MAC address.

Transport Layer

The Transport layer provides end-to-end delivery services, including UDP and TCP, and maps to OSI Transport, Session, and Presentation layers. Included in the Transport layer are Transmission Control Protocol (TCP) and User Datagram Protocol (UDP).

Transmission Control Protocol (TCP) TCP is called a reliable connection-oriented protocol because of the error-detection and correction mechanism that it uses.

User Datagram Protocol (UDP) UDP is an unreliable connectionless protocol due to the fact that it doesn't guarantee delivery of data and has no error-checking routines like TCP. UDP allows very quick transmission of data and works well.

Application Layer

The Application layer provides application services to network users, mapping to the OSI Application layer. The Application layer includes Domain Name Service (DNS), File Transfer Protocol (FTP), Hypertext Transport Protocol (HTTP), Network File System (NFS), and Simple Mail Transport Protocol (SMTP).

Domain Name Service (DNS) DNS provides IP addresses to names on a TCP/IP network. DNS servers are commonly used to map an IP address to a Web site URL (Uniform Resource Locator). Most people can't remember an IP address, but will remember a name. DNS has allowed corporations to advertise their Web site names rather than IP addresses.

File Transfer Protocol (FTP) FTP is a commonly used protocol to transfer files from one host to another. FTP works well, and FTP services allow easy download of files and applications from one host on the Internet to your home PC.

Hypertext Transport Protocol (HTTP) A few years ago, no one knew what HTTP was. Today, everyone that connects to the Internet uses it to transfer text and graphics from an Internet host to a local PC.

Network File Service (NFS) NFS is commonly used in heterogeneous environments where end-users can mount remote host drives on a local machine and use the host drives as if they were locally attached.

Simple Mail Transport Protocol (SMTP) SMTP is used to provide messaging services such as e-mail.

Figure 4-6 shows the differences and similarities between the OSI network reference model and the TCP/IP network reference model.

Summary

TCP/IP is a collection of internetworking protocols. TCP/IP has the ability to interconnect with a variety of vendor applications, networking components, and platforms.

Advantages

The following list summarizes the advantages of the TCP/IP protocol suite:

- Compatible with a variety of vendor applications and platforms
- Routable protocol
- Standard for Internet traffic

Disadvantages

Although the TCP/IP protocol suite is widely used and its interoperability is excellent, IP address assignment and management can be difficult to manage.

OSI Model	Protocols & Specifications	TCP/IP Model
Application	DNS SMTP FTP SNMP NFS Telnet	Application
Presentation		
Session		
Transport	TCP UDP	Transport
Network	ARP ICMP IP (and Routing Protocols) RARP	Internet
Data Link	Physical Media Specifications	Network
Physical		

Figure 4-6 *Comparison between network reference models: OSI versus TCP/IP*

Key Points

Most of the protocol suites in this chapter were developed by corporation to solve internetworking problems with their proprietary hardware. The only exception is TCP/IP, which is probably the most widely used Internet protocol and is capable of working in almost any networking environment.

Here's a summary of the protocol suites that were presented in this chapter:

- AppleTalk was developed by Apple, Inc. to allow network users to share access to printers and files, specifically on Macintosh computers. AppleTalk network capability was built into each Macintosh PC. The early Apple computers were inherently networked and provided network capabilities without end-user configuration or intervention.

- DECnet is a suite of communication technologies developed by Digital Equipment Corporation. DECnet was developed to allow Digital mainframes to communicate with end systems.

- IBM System Network Architecture (SNA) was developed by IBM to perform data communications functions within an IBM mainframe environment. Two key parts of the SNA protocol suite are Synchronous Data Link Control (SDLC) and Advanced Peer-to-Peer Networking (APPN). SDLC is an IBM protocol that manages synchronous, serially transmitted bit information over a data link. APPN is an enhancement to SNA that provides client/server LAN capabilities such as resource allocation and discovery.

- NetWare IPX protocol suite, which includes IPX RIP, IPX SAP, NCP, and SPX, was developed by Novell to integrate internetworks based on the Novell Server 3.x platform. Novell 4.x environments also use IPX to request routing information to NDS servers.

- TCP/IP is a collection of internetworking protocols. TCP/IP has the ability to interconnect with a variety of vendor applications, networking components, and platforms.

Chapter 5

Cisco-specific Protocols and Others

Cisco Systems has developed some noteworthy protocols. These protocols enhance the internetworking capabilities of their current hardware product offerings. Often, Cisco attempts to provide a solution for an interoperability issue, with a Cisco-specific protocol, technology, or implementation. There certainly are times when a proprietary solution will benefit end-users. Today, it's important that companies work together to implement standards that will allow interoperability and effective communication between a variety of vendors and system implementations. An example of this is the work that Cisco and StrataCom did within the Frame Relay environment. During the early days of Frame Relay implementations, StrataCom was a pioneer in implementing effective solutions for Frame Relay networks. Cisco was able to add needed funds, expertise, and technology solutions. The result is a partnership that results in better solutions for end-users and global internetworks.

Cisco-specific protocols are discussed first in this chapter. Later, we discuss switching and bridging protocols that work together within Cisco networks to complement existing routing protocols.

The Cisco-specific protocols we discuss include both proprietary protocols that are Cisco-developed, as well as standard network protocols that Cisco has enhanced to better integrate into a Cisco-centric network:

- Cisco Group Management Protocol
- Cisco Hot Standby Routing Protocol
- Cisco Discovery Protocol

- Cisco Data Link Switching Plus
- Cisco Gateway Discovery Protocol
- Cisco TCP/IP

Many of the protocols discussed in this section are bridging and switching protocols. In addition, we discuss Internet Protocol version 6 (IPv6), the next generation Internet Protocol. At the end of the chapter, some miscellaneous network protocols that are used in a variety of Cisco implementations are listed.

- Internet Protocol version 6 (IPv6)
- Resource Reservation Protocol
- Simple Network Management Protocol
- Source Route Bridging
- Source Route Transparent Bridging
- Spanning Tree Protocol
- Virtual Trunk Protocol
- Miscellaneous Network Protocols

Tip

EIGRP and IGRP are also Cisco-specific routing protocols and are described in Chapter 3.

Each section in this chapter describes a network-particular protocol, followed by information about how the protocol actually works within an internetwork. In addition, the advantages and disadvantages of each protocol are summarized.

Cisco Group Management Protocol

Cisco Group Management Protocol (CGMP) works by managing or limiting the amount of IP multicast traffic that is sent to specific Cisco Catalyst switch ports on an internetwork. When implementing CGMP into your internetwork, you will need to assure that you have a connected router that is running both the CGMP protocol and the Internet Group Membership Protocol (IGMP). The IGMP protocol is used to establish a network host membership in IP multicast groups. IGMP communicates between hosts and multicast routers on a single network. Cisco Catalyst switches require CGMP because they are unable to distinguish between IGMP messages and IP multicast data.

Description

CGMP is configured both on a Cisco router and a Catalyst switch in order to perform group management functions on the internetwork. A router will use CGMP to communicate to a Cisco catalyst switch about all the IGMP packets that are coming across the network. Since the Cisco Catalyst switch can't tell whether the IGMP packets are IP multicast traffic or IGMP report messages, CGMP interprets this information correctly, and the Cisco Catalyst switch processes the information as necessary. When a network host joins or leaves a multicast group, CGMP will provide the information to the Catalyst switches.

How CGMP Works

When a packet of information is sent from one sender to more than one recipient in an internetwork, it's referred to as a multicast packet. The CGMP protocol creates groups that are designated to specifically accept certain types of multicast traffic. When these CGMP groups are created, the flooding of multicast traffic to a specific switch is limited and switch traffic is more efficient on the specific network segment.

To implement CGMP on your network, you will need to enable the CGMP protocol on your Cisco router and your Cisco Catalyst switch.

From the router console, you will enable the operation of the CGMP protocol in two simple steps. First, you will need to enable CGMP with the "set cgmp enable" command at the router prompt. Next, to configure the multicast groups, you will use the "set multicast router" command along with the module and port connection information. If you don't configure the multicast groups with the "set multicast router" command, CGMP will automatically discover all multicast groups that are connected to the router. Next, you will need to configure CGMP at the Cisco Catalyst switch console.

At the Cisco Catalyst switch console, enter the `set cgmp enable` command to enable CGMP. In order to identify modules and ports that have CGMP enabled routers attached to them, use the "set multicast router" command, along with the appropriate module and port information.

 Tip

The Network Management Console on some Catalyst switches allows you to configure CGMP through a menu-driven interface.

A Cisco router that is CGMP-enabled creates CGMP packets based on the IGMP packets that it receives. The router sends this CGMP packet to the Catalyst switch. The CGMP packet contains the multicast group address, the MAC address of the host, and information on whether the host is leaving or joining an IP multicast group.

Network hosts are enabled to change multicast groups dynamically to receive multicast traffic. When a network host is attempting to join a multicast group on a CGMP-enabled network, it will send an IGMP join message to the CGMP router. The router will take the IGMP message and translate the join request to a compatible CGMP command that the Catalyst switch can interpret. The Catalyst switches on the network will then look up the MAC address of the requesting host in its forwarding table and allow the host to join the appropriate multicast group. When the network host decides to be removed from a specific multicast group, it will stop responding to normal router queries. When the router no longer receives responses from the host, it will inform the appropriate Catalyst switch to remove the host from its multicast forwarding tables.

The CGMP-enabled router updates the network switch with the new CGMP group membership information. The network switch will then make appropriate configuration changes to enable proper forwarding of data packets on the internetwork. The following figures show the multicast join and remove process that takes place on a CGMP network.

Figure 5-1 shows the process that takes place on a CGMP-enabled network when a host wants to join a multicast group.

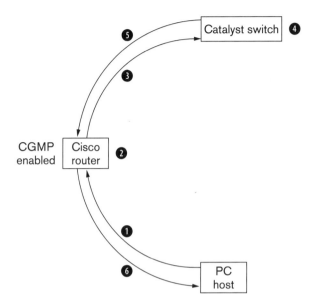

Step ❶–Host sends IGMP request message to CGMP enabled router

Step ❷–Router translates IGMP message to CGMP message

Step ❸–Router sends CGMP join request to catalyst switch

Step ❹–Catalyst switch looks up fast forwarding table lookup for host information

Step ❺–If host information found, join confirmation sent to router

Step ❻–Host begins to receive multicast group traffic

Figure 5-1 *CGMP multicast group join process*

Figure 5-2 shows the process that takes place on a CGMP-enabled network when a host wants to leave a multicast group.

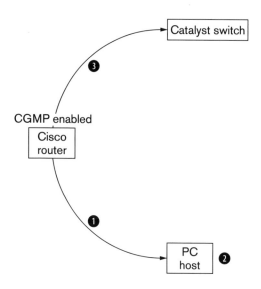

Step **❶**–Router sends multiple multicast queries to host

Step **❷**–Host decides to leave multicast group, so it will not respond to router queries

Step **❸**–Router informs catalyst switch to remove host from its forwarding tables

Figure 5-2 *CGMP multicast group leave process*

CGMP Summary

CGMP works by managing or limiting the IP multicast traffic on individual switch ports on an internetwork. When implementing CGMP into your internetwork, you will need to ensure that you have a connected router that is running both the CGMP protocol and Internet Group Management Protocol (IGMP).

Advantages

The following list summarizes the advantages of CGMP:

■ Provides dynamic changes and updates of IP multicast groups

■ Interprets IGMP information for Cisco Catalyst switches

Disadvantages

The main problem with the Cisco Group Management Protocol is the fact that it has been developed due to the inability of the Catalyst switch to interpret IGMP report messages without confusion. Although this is not a problem, CGMP requires the router to process more information and takes resources from other routing functions.

Hot Standby Routing Protocol

Cisco Hot Standby Routing Protocol (HSRP) was developed by Cisco Systems to overcome the current limitations of processes to provide IP host forwarding fail-over. With Cisco HSRP enabled, hosts can quickly adapt to network topology changes. A default gateway router is required and will allow needed redundancy in a quickly converging network during a router failure or communications link failure. The network components that are involved in the HSRP group are not required to run HSRP software or applications. HSRP is enabled at the router.

 Caution

When implementing Cisco Hot Standby Routing Protocol on your network, it's important to be sure that a routing protocol is in use that allows quick network convergence.

Description

Cisco HSRP allows hosts to adapt to critical network topology changes, such as router outages, very quickly and without specialized applications or hardware. HSRP works together with Cisco routers to create a virtual router on a local area network. To enable HSRP, two Cisco routers share a MAC address and an IP address, thereby enabling fail-over redundancy in an internetwork. Redundancy is a critical component in a fault-tolerant network design. HSRP works in FDDI, Ethernet, and Token Ring environments and is compatible with these routed protocols:

- Novell IPX
- AppleTalk
- Banyan Vines

- DECnet
- Xerox XNS

How Cisco HSRP Works

Cisco HSRP must be configured on each router that is participating in a Hot Standby Group. One router is determined to be the default active router by setting the priority. The priority is a parameter that is set by default to be 100. The router with the highest priority will be the default active router. There are three types of messages that an HSRP router uses to advertise priority settings.

- A *hello message* is used to send a router's priority state information every three seconds by default. If an active router does not send a hello message within three seconds, the standby router with the highest priority assumes responsibility as the active router.

- A *coup message* is used when the standby router with the highest priority assumes responsibility as the active router. When the transition of routing responsibility occurs, it should be transparent to network users. This is why HSRP must be used with a fast converging routing protocol.

- A *resign message* is used by the active router prior to shutdown, or if a higher priority router sends a hello message. A resign message is used to give up active status.

HSRP routers maintain one of several states. When a router is *active*, it's transferring data packets. During the *standby* state, the router is prepared to assume routing functions if the active router fails. *Speaking* and *listening* states refer to sending and receiving hello messages.

Figure 5-3 describes a sample Cisco HSRP configuration.

Cisco HSRP Summary

Cisco HSRP was developed by Cisco Systems to overcome the current limitations of processes to provide IP host forwarding fail-over. HSRP works together with Cisco routers to create a virtual router on a local area network.

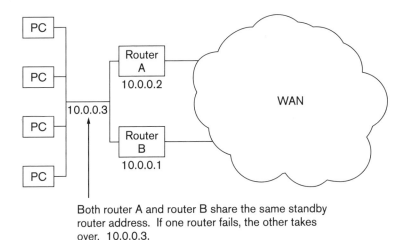

Both router A and router B share the same standby
router address. If one router fails, the other takes
over. 10.0.0.3.

Figure 5-3 *Cisco HSRP configuration*

Advantages

The following list summarizes the advantages of Cisco HSRP:

- Allows hosts to adapt to topology changes immediately; quick convergence
- Works with default gateway
- Provides redundancy in the form of a standby router

Disadvantages

The following list summarizes the disadvantages of Cisco HSRP:

- Not fully compatible with early versions of Cisco IOS
- Not fully compatible with DECnet on all Cisco hardware platforms
- Must be used with fast converging routing protocol for transparent fail-over

Cisco Discovery Protocol

Cisco Discovery Protocol (CDP) is available and runs on all Cisco-manufactured internetworking components at all OSI layers. Cisco switches and routers are CDP-enabled from the factory.

Description

CDP gathers information about neighboring devices on a Cisco network. CDP is a discovery protocol that can collect port and link status information throughout the internetwork. SNMP-enabled network management applications can tie into the information received by CDP and provide detailed and up-to-date network topology information.

How CDP Works

Cisco Discovery Protocol (CDP) is a data link layer (OSI layer 2) protocol that runs on all Cisco internetworking equipment. With CDP, you are able to check out configuration and status information on all attached Cisco equipment. Each Cisco device receives CDP packets with information about other components, and the device processes the information as it pertains to network needs. Each Cisco device that receives a CDP packet will process the packet and then discard the information. CDP packets are not forwarded throughout the internetwork. Some of the information that is included in CDP packets are protocol status, interface configuration data, and Cisco IOS version information.

Cisco Discovery Protocol Summary

Cisco Discovery Protocol (CDP) is a data link layer (OSI layer 2) protocol that runs on all Cisco internetworking equipment. Cisco switches and routers are CDP-enabled from the factory. With CDP, you are able to check out configuration and status information on all attached Cisco equipment.

Advantages

The main advantage to the Cisco Discovery Protocol is that it is standard on all Cisco manufactured equipment and is available on switches, routers, and other internetworking products.

Disadvantages

Cisco Discovery Protocol is not compatible with other vendor switches and routers. Therefore, in a heterogeneous internetworking environment, CDP won't provide complete information on all non-Cisco-internetworking components.

Cisco Data Link Switching Plus

Data Link Switching (DLSw) is an IBM proprietary method to transport Systems Network Architecture (SNA) and NetBIOS over a campus/LAN or WAN network. Cisco has created enhancements to DLSw, and it's referred to as Data Link Switching Plus (DLSw+).

Description

For the purposes of clarity, first we will discuss the functions of the DLSw protocol in general. In the upcoming sections, we will show how the DLSw protocol differs from the specific Cisco implementation of the protocol, DLSw+.

There are three primary functions or components of the DLSw protocol: the Switch-to-Switch protocol (SSP), SNA DLC termination, and local DLC connection mapping. SSP is a protocol that is used to maintain communication between the DLSw nodes on the network. SSP is also responsible for establishing connections between local resources. SSP handles data forwarding, flow control, and error-recovery. SSP is not a routing protocol and does not provide full routing capabilities, but switches data frames at the data link level. Systems Network Architecture (SNA) data-link control (DLC) termination is the principal difference between DLSw and SRB. Since SNA and NetBIOS traffic rely on acknowledgements to ensure communication integrity, DLSw offers local termination in order to eliminate the necessity of link layer acknowledgements having to cross WAN links.

How DLSw Works

There are four basic steps in the operation of DLSw. These include TCP session establishment, the exchange of information between switches, circuit establishment, and flow control.

The first step in DLSw operation is the TCP session establishment between end stations on the network. This TCP session provides the guaranteed reliability of the IP encapsulated SNA traffic.

In the second step, DLSw switches exchange information about communication session specifics. A DLSw switch-to-DLSw switch connection is made. Next, a capabilities message is sent, which provides information about the sending switch, including DLSw version number, NetBIOS information, MAC address table, and receive window size.

The third step of DLSw operation is circuit establishment. Sending and receiving SNA end systems are required to set up a DLC connection to the router, which is the transport mechanism for SNA traffic. To find other SNA devices on the internetwork, SNA devices send out explorer frames that include MAC addressing information. When an SNA device receives an explorer frame, the device will send out a `canureach` frame to each of its DLSw peer nodes. Peer nodes on the network that can reach the sending node will send out an `icanreach` frame to complete the circuit establishment process. The completed circuit establishment process is complete when:

- There are two DLC connections between the two SNA end systems and the network router.
- The TCP connection is established between the two DLSw peer nodes.

The final step of DLSw operation is flow control. Once the capabilities exchange has been processed and the needed circuits have been established, DLSw routers work within a windowing method of creating and changing flow control parameters based on buffer availability and data traffic fluctuations.

How Cisco DLSw+ Differs From DLSw

There are a few differences, or enhancements, that Cisco Systems made to DLSw that allow for increased scalability, load-balancing, and data transport flexibility. DLSw+ creates network environments that can reduce broadcast traffic. With the reduction of broadcasting and multicast traffic, the network can scale to provide more robust network services and resources. DLSw+ reduces broadcast traffic through the reduction of explorer packets. Availability is enhanced by dynamic path selection, allowing load-balancing across data links. Data transport flexibility comes through transport options that allow bandwidth reassignment for specific network applications.

DLSw+, like DLSw, is able to dynamically detect router capabilities on the network. Peer groups are a feature of DLSw+ that creates a less communication-intensive internetwork. Peer routers can help to limit the amount of broadcast traffic and replication. Peer groups have one router that is called the border peer router. All routers within that peer router group communicate through the border peer router. Border peer routers of each group are the only routers that communicate to other border peer routers. This peer router concept limits the explorer frame broadcasting and router resource usage. Figure 5-4 shows a sample DLSw+ internetwork.

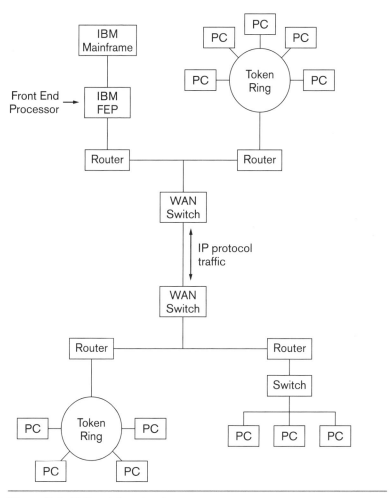

Figure 5-4 *DLSw+ internetwork*

Cisco DLSw+ Summary

Data Link Switching (DLSw) is a method to transport Systems Network Architecture (SNA) and NetBIOS over a campus/LAN or WAN IP network using data link switching and encapsulation. DLSw is an alternative to Source Route Bridging (SRB). SRB is a protocol that enables data transport for SNA and NetBIOS traffic in a Token Ring environment. Cisco created enhancements to DLSw, and it's referred to as Data Link Switching Plus (DLSw+).

Advantages

The following list summarizes the advantages of Cisco DLSw+:

- Reduction in broadcast traffic
- Load-balancing
- Data transport options

Disadvantages

One main disadvantage to using DLSw or DLSw+ does not have to do with the protocol itself, but with the fact that it's used on an IBM SNA environment. IBM SNA is not optimized to operate as efficiently in WAN environments as some other proprietary systems.

Cisco Gateway Discovery Protocol

Cisco Gateway Discovery Protocol (CGDP) is one method whereby router discovery takes place on a Cisco internetwork. CGDP detects routers on the network and provides status information to other networking components.

Description

Router Discovery is the process where the Cisco protocol application translator will learn about routers (or routes to other networks). CGDP is one of the methods used to bring about router discovery. Cisco GDP allows the network routers to be configured to specify a timeout period for down messages to be sent, as well as a priority setting

Cisco GDP Summary

Cisco Gateway Discovery Protocol (CGDP) is one method whereby router discovery takes place on a Cisco internetwork. CGDP detects routers on the network and provides status information to other networking components.

Cisco Transmission Control Protocol/Internet Protocol

The Transmission Control Protocol/Internet Protocol (TCP/IP) suite is the most widely used protocol on the Internet today. Millions of computer systems and end-users connect through unique network addresses. The TCP/IP suite is a collection of internetworking protocols. TCP/IP has the ability to interconnect with a variety of vendor applications, networking components, and platforms. Cisco Systems has developed a TCP/IP subset that is used on all Cisco routers.

Description

The TCP/IP suite is a collection of internetworking protocols. TCP/IP has the ability to interconnect with a variety of vendor applications, networking components, and platforms.

How TCP/IP Works

The networking reference model for TCP/IP is slightly different than the seven-layer OSI model. The TCP/IP model is divided into four layers. The TCP/IP layers are the network layer, the Internet layer, the transport layer, and the application layer.

Network Layer

The Network layer defines access to specific network media and roughly maps to the OSI physical and data link layers. The Network layer of the TCP/IP model works to transmit raw bits across the physical interface. Some of the functions of this layer are to convert the bits into frames to be sent across the network through the Internet layer. Data that is sent from the Internet layer will be converted from frames to bits for transmission across the physical media.

Internet Layer

The Internet layer defines frame format and performs routing functions. IP, ICMP, ARP, and RARP all function at the Internet layer, which maps the OSI Network layer. There are several important protocols that function at the Internet layer of the TCP/IP model.

Transport Layer

The Transport layer provides end-to-end delivery services, including UDP and TCP and maps to OSI Transport, Session, and Presentation layers.

Application Layer

The Application layer provides application services to network users, mapping to the OSI Application layer. TCP/IP Application layer programs include Telnet, SMTP, FTP, DNS, and NFS.

How Cisco TCP/IP Differs

Cisco created a TCP/IP implementation that includes features that enable TCP/IP traffic to perform well on various-speed WAN links. Cisco's main implementation feature is the inclusion of a unique form of the application level service, Telnet. The main feature of Telnet is the ability to connect to a remote terminal. Telnet establishes a TCP connection from one network host to another, and then transmits keystroke information to allow remote access at a console level.

Cisco's implementation adds more features than the traditional Telnet services. Cisco's TCP/IP Telnet features include remote echo, send location, remote flow control, terminal speed, and other useful functions.

Cisco TCP/IP Summary

Cisco created a TCP/IP implementation that includes features that enable TCP/IP traffic to perform well on various-speed WAN links. Cisco's main implementation feature is the inclusion of a unique form of the application level service, Telnet.

Advantages

The following list summarizes the advantages of Cisco TCP/IP:

- Performs well on slow and fast WAN links
- Compatible with all Cisco-manufactured equipment

Disadvantages

Cisco's TCP/IP implementation works well on Cisco hardware implementations. However, it can't be used to control other vendor hardware.

Internet Protocol version 6 (IPv6)

With the explosive growth of the Internet, IPv6 is emerging as a possible successor to the current Internet Protocol, version 4. IPv6 adds to the functionality of IPv4 with increased address size and the ability to be accessed by more than one address. IPv6 is sometimes referred to as *IP Next Generation*.

Description

To help facilitate network management and routing functions, an IPv6 network component can be accessed by more than one address. IPv6 expands the network address from the current IPv4 standard of 32 bits to an expanded address of 128 bits. The IPv6 network address will be noted as eight 16-bit digits, separated by colons. Each digit is represented in hexadecimal format.

How IPv6 Works

IPv6 functions in many ways much like the current IPv4 standard. But IPv6 has the ability to use *anycast* addressing, which enables the end-user to access a group of routers from one IP address, whether it is on the same subnet or not. IPv6 also allows increased flexibility in IP address assignment. There are a variety of IP addressing options that allow internal organizations to have unique IP addresses. Also, multicast addressing and other options will become available. Will it be possible for each home in the world to have its own unique IP address? Certainly. What about the possibility of replacing your social security number with your own IP address?

Those questions are interesting to think about, and IPv6 is the next step in the continued expansion of IP connectivity and communication throughout the world. The transition to IPv6 will be an interesting time, as more and more devices and worldwide components will be addressable and able to communicate with each other.

IPv6 Summary

With the explosive growth of the Internet, IPv6 is emerging as a possible successor to the current Internet Protocol, version 4. IPv6 allows increased flexibility in IP addressing of network components, along with increased address size from the current IPv4 size of 32 bits to the IPv6 specification of 128 bits.

Resource Reservation Protocol

Resource Reservation Protocol (RSVP) is a setup protocol that works with routing protocols to obtain Quality of Service (QoS) information.

Description

RSVP transports QoS requests and sets procedures for Cisco routers to keep current information about resource reservation statistics. RSVP allows Internet-based applications to obtain certain QoS for application data flows. The following list shows the properties of RSVP:

- Creates reservations for unicast and multicast applications
- Initiates and maintains resource reservations
- Works in conjunction with current Internet routing protocols
- Has several different reservation models that allow it to adapt to unique applications
- Is transparent to non-RSVP routers
- Supports IPv6

How RSVP Works

RSVP starts the resource reservation process by querying local routing protocols for routing information. A host will send an RSVP message in an attempt to reserve resources. All RSVP-capable routers pass the incoming packets sent from the RSVP host to a packet classifier. The packet classifier will then determine the route and QoS for each packet. Next, each packet is queued and sent to a packet scheduler that allocates data link layer transmission medium resources. If the data link layer component has its own QoS capabilities, then the packet scheduler works to assure that the QoS capabilities are then fully transferred to RSVP as requested. Any data link layer component that does not have its own QoS capabilities is then accessed by RSVP, and resources are allocated as necessary. RSVP then passes the QoS request back through the router to the source host.

Figure 5-5 shows the RSVP resource allocation process.

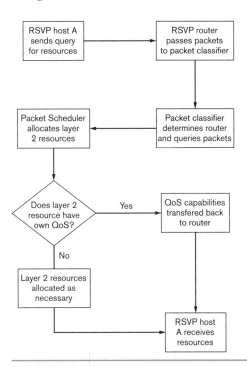

Figure 5-5 *RSVP resource allocation process*

RSVP Summary

Resource Reservation Protocol (RSVP) is a setup protocol that works with routing protocols to obtain Quality of Service (QoS) information. RSVP allows Internet-based applications to obtain certain QoS for application data flows.

Advantages

The following list summarizes the advantages of RSVP:

- Scales well to large multicast groups
- Compatible with routing algorithms currently in use
- Compatible with IPv6

Disadvantages

One of the main disadvantages of using RSVP is in the area of routing resource consumption. With each reservation, CPU and memory requirements increase substantially.

Simple Network Management Protocol

Simple Network Management Protocol (SNMP) allows the exchange of information between network components. SNMP assists network management by providing detailed status information about network services and performance trends.

Description

SNMP operations in a network environment consist of three main components: Network Management Systems (NMS), managed devices, and agents. NMSs are SNMP implementations that allow the network administrator to change, verify, monitor, and analyze SNMP information. Managed devices can be routers, switches, workstations, or other hosts. Agents are application modules that exist on the managed network device.

Agents compare known information about a network component with the status of the network component and send the resulting information to an SNMP-compatible report.

How SNMP Works

SNMP works by the use of simple commands that monitor and control network devices. The trap command "traps" event information and reports the information to the NMS. The read command monitors managed devices. The write command is used to control the operation of managed devices. SNMP also uses a Management Information Base (MIB) that contains information about how the devices on the network are to be managed and controlled. MIBs are programmable components that allow network administrators to create custom network monitoring functions. MIBs are accessed through SNMP. Figure 5-6 shows an SNMP-enabled network.

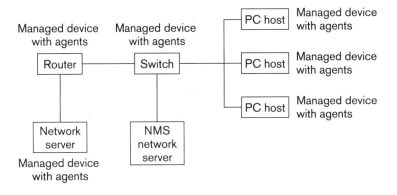

NMS Network Server–host that manages and reports SNMP data

Managed devices–router, switch, network server, PC hosts

Agents–reside in each managed device, reports to NMS

Figure 5-6 *SNMP-enabled network*

SNMP Summary

SNMP operations in a network environment consist of three main components: Network Management Systems (NMS), managed devices, and
agents. SNMP assists network management by providing detailed status
information about network services and performance trends.

Source Route Bridging

Source Route Bridging (SRB) was developed by IBM to provide bridging
between all LAN technologies. SRB is an interior gateway bridging protocol.

Description

In SRB networks, frames are sent that include the complete source-to-destination route. Source route bridges check frames for destination information and store and forward as appropriate. The source will make the routing
choice based on configurable routing metrics. In order to determine the best
path to a destination, the source host sends out explorer frames. There are
three types of explorer frames. Local explorer packets locate devices connected to the local ring. If a device can't be found, the source host produces
either a spanning explorer packet or an all-routes packet. A spanning
explorer packet locates the best route to a destination, and an all-routes
packet locates all routes to a destination. Explorer frames are produced by
the source and updated by each device throughout the internetwork.

How SRB Works

SRB works by using explorer frames to share routing information and
make routing decisions. The following list provides the sequence for data
flow in an SRB network:

1. Source host sends out explorer frames.

2. Bridges receiving the explorer frame copy the frame to all ports.

3. Explorer frame travels through the internetwork, gathering route
   information as it goes.

4. Explorer frame reaches destination host.

5. Destination host replies to all received explorer frames.

6. Source chooses best route path based on predetermined metric based on first frame received (default), minimum number of hops, largest allowed frame size, and a combination metric of all parameters.

7. Source inserts routing information field (RIF) into frames that are sent to the destination host.

Figure 5-7 shows a sample SRB network.

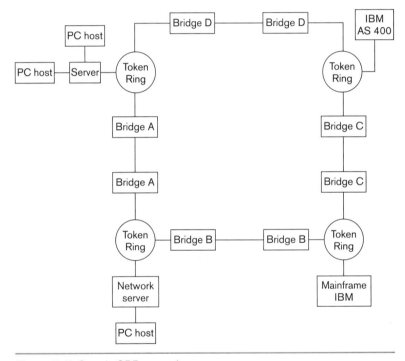

Figure 5-7 *Sample SRB network*

SRB Summary

Source Route Bridging (SRB) was developed by IBM to provide bridging between all LAN technologies. SRB is an interior gateway bridging protocol that works by using explorer frames to share routing information and make routing decisions.

Advantages

SRB works to bridge LAN technologies.

Disadvantages

The following list summarizes the disadvantages of SRB:

- Originally developed for small internetworks
- Not scalable to larger enterprises
- Limit hop count of 7
- Forwards all-routes explorer packets, creating addition LAN traffic

Source Route Transparent Bridging

Source Route Transparent Bridging (SRT) was developed by IBM to overcome the limitations of translational bridging.

Description

SRT is a method to bridge Ethernet networks, using transparent bridging, and Token ring networks, using Source Route Bridging (SRB).

How SRT Works

SRT bridges use a Routing Information Indicator (RII) to distinguish between SRB frames and transparent bridging frames. When the RII bit is set to 1, it represents that the bridge is using the SRB algorithm. When the RII bit is set to 0, it represents that the bridge is using transparent bridging.

SRT bridges combine the functionality of both source route bridges and translational bridges; however, they don't provide translation between the protocols. When an SRT bridge receives source routing frames with routing information, as defined in the presence of an RII bit, it performs source routing. When the SRT bridge receives a frame without routing information defined in the RII bit to zero, the bridge will perform transparent bridging.

SRT Summary

SRT is a method to bridge Ethernet networks, using transparent bridging, and Token ring networks, using Source Route Bridging (SRB).

Spanning Tree Protocol

Spanning Tree Protocol (STP) is a link-management bridging protocol that uses the spanning tree algorithm. STP provides redundancy for networks and also prevents duplicate frames from being forwarded across the network.

Description

The Spanning Tree Protocol is configured throughout the network to find and define all switches that are active. STP creates a tree structure that contains all switches in the internetwork. Once the tree structure has been created, it's used to switch and forward frames to prevent duplicate frame forwarding. The spanning tree structure, or topology, also contains information about redundant paths and alternate routes. If an outage occurs on a switch, or if it otherwise becomes unavailable, STP will use the spanning tree algorithm to reconfigure the spanning tree structure. Redundant paths are then activated and brought into primary status in the spanning tree structure.

How STP Works

Spanning Tree Protocol operation is transparent across the internetwork. LANs participating in the spanning tree structure will send update information in the form of Bridge Protocol Data Units (BPDUs). BPDUs allow all connected LANs and devices access to updated configuration and topology information. BPDU connection messages are sent on a periodic basis to inform the entire STP tree structure of updated topology information including identification of a root switch, cost (or distance) information, and device identification information. If a switch fails and stops sending BPDUs, the switches detect the lack of configuration messages and initiate a spanning tree recalculation.

The STP network is configured so that there is only one path from each switch to the main, or *root*, switch in the network. This process prevents the possibility of looping within the STP tree structure. All alternate paths in the network are placed in a backup state and are available to provide redundancy if a link fails.

STP Summary

STP is a link-management bridging protocol that uses the spanning tree algorithm. STP creates a tree structure that contains all switches in the internetwork. Once the tree structure has been created, it's used to switch and forward frames to prevent duplicate frame forwarding. STP has two very important advantages. First, the root switch is configured so that only one path is enabled to each switch, which prevents looping within the network, and second alternate paths are kept in a standby state to provide redundancy in case of LAN segment failures or hardware failures.

Virtual Trunk Protocol

Virtual Trunk Protocol (VTP) is the protocol used to configure Virtual LANs (VLANs) within specific management domains. VTP is a bridging protocol that operates at the data-link layer.

Description

VLANs are Virtual LANs that are grouped together for ease of management and service distribution. A network administrator can combine workstations and servers into a VLAN for bandwidth and broadcast control. VTP manages VLAN configurations, additions, and deletions.

VTP has two versions. VTP version 2 must be used on Token Ring networks. Each VTP domain must either have all switches running VTP version 1 or all switches running VTP version 2.

Caution

Certain Cisco IOS versions support VLANs but not VTP. Be sure you check Cisco IOS version and VTP compatibility.

How VTP Works

VTP is configured as a VTP domain. VTP domains can be a set of interconnected Cisco switches, or one main switch, such as a Cisco Catalyst 3500.

When a new switch comes up into a VLAN network, the switch will wait to hear a domain advertisement. Once the new switch hears the domain advertisement, it will accept the VLAN management domain name and configuration information. A VTP switch is configured to be in one of several modes:

- VTP Server Mode—Used to modify, create, and delete VLANs. VLAN configurations from a VTP Server are advertised to all other VTP switches in a VTP domain. Within VTP Server mode, global VLAN management domain configuration changes are made to a local VLAN database. If multiple VTP servers are configured, the management domain's redundancy is enhanced.

- VTP Client Mode—Similar to VTP Server Mode but without administrative functions such as modifying, creating, and deleting VLANs. Within VTP Client mode, global VLAN management domain configuration changes can't be made to a local VLAN database. Configuration changes are accepted from other devices within the management domain, but the VLAN global database updates are not authorized.

- VTP Transparent Mode—Used to forward VTP configuration advertisements. VTP switches that are in Transparent Mode don't advertise their own VLAN configuration information. Figure 5-8 shows the VTP switch configuration process.

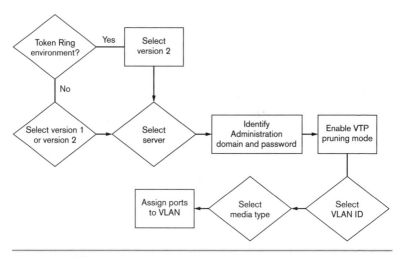

Figure 5-8 *VTP switch configuration process*

VTP Summary

VTP is a bridging protocol that operates at the data-link layer. VTP manages VLAN configurations, additions, and deletions. A network administrator can combine workstations and servers into a VLAN for bandwidth and broadcast control.

Advantages

The following list summarizes the advantages of the VTP protocol:

- Limits broadcast traffic
- Works with a variety of internetworking environments
- Switch configuration changes can be automatically distributed across the network

Disadvantages

VTP is an optional protocol that is used to configure and administer VLANs. The disadvantages are minimal, except for the possible incompatibility with earlier Cisco IOS versions.

Miscellaneous Protocols

This section briefly describes some other protocols that have not yet been discussed in this book, and their purposes. There is no intention to discuss the merit or technical details of each. A brief description of each protocol is presented. The protocols are listed in alphabetical order.

Bootstrap Protocol (BOOTP)

BOOTP is used by a network node to determine the IP address of Ethernet interfaces. BOOTP is part of the TCP/IP protocol suite, and it allows workstations or hosts to boot from a network server. A BOOTP client will request network connectivity information from a BOOTP server. If an IP address is required, the assigned IP address is permanent, unlike DHCP dynamic IP address assignment. Bootstrap methods for booting a system have been in place for many years. The term bootstrap comes from the idea that the Bootstrap Protocol is starting the system from the ground up, as in "pulling you up from your boot straps."

Cisco Duplicate Ring Protocol (DRiP)

Cisco DRiP can be configured on Cisco switches and routers that are running VLAN implementations. DRiP is used to identify Token Ring VLANs in order to prevent duplicate configuration. Each Token Ring configuration on a VLAN is referred to as a Token Ring Concentrator Relay Function (TrCRF). Cisco routers on a Token Ring VLAN that are enabled with the DRiP protocol will send out DRiP advertisements to all neighboring devices every 30 seconds. DRiP routers maintain a configuration database that is checked to prevent duplicate TrCRFs.

Challenge Handshake Authentication Protocol (CHAP)

CHAP is a security authentication protocol that prevents unauthorized access on PPP links. CHAP provides security services by identifying the remote host that is requesting network services from the router. The router then processes the authentication request. CHAP is used only on PPP links and is a good option for use with router-to-router communication since it does not require a secret password to be sent over the internetwork.

Distance-Vector Multicast Routing Protocol (DVMRP)

DVMRP is an interior gateway protocol (exchanges information from with an autonomous network system) that exchanges datagrams with the help of IGMP. When DVMRP receives a data packet, it will flood the data packet to all network paths except on the path that it was received.

Dynamic Host Configuration Protocol (DHCP)

DHCP allows dynamic configuration of IP addresses. DHCP allows IP addresses to be assigned to a variety of hosts on an as-needed basis. Cisco routers can forward DHCP traffic across subnets. If you add an IP helper address to your Cisco IOS router configuration, you will enable protocol forwarding for the BOOTP protocol and the DHCP information that is encapsulated in BOOTP.

High-Level Data Link Control (HDLC)

HDLC is a data-link layer protocol that specifies a data encapsulation process for synchronous data links. HDLC is a bit-oriented protocol that uses frame characters and checksums to provide the encapsulation method.

Multicast Open Shortest Path First (MOSPF)

MOSPF is a multicast routing protocol that is used on Open Shortest Path First (OSPF) networks. MOSPF attaches to OSPF link-state advertisements and is able to learn all of the multicast groups that are on the internetwork.

MultiProtocol over ATM (MPOA)

MPOA is more of a specification rather than a protocol; however, its purpose is to provide a specification for network layer implementations and how they interact and coexist with ATM. MPOA will determine how routers, switches, and network components coexist with ATM in heterogeneous environments running routed and routing protocols.

Next Hop Resolution Protocol (NHRP)

NHRP increases performance on an internetwork by allowing routers to dynamically discover MAC addresses of other network systems or hosts on a, NBMA (Nonbroadcast Multi-access) network. NHRP allows routers to communicate directly with other routers.

Password Authentication Protocol (PAP)

PAP works much like CHAP (Challenge Handshake Authentication Protocol); however, the identification process of a remote host is a little different. CHAP provides security services by identifying the remote host that is requesting network services from the router. PAP allows peer hosts to identify or authenticate each other. PAP does not encrypt access information such as username and password, but it passes the information to the access server or router. The router will then provide the access to network services and resources.

Remote Authentication Dial-in User Service (RADIUS)

RADIUS is both a protocol and a database for authenticating and tracking resource utilization on an internetwork.

Simple Server Redundancy Protocol (SSRP)

Simple Server Redundancy Protocol (SSRP) allows LANE redundancy on ATM networks. There are a few important components in an ATM LANE network that will be briefly discussed before the information about SSRP is presented.

Some of the ATM LANE components are:

- LAN Emulation Clients (LECs) are network components such as workstations and switches. LECs are the emulation interface from an ATM network to a legacy network. LECs provide address resolution and communicate directly with the LAN Emulation Server (LES) to provide MAC registration information.

- LAN Emulation Server (LES) is the main server that provides an administration function for all LECs.

- LAN Emulation Configuration Server (LECS) provides a database function that contains LES addressing information, and it enables communication between the LECs and the LES.

- Broadcast and Unknown Server (BUS) is the main point of broadcast and multicast distribution. BUS was developed to provide ATM broadcasting support.

SSRP configures the LECS configuration structure on an ATM network to provide needed redundancy. With SSRP, multiple LECS are configured on an ATM switch. SSRP will prioritize LECS status based on LECS address. The highest-ranking LECS address becomes the primary LECS. When a LEC requests an ATM address from a LECS, SSRP provides only one primary LECS path to satisfy the query from the LEC. SSRP puts all the other LECS into a backup state and will only allow access to the backup LECS if the primary fails to respond. When a new LECS comes up into an ATM network, it will compare its ATM address against all other LECS addresses, and the highest-ranking address will assume the primary station function and respond to LEC queries.

VLAN Membership Resolution Protocol (VMRP)

VMRP is a protocol that uses Generic Attribute Registration Protocol (GARP) to provide dynamic maintenance procedures for VLAN bridging table information. VMRP also propagates this information to other bridges on the internetwork.

Voice over IP (VoIP)

VoIP allows and supports the transmission of telephone calls over an IP network infrastructure. The early implementation of VoIP was a PC with a modem, a sound card, and Internet access. A user would dial up the Internet and use a software package to connect to other users over the Internet. VoIP in a larger context, as in a corporate environment, will require a conversion application or "blackbox" implementation to connect to a building's PBX switches or at the telephone company's Central Office. This way, end-users will be using VoIP without any manual procedures or implementations at the desktop level.

Summary

Cisco has developed proprietary protocols to enhance its current product offerings. Along with that, there are other internetworking bridging and switching protocols that work together with Cisco routers to complement and enhance data flow in an internetworking environment. Here's a summary of the protocols that were presented in this chapter.

- Cisco Group Management Protocol (CGMP) works by managing or limiting the IP multicast traffic on individual switch ports on an internetwork. When implementing CGMP into your internetwork, you will need to ensure that you have a connected router that is running both the CGMP protocol and Internet Group Management Protocol (IGMP).

- Cisco Hot Standby Router Protocol (HSRP) was developed by Cisco Systems to overcome the current limitations of processes to provide IP host forwarding fail-over. HSRP works together with Cisco routers to create a virtual router on a local area network.

- Cisco Discovery Protocol (CDP) is a data-link layer (OSI layer 2) protocol that runs on all Cisco internetworking equipment. Cisco switches and routers are CDP-enabled from the factory. With CDP, you are able to check out configuration and status information on all attached Cisco equipment.

- Data Link Switching (DLSw) is a method to transport Systems Network Architecture (SNA) and NetBIOS over a campus/LAN or WAN IP network using data link switching and encapsulation. DLSW is an alternative to Source Route Bridging (SRB). SRB is a protocol that enables data transport for SNA and NetBIOS traffic in a Token Ring environment. Cisco has created enhancements to DLSw, and it's referred to as Data Link Switching Plus (DLSw+).

- Cisco Gateway Discovery Protocol (CGDP) is one method whereby router discovery takes place on a Cisco internetwork. CGDP detects routers on the network and provides status information to other networking components.

- The Transmission Control Protocol/Internet Protocol (TCP/IP) suite is the most widely used protocol in use on the Internet today. Millions of computer systems and end-users connect through unique network addresses. The TCP/IP suite is a collection of internetworking protocols. TCP/IP has the ability to interconnect with a variety of vendor applications, networking components, and platforms. Cisco Systems has developed a TCP/IP subset that is used on all Cisco routers. Cisco created a TCP/IP implementation that includes features that will enable TCP/IP traffic to perform well on various-speed WAN links. Cisco's main implementation feature is the inclusion of a unique form of the application level service, Telnet.

- Internet Protocol Security (IPSec)

- Internet Protocol version 6 (IPv6) is emerging as a possible successor to the current Internet Protocol, version 4. IPv6 allows increased flexibility in IP addressing of network components, along with increased address size from the current IPv4 size of 32 bits to the IPv6 specification of 128 bits.

- Resource Reservation Protocol (RSVP) is a setup protocol that works with routing protocols to obtain Quality of Service (QoS) information. RSVP allows Internet-based applications to obtain certain QoS for application data flows.

- Simple Network Management Protocol (SNMP) allows the exchange of information between network components. SNMP assists network management by providing detailed status information about network services and performance trends. SNMP operations in a network environment consist of three main components: Network Management Systems (NMS), managed devices, and agents.

- Source Route Bridging (SRB) was developed by IBM to provide bridging between all LAN technologies. SRB is an interior gateway bridging protocol that works by using explorer frames to share routing information and make routing decisions.

- Source Route Transparent Bridging (SRT) is a method to bridge Ethernet networks, using transparent bridging, and Token ring networks, using Source Route Bridging (SRB).

- Virtual Trunk Protocol (VTP) is a bridging protocol that operates at the data-link layer. VTP manages VLAN configurations, additions, and deletions. A network administrator can combine workstations and servers into a VLAN for bandwidth and broadcast control.

- Bootstrap Protocol (BOOTP) is used by a network node to determine the IP address of Ethernet interfaces.

- Cisco Duplicate Ring Protocol (DRiP) can be configured on Cisco switches and routers that are running VLAN implementations. DRiP is used to identify Token Ring VLANs in order to prevent duplicate configuration.

- Challenge Handshake Authentication Protocol (CHAP) is a security authentication protocol that prevents unauthorized access on PPP links.

- Distance-Vector Multicast Routing Protocol (DVMRP) is an interior gateway protocol (exchanges information from within an autonomous network system) that exchanges datagrams with the help of IGMP.

- Dynamic Host Configuration Protocol (DHCP) allows dynamic configuration of IP addresses. DHCP allows IP addresses to be assigned to a variety of hosts on an as-needed basis.

- High-Level Data Link Control (HDLC) is a data-link layer protocol that specifies a data encapsulation process for synchronous data links.

- IP version 6 (IPv6) is the intended replacement for the current IP addressing scheme, Ipv4, currently used in most internetworks and the Internet.

- IP Security Protocol (IPSec) is a set of standards that provide methods of data security, including authentication.

- Multicast Open Shortest Path First (MOSPF) is a multicast routing protocol that is used on Open Shortest Path First (OSPF) networks.

- MultiProtocol over ATM (MPOA) determines how routers, switches, and network components coexist with ATM in heterogeneous environments running routed and routing protocols.

- Next Hop Resolution Protocol (NHRP) increases performance on an internetwork by allowing routers to dynamically discover MAC addresses of other network systems or hosts on a NBMA (Nonbroadcast Multi-access) network.

- Password Authentication Protocol (PAP) allows peer hosts to identify or authenticate each other. PAP does not encrypt access information such as username and password, but it passes the information to the access server or router.

- Remote Authentication Dial-in User Service (RADIUS) is both a protocol and a database for authenticating and tracking resource utilization on an internetwork.

- Simple Server Redundancy Protocol (SSRP) allows LANE redundancy on ATM networks.

- VLAN Membership Resolution Protocol (VMRP) is a protocol that uses Generic Attribute Registration Protocol (GARP) to provide dynamic maintenance procedures for VLAN bridging table information.

- Voice over IP (VoIP) allows and supports the transmission of telephone calls over an IP network infrastructure.

Part III

Choosing Your Network Components

Chapter 6

Network Hardware

Network hardware components comprise the infrastructure of your network design. Putting them all together into a functioning, productive, and optimized structure can be challenging. Hardware components are constantly being upgraded to provide the latest software technology or feature. The research and development department continues to allow corporations to provide high-quality, quick components at a reasonable cost. Cisco is a leader in the network component industry. Along with Cisco-branded hardware are the cabling and media components that together create the backbone fabric for your network. This chapter covers the main network hardware components that are necessary to complete your network design.

The network components will be covered in this order:

- Media — Cabling and Transmission Media
- Hubs — LAN Components
- Bridges — LAN Components
- Switches — LAN and WAN
- Routers — Core, Distribution, Access
- Miscellaneous — Multiplexers, Modems, and others

Transmission Media

The transmission media and cabling are the physical-layer components that actually carry the data bits. Cabling includes UTP, STP, coax, 10base2, 10base5, and fiber optic. Network transmission media includes T1-type circuits.

How Transmission Media Works

All transmission media basically work the same. Data bits are sent in the lowest common format across the media in bit patterns. Whether it's a 10BaseT cable or a DS-3 high-speed link, you are basically getting ones and zeroes across the line. The difference is the speed of the media, transmission method, cost, and purpose.

Types of Transmission Media

Each type of transmission media has certain advantages, as well as specific use applications. While UTP cabling may be good for the small office, fiber optic media may be more suited for the corporate data center where there are multiple sources of electronic interference to contend with.

Cabling

For most network design projects that you will work on, there will be an existing cabling infrastructure. You will need to assess the cabling system in place and make changes as necessary. Many of the network problems that occur are a result of media problems. Worn interface connections, old cracked cabling, and electrical interference all contribute to a problem network. It's important that if you do have the chance to replace some of the cabling or wiring that you do so with a view of future applications that may be using the infrastructure. It's not at all unlikely that, especially with fiber cabling, you double your cabling capacity for redundancy issues as well as expansion. Cable installation done right and once is very expensive, but done twice is an unnecessary expense when extra wiring can be installed at a minimal extra cost the first time. Generally, the smaller the network environment, the less you should concern yourself with extra cabling. With very large network environments where the cost to run additional cabling is very expensive, be sure you plan for the future. For example, if you have several buildings within a campus location and you want fiber run to each of the buildings, be sure that you have three times the capacity that you need today.

Within each location itself, you may want to consider centralizing the cabling system. This will provide a much more easily managed network environment. To assure network availability, make sure that the cabling system is redundant also.

And finally, cabling and wiring closets should be documented and locked. Shielded Twisted Pair (STP), Unshielded Twisted Pair (UTP), and fiber optic are the main types of cabling that you will find in a LAN environment or campus network.

STP Shielded Twisted Pair (STP) and coax are some of the primary cabling systems implemented in early LAN networks. Due to the physical structure of coax, it's more costly, harder to work with, and less reliable than other cabling standards. But there are certainly miles and miles of coax still running through the floors and walls of network infrastructures across the globe.

UTP Unshielded Twisted Pair (UTP) has taken over as the default cabling for smaller network environments. It is recommended that CAT5 UTP cabling be installed for LAN networks due to its ability to support 100Mbps traffic.

Fiber Optic Fiber optic cabling has been a great addition to the local network as well as to campus networks. Fiber cabling can provide high-speed reliable data transfer. Fiber does not compete and is not affected by electrical signals in the network environment. Fiber optic cable termination is an art. To prevent the possibility of transmission anomalies, it's best to have a qualified licensed electrician or trained professional perform the termination of the fiber cabling. The proper equipment is crucial, as is a keen eye and a great deal of patience.

When installing fiber cabling, you'll find that it's very easy to work with, at least as far as stringing the cabling through the floor. Be careful, though, because the lightness and flexibility can fool you. Be sure that the fiber strand ends are capped and protected when you are laying the cable. Improper handling can cause a fiber strand to crack, making the strand useless unless it's re-terminated.

After you have installed your fiber cabling and before you hook it up to your network component interface, it is important to provide strain relief for the fiber cabling that you are putting in place. Especially if there are a variety of cable types in the same location, it's important to be sure that the fiber cabling is secured to the cabinet chassis and looped in the proper way with strain relief so as not to cause undue pressure on the fiber strands.

As with any media, but especially with fiber, it's important to install redundant strands. If your network environment is constantly in upgrade mode, and you are working with fiber-connected components that require human intervention, it's possible that when connecting the fiber to the component that a strand will crack. Expect it. Plan for it. Lay in at least double the amount of strands that you need for each component.

Data Circuits

Data circuits can be expensive. We will take a look at leased lines and T1 technology. The main difference is that, generally, leased lines are dedicated access for a specific application or business and T1 technology is shared between network services.

Tip

Keep an accurate log of any data circuit activity or anomalies. If a pattern develops, you may want to contact your provider for explanations. Redundancy is also extremely important.

Leased Lines   Leased lines provide a dedicated circuit-enabling reliable data transmission with a guaranteed bandwidth. Many businesses use leased lines as a point-to-point transmission media. Leased line costs can be expensive. Monthly and yearly leases are available depending on the service provider that you work with. There are at least two ways, if not more, to reduce the cost of your leased-line solution. The first is to use a switched carrier circuit that is used only when needed. There is no sense in keeping a dedicated leased line in operation if it's used intermittently. Switched carrier circuits provide a lower cost solution for applications that don't require dedicated access. If you do implement a leased line solution, you will want to configure your leased line modem to run a dial backup procedure when and if the leased line fails for any reason. Dial backup is easily implemented with normal phone lines connected to the leased line modem.

Caution

Leased lines that run a dial backup solution may not automatically restore the link from a dial backup state. Be sure that you monitor any leased line for dial backup status. You can run up some very high phone bills if you're not careful.

The next way to reduce the cost of your leased line solution is to monitor your dial backup lines. A visual display can notify network personnel of dial backup status for any leased line. If a circuit goes down, you may need to verify that the dial backup lines are operational. Although the circuit may need testing, depending on the application, it may be worth it to have the Web to restore the leased line immediately without testing from the service provider. Dial backup costs versus customer expectations and service-level agreements come into play during this decision. The only other thing is to not let anyone take your dial backup lines when they are not in use. They are a favorite choice for those network personnel looking for a dial tone.

T1 The term T1 is actually not a technical term. The signaling standard for the T1 line is called Digital Signal 1 (DS-1). Table 6-1 shows the line signaling speeds for North America.

Table 6-1 *Line Signaling Speeds*

Name	Signal	Approx. Speed	Number of T1s
T1	DS-1	1.54Mbps	1
T3	DS-3	44.74Mbps	23
T4	DS-4	274.18Mbps	177

Transmission Media Configuration Examples

Most LAN implementations that were installed early-on during the information technology boom were based on 10Base2, coax cabling with a BNC connector and NetWare 2.x. Then came 10BaseT Ethernet UTP cabling, then CAT5 cabling. Of course now, fiber cabling to the desktop is not common, but 100Mbps is becoming common. Fiber is more common on internetworking connections between switches or between switches and routers. Data centers have used fiber optic cabling for many years to take advantage of the speed and simplicity of fiber. There is quite a bit of fiber running throughout the U.S., and it generally is laid or strung where railroad tracks are laid. What's the quickest point between two lines? Well, the railroads already have a presence, so why not use that? T1 lines or DS-1 lines are used to connect WAN switches to each other, which connect to DS-3 circuits, connecting to ever-larger pipes of data.

Caution

Be sure that you have redundancy on your WAN circuits. Even having multiple vendors does not ensure that there is no single point of failure. Satellite links do offer U.S. domestic redundancy; however, once the data path leaves the U.S., you have no guarantee of redundancy.

The one thing to be sure of when using a transmission media such as data circuits, T1s, leased lines, or anything of that type, is to be sure you know where your data is going. This is especially important when you don't own the transmission media. Many times when there is a circuit outage, your individual data circuit may be switched to a backup path that may compromise your circuit redundancy. You should be aware if there are any common points of failure in your data circuit paths.

Selecting the Appropriate Transmission Media

The appropriate transmission media for your network will depend on three very simple questions.

What Do You Have Installed Today?

More than anything, the current state of the network will determine what you need to move on to the next level of your network design. If you can build on the current transmission media in place, then do it. When you design a network, you will first take into account the applications and tasks that the network must serve, but when you build the network, you need to take into account if the physical transmission media can handle the infrastructure that you place "on top" of it. Certainly, old cabling lying around the floor would be easily replaced by a well-documented and installed CAT5 solution for a LAN. But replacing a coax cabling system on a massive LAN is much more costly. It's not an easy decision to decide what to replace and when. There is much more at stake than the technology when corporations and businesses decide to reinvent or upgrade the technology infrastructure. The key point here is to use what you can and what you have already invested in. If the underlying physical infrastructure — in this case, transmission media — can't support the applications that will be deployed over the next five years, it's time to replace or upgrade it.

What Do You Need to Implement the Immediate Solution?

In other words, if you had to get the bare-bones solution to just get it up and running, what would you need? Unfortunately, we have all learned that bare-bones solutions are cut and whittled down until they no longer have any existence when presented as a solution. But it's important for you to know exactly what you do and don't need to make it work. Whether or not you present this information is your decision, but you need to know.

What Do You Need to Implement Future Enhancements Within the Next Five Years?

Depending on the corporation, the industry, the players, and the project, you may be involved in a solution that has long-term effects. Try and get as much information as possible about your corporation or client's long-term strategy. You will be much more helpful if you can implement an immediate solution that will provide long-term benefits and that will support not only the current and soon-coming applications, but also the network services planned for the future.

Be careful about using any transmission media that is shiny, new, and unproven. For instance, satellite communication does have its advantages. But, it's important to know the limitations of the media, as the following example shows. One company, which we'll call Silly String Networks, elected to use a satellite technology known as VSAT (Very Small Aperature Terminal). Silly Strings used VSAT for branch office access to the core network. VSAT technology used very small satellite terminals that stood about six feet tall and were generally placed on top of buildings to communicate with the main satellite system. It was great, when it worked. Unfortunately, at the time that the VSAT satellite nodes were implemented, the technology was very susceptible to rain and adverse weather patterns. You could predict the network availability based on the weather patterns across the country. Silly String was wise enough to use the technology, but not to rely on it completely. It was an investment that had potential, but it was unrealized at the time.

On the other hand, Silly String decided to invest money and infrastructure in Frame Relay technology. It was a great decision. Even before Cisco bought StrataCom, it was using StrataCom Frame Relay WAN switches, which worked well.

The lesson in this case is that a person with a diverse technical background who has a keen eye for future technologies should be involved in the decision-making process for any new infrastructure implementation. You would, of course, think this is common sense and done all the time. It's not.

Hubs

Hubs were originally used to connect small LANs and workgroups with limited need for dedicated bandwidth. Hubs are passive devices that are used in situations where shared bandwidth is an acceptable method to pass data traffic.

How Hubs Work

Although hubs do regenerate the signal as it passes through them, they should be used in limited situations due to the signal delay. Hubs operate at the physical layer, or Layer 1, of the OSI reference model.

Hub Configuration Examples

Really, hubs are hubs. They are shared media devices that connect a small workgroup or office. Since they don't segment broadcast or collision domains, their usefulness is limited. Most of the configurations for hubs are connecting workstations together that need limited bandwidth. One thing to be careful of: When connecting hubs together, keep in mind that a 10Mbp port will be shared among all the ports or workstations that it's connected to. Sometimes hubs are used as repeaters to connect one faraway workstation to the main server room, and life is good. Then more and more workstations connect to that measly 10Mbps port, and life is not so good. So hubs are limited, but it's hard not to like them. Almost everyone has come home with one, and no matter how many years ago it was, were excited when they connected their hub to another, and presto, they had a network!

Cisco Hub Hardware Products

An attempt to give you an accurate list of the latest Cisco hub hardware product specifications would be doomed to failure. Software features and hardware change so quickly that no one can possibly keep up with the features of each new hardware model. This section will give an overview of the types of features that are available in each Cisco hub family.

Cisco Hub Family

The Cisco Hub Family consists of several hardware products. There is no attempt to cover every hub product that is available from Cisco. This information should be used as a general guide to show how Cisco hardware and features are available within the hub product line. We will cover an overview of most of the Cisco hubs and the general purposes of each.

HP 10BaseT The Cisco HP 10BaseT hub was developed by HP and Cisco and can be fully integrated in a Cisco Catalyst switch environment. It also works in small stand-alone LAN environment. You can connect up to four of these hubs in a stackable solution. The following list describes some of the important features of the HP 10BaseT hub:

- Ethernet fixed-configuration managed hub
- 16 10Base T ports
- SNMP-enabled, Telnet support
- Shared media environment, not dedicated bandwidth
- Redundant power supply
- Port level security

1500 Series Micro Hub The Cisco1538 Micro Hub provides auto-sensing for 10/100 environments. This is good for small-office connectivity. This hub is also part of the "Cisco Networked Office" product line for smaller businesses. You can connect up to five of these hubs in a stackable solution. The following list describes some of the important features of the Cisco 1500 Series Micro Hub:

- Ethernet hub
- Eight 10/100 auto-sensing ports
- Throughput limited to 100Mbps

- Shared media environment, not dedicated bandwidth
- Auto configuration
- CiscoWorks management on some models

FastHub 400 10/100 Series The FastHub 400 Series hub has 12-port and 24-port models that auto-sense 10/100 speeds. You can easily connect these to Catalyst switches. You can get these hubs either managed or not, with varying amounts of ports per hub. The following list describes some of the important features of the Cisco FastHub 400 10/100 Series hubs:

- Ethernet hub auto-sensing 10/100 speeds
- Shared media environment, not dedicated bandwidth
- Up to 24 ports
- Compatible with Catalyst switches
- SNMP and Telnet support
- RMON software support
- Lower cost small-office solution
- Redundant power supply

Cisco Hub Family

Table 6-2 compares the major features of the Cisco Hub Family of products that were discussed in this section. Listed here are the comparisons and major uses of each hub series and how they might fit into your network design:

Table 6-2 *Cisco Hub Family – Use Comparison*

Series	100Mb	SOHO	Branch Office	Ports
HP10BaseT		X		16
1500	X	X	X	8
FastHub400	X	X	X	24

Selecting the Appropriate Hub

When looking for a hub, picking one that will last is important. There are plenty of cheap "office solution" hubs and four-port hubs that won't last and are not in any way manageable. For newer implementations, if you need to use a hub, an auto-sensing 10/100Mbps hub may be your best bet.

Bridges

Bridges operate at the data-link layer of the OSI reference model. Bridges forward data frames based on the destination MAC address.

How Bridges Work

Bridges work at the physical- and data-link layers of the OSI reference model. Bridges forward frames based on frame header information. Bridges work to separate collision domains, so in a smaller network environment, bridges are good to separate traffic. Bridges don't stop broadcast traffic; in fact, they forward them out every port of each bridge device. Newer technologies such as VLANs can keep broadcast traffic within a specific domain of network users. Each port on a bridge has a separate bandwidth domain, but all ports are on the same broadcast domains.

Types of Bridging

In Chapter 5, we discussed several types of bridging used in Cisco networks. This section is a quick review of some of the bridging technologies that we have already talked about and some additional ones that haven't been discussed yet. We discuss source-route bridging, transparent bridging, and mixed-media bridging

Source-route Bridging

In source-route bridging (SRB) networks, frames are sent that include the complete source-to-destination route. Source-route bridges check frames for destination information and store and forward as appropriate. The source will make the routing choice based on configurable routing metrics. There are three types of explorer frames that the source will send out to determine the best path to a destination.

Transparent Bridging

Transparent bridging is used to connect two or more LAN segments so that they can communicate in a transparent fashion. When a remote LAN sends data to a specific destination, it does not look to see where on the bridging LAN the data is. The transparent bridge will read the source frames and forward the data as appropriate. To effectively bridge traffic, a transparent bridge will listen for data traffic and learn the destinations of the data. When this happens, the bridge will begin to build a table of MAC addressing destination information. The bridge will cache the table entries and update the table when frames are sent through the bridge.

Mixed-media Bridging

Mixed-media bridging is used when you need to connect networks that are running different types of bridging technologies. Translational bridging works within the mixed-media bridging network environment. Translational bridging simply is used to translate one data link protocol to a different data link protocol. For instance, a situation where you are connecting an Ethernet bridge to a Token Ring bridge is a use for translational bridging.

Selecting the Appropriate Bridge

When selecting a bridge component or software solution, it's important to look at the several areas of specification listed here:

- What is the cost of the solution?
- What type of frame filtering or forwarding is performed?
- Can the bridge solution be used for LAN and WAN implementations?
- Is the bridge solution compatible with your current network infrastructure investment?
- How reliable is the history of the bridging solution?
- What is the capacity of the bridge solution?

Switches

LAN switches are used to connect a common broadcast domain and to provide frame-level filtering as well as dedicated port speed to specific end-users. WAN switches work at the core level of enterprise networks to switch high-speed data traffic to specific parts of the network. Some switches have limited routing capabilities and can provide Layer 3 routing functions at the most basic level. Some of the benefits of using switches for your network design are higher bandwidth to the desktop and ease of configuration. With more and more bandwidth-intensive applications being used at all levels of a corporation, it makes sense to selectively replace hubs and bridges with switches.

How Switches Work

Switches transfer data on an internetwork by receiving data frames from a source destination and forwarding them out to the destination through a different port on the switch based on the frame information. Traditional Layer 2 switching works by looking at the MAC addressing information in the data frames and forwarding the data according to the switching table information. If the switch looks at the MAC addressing information and still doesn't know from which port to send out the frames, it will broadcast the frames out all of the switch ports (referred to as flooding) to determine the destination. Once the destination address is found, the information is added to the switching table.

Switches work by providing a higher bandwidth per port to an end-user or application. Switches allow fewer users in each network segment, but they provide dedicated bandwidth—which is increasingly important with graphics and multimedia applications.

Switches allow network users the ability to transfer data traffic in a network environment free of collisions and bandwidth contention. There are several types of switching technologies that enable quick and scalable network transmission.

Most switches can be deployed in a network infrastructure without fully redesigning the network. There are several ways to implement switches depending on your network needs. Newer switches are capable of operation at OSI Layer 3, referred to as Layer 3 switching. These devices can replace some, but not all, of the traditional features of routers.

Types of Switching

The switch itself can be configured in a variety of ways to allow certain network services and features to be available within your network. Some of the types of switching are distributed switching, fast switching, Layer 3 switching, netflow switching, optimum switching, process switching, and tag switching. We will also discuss some of the features of LAN switching and WAN switching.

Fast Switching

Fast switching is the process of copying data packets into packet memory. The switching path to the destination host is determined by looking up the location in the fast-switching cache. After the destination host path is determined, subsequent data packets will use that switching path, thereby reducing path determination time.

LAN Switching   There are two basic types of LAN switching: Store and Forward switching. and Cut-through Switching.

Store and Forward Switching   A Store and Forward switch works by reading and copying the entire data frame into its buffers. Error checking is performed, and the destination address is looked up in the MAC address table. Once the switch has determined which interface the frame should switch to, the frame is forwarded to the appropriate destination.

Cut-through Switching   Cut-through switching allows faster processing than Store and Forward switching. A switch using Cut-through switching will copy the destination address and a small portion of the frame to its buffers before checking for the destination address interface in its MAC address table. As soon as the destination is found, the frame is sent out the appropriate port on the switch. Increased switching speed is realized because the Cut-through switch does not copy the entire frame to the switch buffers.

Layer 3 Switching

Layer 3 switching differs from the traditional Layer 2 switching by enabling data frames to be switched based on network addressing information. Traditional Layer 2 switching will look at the frames for the MAC address information for the destination address.

Layer 3 switching actually can use some routing functions, such as addressing. Switches can be configured like routers into an addressing mechanism, but are still bound by a flat-network addressing scheme. Switches that operate at Layer 3 still can't offer features such as path optimization and load balancing.

NetFlow Switching

Cisco Netflow switching is basically a process that allows you to collect network management information on higher-level routers. This information can be used to track network utilization for specific applications and network segments. NetFlow works somewhat like a Web counter. When users access a Web page enabled with a tracking counter, the counter will pull up statistical information. This usually includes the time zone the users are in, the browsers they use, display settings, whether the users have been to the site before, and many other details about traffic on the Web site. NetFlow maintains records of traffic statistics for accounting purposes, planning, and management.

Optimum Switching

Optimum switching is very similar to the fast switching process of copying data packets into packet memory. Optimum switching is a faster switching process. The destination host switching path is determined by looking up the location in the optimum-switching cache.

Process Switching

Process switching can be described as a router processor repackaging a frame after the frame has been processed. Process switching occurs when encapsulated frames are being sent across a WAN link. Encapsulation takes place in the router's processor, so when encapsulation is being used and switching is needed, process switching occurs.

Tag Switching

Tag switching allows network designers to use some of the existing infrastructure while providing higher-level networking services such as ATM and Internet technologies. Tag switching works by combining the data-link layer (OSI Layer 2) capabilities with the network layer (OSI Layer 3) services. Tag switching allows a more scalable network design by incorporating combinations of data-link layer services and network layer protocols.

The process of tag switching involves assigning labels or tags to data packets that provide switching information to components on the network

WAN Switching

WAN switching is probably one of the faster growing areas of network component deployment. WAN switches enable service providers and corporate networks to switch data traffic at very high speeds. To gain some perspective on the speed of WAN switching, in 1985 a major service provider was switching WAN traffic at speeds of 56k. Now, that may seem long ago, but this provider was the largest commercially available network in the world besides the telephone company. Since then, and since enterprise networks have developed in all major corporation network infrastructures, the speed that used to switch WANs is now the default modem speed for end-user dial-up access to the Internet from their homes. Today, WAN switches are capable of providing multiple services and protocols. In 10 years we'll see a phenomenal growth in home-subscriber access to the Internet and network services. WAN switches will play a major role in distributing sufficient bandwidth to run these new network service applications.

Switch Configuration Examples

When designing your network with switches, it is, of course, important to retain the infrastructure that is currently in place. You could, of course, pull out all your hubs and replace them with switches. But realistically that won't happen without a very large budget or a company that is overhauling its entire network.

Dedicated Bandwidth to Specific Users

One way to implement a switch into an existing network is to install the switch only where needed. This sounds simple, but it could cause some political infighting if people are even aware that the upgrade is being done. Once people get wind of an upgrade, they will complain that they just can run WordPerfect because the "network is slow." Well, enough about that. If you have a bandwidth-intensive application such as a financial, multimedia, or engineering package that needs certain bandwidth to operate properly, then a switch is necessary. You can install the switches on the network where they are needed to provide dedicated bandwidth. It's important to realize that when a major application is deployed, you will need to create a network environment that has as few obstacles as possible to transmitting the data. Historically, a "slow network" has been a finger-pointing episode as everyone scrambles to figure out the problem. With dedicated access for the new application, especially in the beginning of the deployment, you can prove that the network is not the problem. Also, before you install the network switch, be sure that you take a brief network analysis of the situation and document your results. Then analyze the results after the switch is installed and document your results.

Adding High-speed Switches

Another implementation of switches in your network is to install a high-speed switch between your router and your local LAN switch. This implementation will provide equal bandwidth from the backbone routers to the desktop.

You can go a step further and install routers between your high-speed switch and your local LAN switch if needed. A mission-critical multimedia application may be a good example of when you would want to use a router between your LAN switches and your high-speed backbone switch.

Cisco Switch Hardware Products

Software and hardware features change so quickly that keeping up with new features of each specific hardware model is certainly a challenge This section gives an overview of the types of features that are available in each Cisco switch family.

Cisco Catalyst and LAN Switches

The Cisco Catalyst family consists of a wide variety of hardware products. Each series type includes several model numbers and types. There is no attempt to cover every switch product or series that is available from Cisco. This information should be used as a general guide to show how Cisco hardware and features are available throughout the switch product line. We cover an overview of most of the Cisco series switches and the general purposes of each.

Cisco 1548 Switch   The Cisco 1548 switch is a good choice for smaller businesses or offices that need one or two workstations to have dedicated bandwidth to the desktop. This would be a good step up from 10BaseT in a small office. You could use this in a small office or business to connect to all the workstations or desktops and even to the server. The ports are 10/100 auto-sensing, so you can have 10Mbps workstations along with 100Mbps workstations, while still keeping your 10Mbps cards in your PCs working for you. The switch is part of the "Cisco Networked Office" stack that is a line of products geared for the small office or business. The following list describes some of the important features of the Cisco Catalyst 1548 switch:

- Fixed configuration, Ethernet
- Eight 10/100 auto-sensing ports
- SNMP-enabled, Cisco IOS-compatible on some models.
- VLAN compatibility (for some models)
- Auto Configuration
- Works as stand-alone or connected to other hubs
- Part of Cisco Networked Office stack of products

Catalyst 1900 Series   There are a few models in this series. These switches work well when you need high-speed connectivity from desktop to servers or routers. This switch has both the standard and enterprise editions. The standard edition is basically an alternative to the 10BaseT hub with some 100Mbps switched ports. When you get into the Enterprise edition, you start looking at VLAN support, Cisco IOS compatibility, and the ability to configure the unit at a more detailed level. The following list describes some of the important features of the Cisco Catalyst 1900 Series switches:

- Ethernet switch, 12- and 24-port capacity
- Web-based management console
- VLAN compatibility
- Cisco IOS command-line interface management (some models)
- Telnet and SNMP-enabled
- CiscoWorks Web browser interface management
- RMON software support
- Standard Edition can be upgraded to Enterprise Edition

Catalyst 2820 Series The Catalyst 2820 series is also for switched Ethernet environments and is a higher-end switch for dedicated bandwidth to the desktop. The Catalyst 2820 is seen as more flexible because of the availability of ATM, FDDI, 100BaseT, and fiber optic modules. An Enterprise edition is also available that does basically what the Catalyst 1900 Enterprise edition does, with added VLAN support, easier management, and configuration abilities. The following list describes some of the important features of the Cisco Catalyst 2820 Series switches:

- Ethernet switch
- Managed by Web browser interface
- VLAN compatibility (for Enterprise edition)
- ATM and FDDI compatibility for modules
- Telnet and SNMP support
- RMON software support
- Flexibility with add-on modules
- Used for larger workgroups or higher bandwidth needs

Catalyst 2900 Series The Catalyst 2900 Series switch is a good choice if you are upgrading your network to provide some workstations the dedicated 100Mbps speed, while keeping others at 10Mbps. The 2900 Series moves you more into the wiring closet arena for larger LAN implementations. You can implement over 1,000 VLANs with this switch. There are several models of the Catalyst 2900 switch with varying features. There are a few different types of Catalyst 2900 switches, and each one offers something a little bit different. Basically, it gets down to what you will pay; there are separate models for each price range, with different features for a variety of networks. The following list describes some of the Cisco Catalyst 2900 Series switches:

- Ethernet switch
- Capable of interfacing with 1000Mbps uplinks
- All models offer VLAN compatibility
- All models SNMP-enabled
- Greater management capabilities with CiscoWorks
- Web-based management interface
- Enhanced security features

Catalyst 3500 Series The Catalyst 3500 Series is used to connect the lower-end Catalyst switches together in a stackable solution as well as to provide 1000Mbps-dedicated ports on some models. You can integrate your voice and IP applications with this switch. The following list describes some of the Cisco Catalyst 3500 Series switches:

- Ethernet switch
- Some models are available with 1000Mbps ports.
- All models VLAN-compatible
- All models SNMP-enabled
- Implements Cisco Switch Clustering technology to provide communication between the Catalyst 3500 switch and downstream switches such as the Catalyst 2900 or Catalyst 1900 switches
- IP Telephony support

Catalyst 3900 Series The Catalyst 3900 Series consists of Token Ring switches. The following list describes some of the important features of the Cisco Catalyst 3900 Series switches:

- Token Ring switch
- Stackable, up to 224 ports

- All models VLAN-compatible
- All models SNMP-enabled
- Supports CDP

Catalyst 4000 Series The Catalyst 4000 Series switches move you from out of the realm of playing with switches into serious effect. This switch is designed to offer up to 24Gbps of bandwidth. You can use this to get dedicated bandwidth to the desktop, but there's a whole lot more. The following list describes some of the important features of the Cisco Catalyst 4000 Series switches:

- 10/100/1000 capable switching
- Up to 36 1000Mbps ports capacity
- Capable of supporting 1,000 VLANs
- Offers security and QoS features
- Modular supervisor engine (can be upgraded)
- Up to 96 ports of 10/100Mbps

Catalyst 5000 Series The Catalyst 5000 Series is Cisco's baby, and is probably one of the more popular switches as far as number of implementations in networks. There are quite a few Catalyst 5000 models, all offering different levels of configuration and management features. You can get a Catalyst 5000 switch with Gigabit modules, or ATM for the WAN. The following list describes some of the important features of Catalyst 5000 Series switches:

- Compatible with Ethernet, Token Ring, FDDI, or ATM depending on model
- VTP protocol support for VLAN implementation and management
- Advanced Cisco IOS switching support
- Redundant power supplies as well as other optional redundant components
- Can scale to Gigabit environments
- Modularity allows use of existing infrastructure investment
- Very high throughput

Catalyst 6000 Series The Catalyst 6000 Series provides a higher-level capacity as compared to some of the other switch series. The main feature of this switch is the ability to increase the backplane bandwidth capacity of your switch depending on your network needs. The Catalyst 6000 Series provides multilayer switching support along with higher performance. This unit is also designed to be scalable and has quite a few options that you can add. The following list describes some of the important features of Catalyst 6000 Series switches:

- High bandwidth capabilities for all models
- Supports up to 130 Gigabit ports
- Multilayer switching support
- QoS features
- Cisco IOS integration
- Enhanced security features

Catalyst 8500 Series The Catalyst 8500 Series is what Cisco calls a multiservice switch, able to provide ATM switching as well as support for multiple protocols. Basically, Cisco took the LightStream 1010 ATM Switch and branded it with the Cisco name. Now the LightStream 1010 is the Cisco Catalyst 8500 Series switch. You will also find that the LightSteam name is still being used and supported, but Cisco will eventually drop the name entirely. The following list describes some of the important features of Catalyst 8500 Series switches:

- ATM switching support
- Multiprotocol support
- QoS features
- Cisco IOS integration

Cisco ATM Switches

Cisco has developed some hardware solutions that will enable networks to provide high-quality ATM services. Not every Cisco ATM solution is represented in this section. This section provides an overview of some of the Cisco ATM hardware solutions available to you as you implement ATM technology.

Lightstream 1010 The LightStream 1010 is a multiservice switch, able to provide ATM switching as well as support for multiple protocols. Cisco took the LightStream 1010 ATM Switch and branded it with the Cisco name. Now the LightStream 1010 is the Cisco Catalyst 8500 Series switch. You will also find that the LightSteam name is still being used and supported, but Cisco will eventually drop the name entirely. The following list describes some of the important features of LightStream 1010 switches:

- ATM switching support
- Multiprotocol support
- QoS features
- Cisco IOS integration
- ATM switching support
- High-speed switching
- Cisco IOS integration with QoS features

BPX 8600 The Cisco BPX 8600 is able to provide ATM switching as well as support for multiple protocols. This is one of the StrataCom switches that Cisco got when they bought StrataCom. The BPX 8600 is targeted toward the service provider networks. You can run both IP and ATM from the same switch platform. There are a variety of configuration choices that you can get on this unit, depending on how your network is configured and how you plan to use it. When StrataCom owned this series, it was a stable unit with minimal problems on the hardware side. There were some problems early on with the firmware versions of the CPU boards, and slight glitches with the StrataView network management software. The following list describes some of the important features of BPX 8600 Series switches:

- ATM and IP integrated support
- Multiprotocol support
- QoS features
- Cisco IOS integration
- Developed for service provider network
- Scales well
- StrataCom hardware

MGX 8220 The Cisco MGX 8220 is a concentrator switch that brings ATM switches together on a network. This unit has a good bit of redundancy built in to it. This is another StrataCom unit that Cisco got with the purchase of StrataCom. This unit concentrates ATM traffic for a variety of hardware platforms. This was designed for service provider networks, which makes sense for a backbone ATM switch. The following list describes some of the important features of the Cisco MGX 8220 concentrator:

- Support for multiple protocols
- ATM support
- Redundancy at critical component level
- CiscoView network management
- Concentrates multivendor ATM traffic
- StrataCom hardware

IGX 8400 The Cisco IGX 8400 is a high-level backbone switch. This switch offers a good bit of networking power and features for the WAN backbone. Another product from StrataCom, this is also designed for service provider networks. The following list describes some of the important features of the Cisco IGX 8400 WAN switch:

- Unit can be scaled as needed
- Multiservice support
- Capable of backbone switching
- StrataCom hardware
- Designed for service provider networks

MGX 8800 The Cisco MGX 8800 WAN switch integrates ATM and IP network services. This unit is designed to be a flexible part of a service provider's network. This unit is targeted toward the service provider that is offering multiple network services such as Internet, e-commerce, and multimedia applications. Cisco has positioned this switch to be the answer to any technology that comes up in the future. The following list describes some of the important features of the Cisco MGX 8800 WAN switch:

- ATM and IP integration
- VPN support

- Many redundant features; 100 percent redundancy option
- Cisco IOS integration
- Multiservice platform

Cisco Internet Hardware

Cisco has developed a few Internet hardware products that will allow you to manage Web site traffic and provide high levels of network availability. Not every Cisco Internet hardware solution is represented in this section. This section provides an overview of some of the Cisco Internet hardware solutions available to you to implement in your network.

Cisco LocalDirector The Cisco LocalDirector is more of a traffic cop than anything else. This unit can direct TCP traffic and monitor and control functions at a network operating system level. LocalDirector was developed to help manage Web site traffic. LocalDirector can perform load balancing on your network. For instance, if you have multiple NT Servers running IIS and the traffic increases beyond the capabilities of the servers that you have running, LocalDirector can request services from a spare server that is part of the server cluster. You can set LocalDirector to move to a server within a specific set of parameters, or you can put a server in service or out of service based on load or time of the day. The following list describes some of the important features of the Cisco LocalDirector network component:

- Redundancy at critical components
- Has ability to configure network server access
- Provides load balancing
- Can scale to large Web site implementations
- Supports SSL
- Compatible with a variety of operating systems
- Has a hot standby capability
- Supports a full suite of TCP/IP Internet protocols

Cache Engine 500 Series The Cisco Cache Engine 500 Series components work by caching Internet- or intranet-related Web traffic and thereby increasing available bandwidth on the rest of the network. The

Cache Engine 500 Series works with a Cisco proprietary protocol called Web Cache Communication Protocol (WCCP). This unit works much like any other caching system for Internet use; the cached content is stored locally and when requests for the information come in from Internet traffic, the request is fulfilled from the cache system instead of traversing the network and increasing bandwidth. It is compatible with a wide variety of operating systems and infrastructures. The following list describes some of the important features of the Cisco Cache Engine 500 Series components:

- Cache engine to increase bandwidth
- Cisco IOS compatibility
- Cisco Web Cache Communication Protocol (WCCP)
- Easily integrated into existing network
- Targeted for ISP
- Compatible with a variety of network operating systems

Cisco 6510 Service Selection Gateway The Cisco 6510 Service Selection Gateway is a network component that enables service providers to present network services to customers within a browser-based interface. The following list describes some of the important features of Cisco 6510 Service Selection Gateway:

- Customers can select services from a browser window
- Capable of handling heavy user load

Cisco Switch and Internet Family

Table 6-3 compares the major features of the Cisco Switch and Internet Family of products that were discussed in this section, and how they would fit into your network design:

Table 6-3 *Cisco Switch and Internet Family – Use Comparison*

Series	LAN	VLAN	WAN	ATM	Internet
Cisco 1548	X				
Catalyst 1900	X				
Catalyst 2820	X	X		X	

Series	LAN	VLAN	WAN	ATM	Internet
Catalyst 2900	X	X		X	
Catalyst 3500	X	X		X	
Catalyst 3900	X	X			
Catalyst 4000	X	X			
Catalyst 5000	X	X	X	X	
Catalyst 6000	X		X	X	X
Catalyst 8500			X	X	X
LightStream 1010			X	X	X
BPX 8600			X	X	X
MGX 8220			X	X	X
IGX 8400			X	X	X
MGX 8800			X	X	X
LocalDirector					X
CacheEngine500					X
6510 Gateway					X

Selecting the Appropriate Switch

There are a variety of switches based on your unique network needs. Cisco offers a hardware selection tool that you can use to better define which model of switch that will work within your network design. There are, however, differences between Layer 2 and Layer 3 switches that are important to consider when choosing a switch.

A Layer 2 switch provides dedicated bandwidth to individual end-users who need specific network services at specific bandwidth levels. Layer 2 switches offer micro-segmenting that allows each individual user to be located on his or her own network segment. Layer 2 switches also allow you to set up Virtual LANs (VLANs), segmenting specific ports to specific broadcast domains.

Layer 3 switching actually can use some routing functions, such as addressing. Switches can be configured like routers into an addressing mechanism, but they are still bound by a flat network-addressing scheme. Switches that operate at Layer 3 still can't offer features such as path optimization and load balancing.

When selecting a switch component or switching software solution, it's important to look at the several areas of specification listed here:

- What is the cost of the solution?
- What type of switching is supported?
- Can the switch solution provide adequate throughput for your network?
- Will the switch provide adequate throughput for a while to come, or put another way, is it able to be upgraded?
- How reliable is the history of the switching solution?
- Does the switch support VLAN technology?
- Is the switch easily managed?
- Does the switching solution make use of your current infrastructure investment?
- Do you or your staff have adequate training or knowledge to implement the switching solution?

Routers

Routers provide networks with the ability to interconnect multivendor networks, limit access with security features, and provide network management functions along with additional software components. This section covers understanding how a router works, types of routing, router configuration examples, Cisco router types, and the process of selecting an appropriate router for your network.

How Routing Works

Routers are used to connect separate networks into separate broadcast domains. Routing is done by looking at the network layer address (OSI Layer 3) and sending packets to their appropriate destinations. Routers are used at various layers of a hierarchical network design and are used for higher-level network services. Routers are necessary when implementing security, QoS features, load balancing, and other network services. On a router, each port has a separate bandwidth domain and broadcast domain.

Types of Routing

The types of routing discussed here are some of the features of Cisco routers and also include some generic routing types that can exist in any network.

Dial-on-Demand Routing

Dial-on-Demand Routing (DDR) is the process of enabling network connections across public telephone networks. DDR will be activated on a router when specific data is sent to the router with the destination to be the remote network. DDR is like a switched carrier modem that brings up the line signal when data is ready to be sent.

Dynamic Routing

Dynamic routing is the process of adapting to changes in the topology as they happen. Optimal path selection is a result of routing protocols processing path and cost information and dynamically routing information according to the best path solution.

Policy Based Routing

Policy based routing is a Cisco IOS Quality of Service (QoS) feature that enables traffic classification and implementations of specific policies based on that classification.

Redistribution Redistribution is an option available to enable a border router on the edge of an autonomous system to exchange route information with another autonomous system. If the autonomous systems have different routing protocols, which would be likely, there might possibly be the occasion for route selection anomalies. Each routing protocol has different methods to compute the best path selection, and they converge when there are network changes.

Static Routing

Static routing is fairly common sense, just like dynamic routing. With static routing, the path to the destination is predetermined within the router software. The router makes no best path selection and does not calculate costs to alternate routes. Static entries in the routing table provide path information.

Cisco Router Hardware Products

This section gives an overview of the types of features that are available in each Cisco router family. Feature sets, software, and hardware change so quickly that no one can possibly keep up with the latest features of each hardware model.

Cisco Router Family

The Cisco Router Family consists of a wide variety of hardware products. Each series type includes several model numbers and types. There is no attempt to cover every router product or series that is available from Cisco. This information should be used as a general guide to show how Cisco hardware and features are available throughout the router product line. We cover an overview of each series and the general purposes of each.

Cisco 700 Series The Cisco 700 Series router is for a small ISDN implementation. If you are connecting an office of five people or so to the Internet, this may be a solution to take a look at. But before you do, also check out the Cisco 800 Series, too. This router can be used with multiple protocols and is fairly easy to manage. The unit comes with the Cisco IOS software already installed. The following list describes some of the important features of the Cisco 700 Series router:

- NAT-compatible for private addressing
- ISDN router for small office or home
- Works with DHCP to address workstations
- Multiple Ethernet ports available
- Easy configuration with FastStep software
- Solution for small office or small business

Cisco 800 Series The Cisco 800 Series is also an ISDN solution along with the 700 series, but this router is for an office with about 20 people or so. Cisco IOS compatibility is important for companies that have other Cisco technology solutions in place in other parts of their networks. This product is also for the reseller who is implementing a quick ISDN solution for a small business. The Cisco 800 series of routers can also provide connections to Frame Relay networks, X.25, leased line connections, and dial-up to the small-office customer at a fairly reasonable price. Cisco introduced this unit at a cut-rate price, but the price is still under $1,000. The following list describes some of the important features of the Cisco 800 Series router:

- NAT-compatible for private addressing
- ISDN router for small office or telecommuter
- Works with DHCP servers
- Multiple Ethernet ports available
- Cisco IOS feature set-compatible
- X.25-compatible
- Frame Relay support
- Low cost

Cisco 1000 Series The Cisco 1000 Series routers are for small office connectivity to a WAN or Enterprise network environment. These routers are fairly simple to install and have a fixed Cisco IOS configuration for ease of management. Optional WAN interfaces can get your office connected without much trouble; it would even fit on your desk. The following list describes some of the important features of Cisco 1000 Series routers:

- Compatible with multiple WAN environments
- Able to be remotely managed
- Works with DHCP servers
- Multiple Ethernet ports available
- Cisco IOS feature set-compatible
- ClickStart utility for easy configuration

Cisco 1400 Series The Cisco 1400 Series routers are provided for WAN connectivity from branch offices to Enterprise networks. ATM and DSL compatibility are the main features of this router. Along with multiple services, the Cisco 1400 Series can provide increased security and QoS features. But more than anything, this router is targeted for DSL applications and service providers. The following list describes some of the important features of Cisco 1400 Series routers:

- ATM WAN network-compatible for certain models
- DSL-compatible for certain models

- VPN capability
- QoS features
- Modular

Cisco 1600 Series The Cisco 1600 Series routers marketed by Cisco are the routers for intranet/Internet access from the branch office. You can connect to a variety of networks such as Frame Relay, and if you have to, you can connect to X.25 networks. These routers have modular components and are sold as part of the "Cisco Network Office" product line. The following list describes some of the important features of Cisco 1600 Series routers:

- Able to use Cisco IOS feature sets
- Support for various WAN environments, depending on WAN interface card
- Leased line solution
- Comes with Cisco ConfigMaker for easy network configuration, and includes the FastStep configuration utility
- ClickStart utility for easy configuration
- Part of Cisco Network Office product line
- VPN options available
- Integrated CSU/DSU

Cisco 1700 Series The Cisco 1700 Series routers are placed in the "all-in-one" solution for the small business. Smaller businesses can use this to connect to a VPN, access the Internet, communicate with multimedia applications, and generally run their businesses. The Cisco 1700 is also modular to allow upgrades, an important factor when choosing a router for small-business applications. The following list describes some of the important features of Cisco 1700 Series routers:

- Able to use Cisco IOS feature sets
- Cisco IOS firewall available as an option
- ISDN-compatible
- Intranet/Internet solution for small business
- VPN support

- Security features for Extranet access
- Modular

Cisco 2500 Series   The Cisco 2500 Series router has to be the favorite son (or daughter). Based on use alone, this router is probably the most popular router for branch offices. With a variety of features, this is the router for everyone. And this one can also fit on your desk. The following list describes some of the important features of the Cisco 2500 Series router:

- Ethernet and Token Ring configurations, based on model
- Great for branch office access to WAN
- Can be configured to connect to a wide variety of WAN technologies
- Relatively easy to configure
- Full Cisco IOS and feature set availability
- ClickStart utility for ease of configuration
- Reliable
- Can upgrade flash memory

Cisco 2600 Series   The Cisco 2600 Series router is billed as being the router that can help you use your current infrastructure investment because of its modularity. This router has multiservice options such as VPN and multimedia. You can use this router in a Token Ring or Ethernet environment, and some of the models, depending on options, have ATM and ISDN components. The following list describes some of the important features of the Cisco 2600 Series router:

- Modular design and architecture; able to be upgraded and enhanced
- Cisco IOS QoS features available
- ATM and ISDN available on certain models
- Ethernet and Token Ring supported
- Powerful RISC processor
- Integrated CSU/DSU
- Redundant power supply optional

Cisco 3600 Series   The Cisco 3600 Series routers are developed for the smaller ISP. This router is highly modular with many options for voice, data, and routing. This series supports VPN technology along with multi-protocol routing. The following list describes some of the important features of Cisco 3600 Series routers:

- Support for VPNs
- Cisco IOS Firewall feature set
- Higher density router
- Single-solution router for ISP
- Numerous modular interface options

Cisco 3810 Series The Cisco 3810 Series is marketed as a concentrator solution, rather than a typical router. These concentrators are used as a solution to integrate voice and data traffic over a single backbone. The following list describes some of the important features of Cisco 3810 Series concentrators:

- Integrates voice, data, and video
- Compatible with ATM
- Compatible with all Cisco IOS-enabled routers

Cisco 4000 Series The Cisco 4000 Series routers are suited for the environment that is moving from a shared to a switched environment. The 4000 series is also very capable of handling multimedia applications at the access level. The following list describes some of the important features of Cisco 4000 Series routers:

- ATM, ISDN, FDDI, Ethernet, and Token Ring compatibility
- Powerful RISC processor
- Integrates well with legacy systems
- Cisco IOS QoS and security features available

Cisco Access Servers Cisco has a group of access servers that can be used in large WAN implementations or in carrier networks. The following list describes some of the important features of the Cisco AS5300 gateway:

- Easily scaled for future growth
- PBX interface-compatible
- Integrated voice recognition system
- SNMP-enabled

- Powerful RISC processor
- Scalable
- ISDN support

Cisco 7000 Series The Cisco 7000 Series is a multiprotocol router. The following list describes some of the important features of the Cisco 7000 Series router:

- Multiprotocol support
- Modular design

Cisco 7100 Series The Cisco 7100 Series routers are a higher-end solution for a VPN. The following list describes some of the important features of Cisco 7100 Series routers:

- Cisco IOS with QoS features
- Good set of VPN features to run the network efficiently
- Security features
- Powerful RISC processor

Cisco 7200 Series The Cisco 7200 Series routers are high-end multi-service routers that can crunch, or should I say switch, some packets. The following list describes some of the important features of the Cisco 7200 Series routers:

- Full Cisco IOS and QoS features
- Dual power supply option (recommended!)
- Multiple processors
- Hot-swappable power supply and port adapters, otherwise referred to as "online insertion and removal"

Cisco 7500 Series The Cisco 7500 Series routers are the high-end multiprotocol routers. This group of routers is sold as a data center solution or backbone solution. You can't fit one of these on your desk. The following list describes some of the important features of Cisco 7500 Series routers:

- High performance switching
- Full Cisco IOS and QoS features
- Wide variety of LAN and WAN port adapters

- Backbone routing solution
- ATM support
- Multiprotocol support

Cisco 12000 Series The Cisco 12000 Series routers are called the Gigabit Switch Router (GSR). This really is a solution for service provider networks. Of course, over time everyone will want one in their network because this router can do it all. This is a core backbone router that switches traffic at extremely high rates on IP networks. The following list describes some of the important features of Cisco 12000 Series routers:

- Scalable platform for upgrades and enhancements
- Powerful processor
- Redundancy at critical component level
- Full Cisco IOS and QoS features
- Designed for service providers

Cisco AGS+ The Cisco AGS+ Series routers are Cisco legacy core routers that have been around for quite a long time. Some of the components of this router have been retired and are no longer being manufactured. The following list describes some of the important features of Cisco AGS+ Series routers:

- Scalable
- Modular
- Limited processing power
- Retirement of some parts

Cisco Router Family

Table 6-4 compares the major features of the Cisco Switch and Internet Family of products that were discussed in this section. Of course, every router could somehow fit into a WAN and VPN, but listed here are the comparisons, major uses of each router series, and how they might fit into your network design:

Table 6-4 *Cisco Router Family – Use Comparison*

Series	SOHO	Branch Office	Telco or Carrier	WAN	VPN
700	X				
800	X	X			
1000	X	X			
1400	X	X			X
1600	X	X			X
1700	X	X			X
2500		X		X	X
2600		X		X	X
3600				X	X
3810				X	X
4000				X	X
AccessServers			X	X	X
7000			X	X	X
7100			X	X	X
7200			X	X	X
7500			X	X	
12000			X	X	
AGS+		X		X	

Router Configuration Examples

Most networks that are hierarchically designed use one or more of the core, distribution, or access layers. Each layer of the hierarchical design is discussed in this section.

Core Layer Routers

The core routers of a network are used to switch data traffic. If possible, limit the amount of traffic filtering at this level. For your core layer, you will want to have high availability, redundancy, and performance. This is where you spend your money. Get a good solid solution that is scalable and reliable.

Distribution Layer Routers

Distribution routers on a network provide the boundary or point when packet filtering and manipulation will begin. The distribution routers divide the core and access layers and allow the core routers to focus processing power and resources to core data-switching functions. You will still want to have redundancy and power, but not to the degree that you would on the core layers. Distribution layer routers will be performing more specific tasks and will be more limited in power, although unique in service offerings.

Access Layer Routers

The access layer of a network involves the end-user's attachment to the network. This can include switching as well as routing. Most of the access layer components include switches and bridges. Of course, Layer 3 switching can be included in this layer. As far as routing is concerned, you can use Cisco routers that are specifically built to be access routers in this area of your network.

Selecting the Appropriate Router

Cisco has a product selection tool that will allow you to make a decision on what model and type of router that you need depending on the parameters that you set. Check the Cisco Web site for more details. But one thing you should definitely get when selecting a router is a hot-swappable dual power supply, if available. When selecting a router component or routing software solution, it's important to look at the several areas of specification listed here:

- What is the cost of the solution?
- What types of routing features are supported?
- Can the router solution provide adequate throughput for your network?
- Can the router be upgraded if needed?
- How reliable is the history of the routing solution?
- Is this router model or routing solution new or proven?
- Does the routing solution make use of your current network infrastructure investment?

- What types of features are available on this router model?
- Is the router easily managed?
- Is the router being used as a core router, distribution router, or some type of access router?
- Do you or your staff have adequate training or knowledge to implement the routing solution?
- What Cisco IOS feature set is needed to implement this router solution?

Miscellaneous Hardware Components

The network hardware components listed in this section can be used, and will be needed, in a variety of network designs. Each component is discussed in general as to how it will work within a generic infrastructure. We won't use the Web to discuss these components in detail.

Multiplexers

A multiplexer can be a variety of networking components that split signals and resources to provide needed bandwidth for a variety of network applications. One example is a fiber optic multiplexer (mux) that splits a signal out into various network device channels. T1 lines employ multiplexing technology to split the T1 signal into smaller units for individual application use. There are two main types of multiplexing. Time-division multiplexing allocates each channel or application a specific time slice to process and/or transmit data. Frequency-division multiplexing separates bandwidth by frequency, allocating proper bandwidth needs for specific network services.

Modems

Remote access technology has moved rapidly and has been enhanced by new technologies. The standard dial-up modem has moved from a 300-baud, data set modem, used in corporate data centers, to a 56kbps standard for home use. Dial-up still remains the most popular (due to amount of use, not preference) access method for remote users to access corporate networks or the Internet. Newer technologies such as Digital Subscriber Line (DSL) can offer higher speeds than ISDN. Also, cable modem is another technology that promises higher speeds to access the Internet or remote networks. Realistically, corporate network users still will continue to use a dial-up solution to access their data. The remote solution does not have to be the latest technology; it just needs to work reliably and cost-effectively. It may be best to select a proven dial-up access solution for your network, not a recently released new technology that promises everything but doesn't work. Let someone else be the beta tester. Although there is limited bandwidth due to the shared nature of most of these remote access solutions, it's sufficient for today's network applications such as e-mail and Internet access.

Network Analyzer

One of the most important tools that you can have as a network designer or support personnel is a network analyzer. With a network analyzer, you can determine network bottlenecks, traffic problems, broadcasting information, protocol conversations, and generally just about anything that is going on in your network. Good network analyzers are expensive, but for the most part, you can use a cheaper tool for in-house use. If you were at a client site, it would be best to invest in a well-documented and known network analyzer tool. When you are charging your client a high hourly rate for your expertise and network analysis equipment, it's important to have a good network analyzer.

When analyzing network traffic, you can define information filters by IP address, the data pattern of the traffic, protocol, traffic type, packet type, packet size, and many other ways.

With a good network analyzer, you can capture network traffic for a detailed analysis, diagnose problems, monitor real-time network traffic, collect error statistics, create a network baseline for later comparisons, and develop notification services for network personnel based on configurable parameters. You can also use a network analyzer to generate traffic and develop load-testing and trend analysis.

Key Points

In this chapter, we talked about the hardware components that are critical to building your network. It's important for most network design projects to assess the current environment and Web in order to use the technology investment in network hardware that has already been installed. There are times when this is not necessary, practical, or recommended. Most corporations, however, are not building a network from scratch and just want you to implement a platform for an application that is being upgraded, enhanced, or installed for the first time. There is so much that goes into the decision on what type of hardware to buy. It seems that corporate politics plays so heavily into the decision when the prices reach the level that a lot of routers do.

In one situation that I encountered, I assessed the network and made the recommendations. They were reviewed. I was asked to make changes, not once, but several times. It had nothing to do with the technology; it was just a strategy to get the correct vendor to provide the hardware and get the contract. Six months later, the hardware appeared. The project finally took off and did get completed in time. But it can get frustrating when this happens. Depending on your position as a contractor, consultant, manager, or engineer, your experiences will vary widely. It just seems that when hardware purchases are involved, there are a lot of hands in the pot and more than technology decisions being made. It's important to take a step back and understand that sometimes your technologically sound network design may not be part of the overall plan for the business that you are working with.

This chapter covered hubs, bridges and bridging methods, switching and switching methods, routing and routing methods, and some miscellaneous network components. Each network component plays a part in providing your network users the services and quality that they expect. Probably one of the most important parts of making a good hardware choice is to get opinions from other network personnel that you know. You will have to admit that you don't know everything when you do this. But when you decide that the Cisco 2500 router is the best solution to connect all the schools in the school system together, you may be right. But there are other solutions, and maybe one might be right for you. With the amount of information on new technologies being brought out daily, it's impossible to know it all. You don't have to know everything, but you need to know how to get the answers. Some of these will come from other engineers and consultants, and some will come from vendor contacts and information. Use your resources and use them well.

Chapter 7

Network Software

This chapter covers the software features and applications that you can use to develop, maintain, secure, and optimize your network design. The three main areas of discussion are the Cisco Internetworking Operating System (IOS), network optimization methods, and Cisco product offerings. The first section, Cisco IOS, will cover an overview of the operating system, some frequently used commands, and different types of Cisco IOS feature sets. The network optimization methods section covers topics such as queuing and detection methods. Finally, we cover some Cisco-specific product offerings that are available for your network environment.

Cisco IOS

The Cisco Internetworking Operating System (IOS) is the pulse of the Cisco network. Cisco has developed this operating system to be included in each Cisco network product. With it, you can configure, test, maintain, design, and optimize your network.

Overview

The Cisco IOS is part of each and every hardware component that Cisco sells. The Cisco IOS integrates a network to provide scalable, optimized, secure network infrastructures. All Cisco network components work together through the IOS operating system. This section covers the Cisco IOS command line interface (CLI) and how it works.

The Cisco IOS operating system allows you to configure and manage a variety of network components. In this section and the remainder of this chapter, we use a network router as the sample network component to be configured or managed.

Command Modes

The major command modes within the Cisco IOS are User Exec mode, Privileged Exec mode, Global Configuration mode, Interface Configuration mode, and Boot mode.

User Exec Mode User Exec mode is the first mode that you will enter when your router comes up. More than likely, you will have to enter a console password to get to the User Exec mode. Only certain commands are available from this mode. Generally, you can list basic system information and perform some limited testing.

You can recognize User Exec mode from the router prompt. You will see the router host name followed by the >. It will look something like this:

```
routerhostname>
```

Table 7-1 is an alphabetical listing of some of the commands that are available from the User Exec mode and their purpose. The commands that are available to you may be different depending on the software feature set that is loaded on your router.

Table 7-1 *User Exec Commands*

Command	Purpose
access-enable	Create a temporary Access-List entry
clear	Reset functions
connect	Open a terminal connection
disable	Turn off privileged commands
disconnect	Disconnect an existing network connection
enable	Enter Privileged Exec mode
exit	Exit from User Exec mode
help	Description of the help system
lat	Open a LAT connection
lock	Lock the terminal

Command	Purpose
login	Log in as a particular user
logout	Exit from the EXEC
mrinfo	Request neighbor and version information from a multicast router
mstat	Show statistics after multiple multicast trace routes
mtrace	Trace reverse multicast path from destination to source
name-connection	Name an existing network connection
pad	Open an X.29 PAD connection
ping	Send echo messages
ppp	Start IETF Point-to-Point Protocol (PPP)
resume	Resume an active network connection
rlogin	Open an rlogin connection
show	Show running system information
slip	Start Serial-line IP (SLIP)
systat	Display information about terminal lines
telnet	Open a telnet connection
terminal	Set terminal line parameters
tn3270	Open a tn3270 connection
traceroute	Trace route to destination
tunnel	Open a tunnel connection
where	List active connections
x3	Set X.3 parameters on PAD
xremote	Enter XRemote mode

Some of these commands (as you may have figured out) will be of little use to you, but you'll want to use others on a daily basis.

Privileged Exec Mode Privileged Exec mode allows you to make configuration changes to your router. Once you have entered Privileged Exec mode, you can move into other configuration modes that change configuration values and parameters. To enter Privileged Exec mode, enter the enable command at the User Exec mode prompt. Once you have entered the enable command, you will probably be prompted for a password. If you enter the correct password, you will see the new router prompt that indicates that you are now in Privileged Exec mode. You will see the router host name followed by the #. It will look something like this:

```
routerhostname#
```

Privileged Exec mode allows you access to all the different configuration modes available to you, depending on your router's particular Cisco IOS feature set. As you can easily tell from Table 7-2, there are many Privileged Exec mode commands that are also available in User Exec mode. Commands in **bold type** are not available in User Exec mode.

Table 7-2 *Privileged Exec Commands*

Command	Purpose
access-enable	Create a temporary Access-List entry
access-template	**Create a temporary Access-List entry**
bfe	**For manual emergency modes setting**
clear	Reset functions
clock	**Manage the system clock**
configure	**Enter configuration mode**
connect	Open a terminal connection
copy	**Copy configuration or image data**
debug	**Debugging functions**
disable	Turn off privileged commands
disconnect	Disconnect an existing network connection
enable	Turn on privileged commands
erase	**Erase flash or configuration memory**
exit	Exit from the EXEC
help	Description of the interactive help system
lat	Open a LAT connection
lock	Lock the terminal
login	Log in as a particular user
logout	Exit from the EXEC
mrinfo	Request neighbor and version information from a multicast router
mstat	Show statistics after multiple multicast trace routes

Command	Purpose
mtrace	Trace reverse multicast path from destination to source
name-connection	Name an existing network connection
ncia	**Start/Stop NCIA Server**
no	**Disable debugging functions**
pad	Open an X.29 PAD connection
ping	Send echo messages
ppp	Start IETF Point-to-Point Protocol (PPP)
reload	**Halt and perform a cold restart**
resume	Resume an active network connection
rlogin	Open an rlogin connection
rsh	**Execute a remote command**
sdlc	**Send SDLC test frames**
send	**Send a message to other tty lines**
setup	**Run the SETUP command facility**
show	Show running system information
slip	Start Serial-line IP (SLIP)
start-chat	**Start a chat-script on a line**
systat	Display information about terminal lines
tarp	**TARP (Target ID Resolution Protocol) commands**
telnet	Open a telnet connection
terminal	Set terminal line parameters
test	**Test subsystems, memory, and interfaces**
tn3270	Open a tn3270 connection
traceroute	Trace route to destination
tunnel	Open a tunnel connection
undebug	**Disable debugging functions**
verify	**Verify checksum of a Flash file**
where	List active connections
which-route	**OSI route table lookup and display results**
write	**Write running configuration to memory, network, or terminal**
x3	Set X.3 parameters on PAD
xremote	Enter XRemote mode

Global Configuration Mode Global Configuration mode allows you access to all the other configuration modes on your router. Global Configuration mode commands will change system-wide parameters. To enter Global Configuration mode, enter the `configuration terminal` command. Your router prompt will change again and will look something like this:

```
routerhostname(config)#
```

This prompt shows you that you are in Privileged Exec mode/Global Configuration mode. Table 7-3 gives an alphabetical listing of commands available from Global Configuration mode. The commands available to you will be different depending on the feature set of your router. The commands in **bold type** are not available in either User Exec mode or Privileged Exec mode.

Table 7-3 Global Configuration Commands

Command	Purpose
aaa	Authentication, Authorization and Accounting
access-list	Add an access list entry
alias	Create command alias
apollo	Apollo global configuration commands
appletalk	Appletalk global configuration commands
arap	Appletalk Remote Access Protocol
arp	Set a static ARP entry
async-bootp	Modify system bootp parameters
autonomous-system	Specify local AS number to which we belong
banner	Define a login banner
boot	Modify system boot parameters
bridge	Bridge Group
bstun	BSTUN global configuration commands
buffers	Adjust system buffer pool parameters
busy-message	Display message when connection to host fails
cdp	Global CDP configuration subcommands
chat-script	Define a modem chat script
clns	Global CLNS configuration subcommands

Command	Purpose
clock	Configure time-of-day clock
config-register	Define the configuration register
decnet	Global DECnet configuration subcommands
default	Set a command to its defaults
default-value	Default character-bits values
dialer-list	Create a dialer list entry
dlsw	Data Link Switching global configuration commands
dnsix-dmdp	Provide DMDP service for DNSIX
dnsix-nat	Provide DNSIX service for audit trails
downward-compatible -config	Generate a configuration compatible with older software
dspu	DownStream Physical Unit Command
enable	Modify enable password parameters
end	Exit from configure mode
endnode	SNA APPN endnode command
exception	Exception handling
exit	Exit from configure mode
frame-relay	Global frame relay configuration commands
help	Description of the interactive help system
hostname	Set system's network name
interface	Select an interface to configure
ip	Global IP configuration subcommands
ipx	Novell/IPX global configuration commands
kerberos	Configure Kerberos
key	Key management
keymap	Define a new keymap
lat	DEC Local Area Transport (LAT) transmission protocol
line	Configure a terminal line
lnm	IBM Lan Manager
locaddr-priority -list	Establish queuing priorities based on LU address
location	Network Management Router location command
logging	Modify message logging facilities

Continued

Table 7-3 *Continued*

Command	Purpose
login-string	Define a host-specific login string
map-class	Configure static map class
map-list	Configure static map list
menu	Define a user-interface menu
modemcap	Modem Capabilities database
mop	Configure the DEC MOP Server
multilink	PPP multilink global configuration
ncia	Native Client Interface Architecture
netbios	NETBIOS access control filtering
no	Negate a command or set its defaults
ntp	Configure NTP
partition	Partition device
printer	Define an LPD printer
priority-list	Build a priority list
privilege	Command privilege parameters
prompt	Set system's prompt
queue-list	Build a custom queue list
resume-string	Define a host-specific resume string
rif	Source-route RIF cache
rlogin	Rlogin configuration commands
rmon	Remote Monitoring
route-map mode	Create route-map or enter route-map command
router	Enable a routing process
rsrb	RSRB LSAP/DSAP filtering
rtr	RTR Base Configuration
sap-priority-list	Establish queuing priorities based on SAP and/or MAC address(es)
scheduler	Scheduler parameters
service	Modify use of network-based services
sgbp	SGBP Stack Group Bidding Protocol configuration
smrp	Simple Multicast Routing Protocol configuration commands
sna	Network Management Physical Unit command

Command	Purpose
`snmp-server`	Modify SNMP parameters
`source-bridg`	Source-route bridging ring groups
`state-machine`	Define a TCP dispatch state machine
`stun`	STUN global configuration commands
`tacacs-server`	Modify TACACS query parameters
`tarp`	Global TARP configuration subcommands
`terminal-queue`	Terminal queue commands
`tftp-server`	Provide TFTP service for netload requests
`tn3270`	tn3270 configuration command
`translate`	Translate global configuration commands
`ttycap`	Define a new termcap
`username`	Establish User Name Authentication
`vines`	VINES global configuration commands
`vpdn`	Virtual Private Dial-up Network
`vty-async`	Enable virtual async line configuration
`x25`	X.25 Level 3
`x29`	X29 commands
`xns`	XNS global configuration commands
`xremote`	Configure Xremote

Interface Configuration Mode The Interface Configuration mode allows you to make configuration changes on a per-interface level. Interface Configuration mode commands only affect the interface that is being accessed. Once you have entered the Global Configuration mode, you enter the `interface` command with the appropriate interface that you wish to access. You will then see a new prompt that looks something like this:

```
routerhostname(config-if)#
```

This prompt shows you that you are in Privileged Exec mode/Global Configuration mode/Interface Configuration mode. There are a host of commands that are available once you enter the interface that you wish to configure.

ROM Monitor Mode (Boot Mode) ROM Monitor mode is one mode that you don't want to be in unexpectedly if you are upgrading your router configuration files. If the system can't find a valid image to upload, the router will default to ROM Monitor mode, or Boot mode as it is sometimes called. In Boot mode, you have limited capabilities to configure or manage your router. Boot mode is a small subset of the Cisco IOS. You will see a prompt that looks something like this:

```
boot>
```

Optionally, you can enter Boot mode if you interrupt the normal boot sequence on your router.

Online Editing

The Cisco IOS provides a few important and helpful tools to help you view, change, and edit basic commands and tasks. A few of the more common editing tools are discussed. We include help, cursor movement, history, and menu editing features in this section.

Help The Cisco ISO offers some great online help features. In each of the command modes that are available on your router, there is a help system that you can use to both complete command sequences and see what's available to configure and maintain the router. Just enter the help command to list the help system information.

A unique feature of the Cisco IOS is called *context-sensitive help*. This feature allows you to complete command sequences with little knowledge of the command syntax. When you enter a portion of a command and a question mark, the system will list all possible commands with that beginning portion that you've entered. Suppose you know that there is a command that copies a system image from a tftp server to a router. You can enter co ? at the router prompt, and the system will list all commands that begin with co. You can continue this type of sequence with the copy command by entering copy ?. The system will then prompt you with all the keywords associated with the copy command. You can continue this process until you have found all the commands that enable you to copy a system image from a tftp server to a router.

Keystroke Commands To move around within the Cisco IOS system, there are many keystroke commands that will enable you to navigate around in the IOS environment. Following are partial lists of the keystroke commands available.

Backward cursor movement commands:

- Ctrl-B — Moves the cursor back one character
- Esc-B — Moves the cursor back one word
- Ctrl-A — Moves the cursor to the beginning of the line

Forward cursor movement commands:

- Ctrl-F — Moves the cursor forward one character
- Esc-F — Moves the cursor forward one word
- Ctrl-E — Moves the cursor to the end of the line

Deletion cursor commands:

- Delete — Erases the character that was just entered
- Ctrl-D — Deletes the character that is at the cursor
- Ctrl-K — Deletes all the characters from the cursor location to the end of the line

Recall cursor commands:

- Ctrl-P — Recalls most recent command; repeat recalls older commands
- Ctrl-N — Use in conjunction with Ctrl-P keystroke sequence to recall new commands

There are many more keystroke commands available. It's a good idea to become familiar with keystroke commands for ease of navigation.

History The history feature is a timesaving option that allows the administrator to recall commands during a console session. A configurable number of commands are saved in a history buffer, the default being 10. If you reboot the router, the command line history function does not save the previous session's history. This is a good security feature, and it also keeps your mistakes to yourself!

Menus Creating menus is a good way to control access to certain functions within the Cisco IOS. If you have personnel who need access to router functions, but who don't know or don't want to know, how to navigate through the router commands, then the menu option is a nice feature to enable on your routers. Menus are created from within the configuration mode of the router. It's a good idea to restrict access to menu creation for your own sanity.

Configuration Tools

There are alternatives to using the command line interface (CLI). When installing software, you can use automated configuration tools. One example is the Remote Software Loader (RSL) that allows you to load a new system image without even knowing one Cisco IOS command. However, should RSL fail to work, it's important to know what IOS commands can replace the configuration tool process. Automated tools are great; however, as we all know too well, there are circumstances that prohibit the use of them. When they don't work, we do. Understanding the IOS commands behind the automated configuration files goes a long way when you are faced with an unruly router, laptop problems, or bad cabling as the sun fades in the background and interstate traffic begins to mount.

With that in mind, here are a few of the configuration tools that Cisco offers to help automate basic configuration tasks.

Autoinstall Autoinstall is a configuration tool that allows you to install a Cisco IOS operating system without manual intervention. When you install a new router into your network, you can use the autoinstall configuration tool to automatically load and configure your new router from a TFTP server. Autoinstall requires that you have another router up in your network before you bring the new one online to complete the configuration process.

Setup Setup is a Cisco IOS feature that enables you to configure a new router when it comes up into the network for the first time. Setup can also be used to automate certain administrative functions once the router has been configured and is operating in the network.

When you use the setup feature for a first-time installation, be sure that you have all your router configuration data available to you. Setup will prompt you to provide interface configuration data, protocol information, network addressing, and password information.

Using setup after the initial configuration is a good idea when you have to make major changes to your router configurations. When you invoke setup, the System Configuration dialog box will open and walk you through the process of making configuration changes to your routers. Setup will continue to prompt you for configuration information. As you make your changes, setup writes a script file that will hold the changes until you verify them at the end of the process.

ConfigMaker ConfigMaker is an application that runs from a Windows Intel system to allow you to configure your network routers. ConfigMaker is generally used for smaller networks.

ConfigMaker is a good tool for experienced network administrators who know and understand their network environment. With ConfigMaker, you can create a diagram of your proposed network, and the configuration files will automatically be generated with the most common interface commands and features.

There are several options that are included with ConfigMaker that help you in your network design.

- AutoDetect Device Wizard detects devices and network interface cards on your network.

- VPN Wizard — Virtual Private Network (VPN) links are discovered using the VPN Wizard.

- The Firewall Wizard allows you to figure out how to implement a firewall between you and the Internet.

- The Network Address Translation (NAT) feature defines static translations to your network devices.

- The Deliver Wizard uses the host COM port to deliver device information.

Remote Software Loader Remote Software Loader (RSL) is an easy-to-use software image loader application that runs from a remote network host. You can upgrade system image files to your router. RSL requires certain prerequisites before it will work correctly. You will need a Windows-based machine to host the RSL application. Of course, TCP/IP must be correctly configured for access to your router. On the hardware side, you will need a Token Ring or Ethernet adapter from your host machine and the appropriate cable to attach to the router Ethernet port. Use the Ethernet crossover cable that was supplied with your router for an Ethernet adapter. Next, you will need a serial cable to connect from your console port on your router to the serial port on your host machine. You can use RSL to upgrade routers with an existing configuration or to set up a new router with no configuration. There are a few options that you may want to change depending on your unique configuration and needs, but basically RSL works very well.

The next section covers some configuration information to help you get your router up and running.

Router Configuration

Although the number of Cisco IOS operating system commands is numerous, there are some very common commands that are used on a continuing basis to perform daily tasks and maintenance functions. This listing is not exhaustive, but it will explain each command, how it is used, and how it works together with other commands to complete your network design and maintenance tasks. We cover areas such as maintenance tasks and interface configuration.

Maintenance Tasks

Maintenance tasks take on a variety of forms, from network upgrades, documentation, preventative maintenance, and everything in between. Many times, it seems that there is not enough time to get all the things done with projects, deadlines, new projects, new deadlines, politics, network "disasters," firefighting, and everything else that we deal with on a daily basis. Here are a few basic maintenance tasks that need daily attention.

Router status It's important that you know the status of your router interfaces and configurations on a daily basis. There are a variety of show commands that will allow you to verify the status of your router interfaces and configuration.

Tip

You can display a long list of router status information including buffers, protocols, stacks, and other important configuration data with the show tech-support command.

Here are a few of the more common show command options and their uses.

- buffers — Displays more buffer information than you'd care to know. Included are buffer elements, public buffer pools, and interface buffer pools.

- configuration — Displays the configuration information for each of the router interfaces, including console, aux and vty.

- interfaces — Displays interface information, including hardware port status, protocol line status, interface network address, queuing strategy, and error counts.

- protocols — Displays each of the interface protocols that are running on the router and their status.

- running-config — Displays current configuration that the router is using, including all the configuration information for each of the router interfaces, including console, aux, and vty.

- version — Displays version number, router uptime, system image file name, memory types and sizes, interfaces available, and configuration register setting.

Upgrading Memory Upgrading memory hardware should be a very simple and straightforward process. Check with your router documentation on the correct way to disassemble the router to easily access the memory components that you are to upgrade. Main memory, flash memory, and shared memory can all be upgraded within minutes. Be sure that you have some type of electrostatic discharge equipment available. Although most of the time it's not necessary, that one-in-a-hundred time is worth the effort. The first question that will come up during a failure is, "Did you wear your wrist strap?" If you don't have a wrist strap available, you can use an electrostatic discharge bag that many network components are shipped in. Just hold the memory chip with the bag and discharge any static on the router before installation. Weather conditions and building environment conditions can also contribute to excessive electrostatic charge. And, don't wear polyester!

Testing and Troubleshooting One of the most important things that you can do is perform preventative maintenance tasks on your router configuration. Here are a few commands that can help you verify your router configuration and network connectivity.

Ping—The `ping` command is probably one of the better-known commands for network connectivity verification. You can enter a simple `ping` from the User Exec prompt. You are probably familiar with most of the options. There is an interactive `ping` command that is available in Privileged Exec mode. The extended `ping` command is an interactive command that will prompt you for extended host information. Table 7-4 shows an example of the prompts for the interactive `ping` command:

Table 7-4 *Interactive Ping Command Prompts*

Prompt	Example
Enter the ping command	`routerhostname#`**`ping`**
Enter protocol type; default is IP	`Protocol [ip]`
Enter target IP address for ping	`Target IP address:` **`10.1.1.0`**
Enter number of repeats; default is 5	`Repeat count [x]:` **`25`**
Enter datagram size	`Datagram size [xxx]:` **`200`**
Enter timeout value	`Timeout in seconds [xx]:` **`10`**
Enter additional commands	`Extended co)mands [n]:`**`y`**
	`Source address or interface:` **`0.0.0.0`**
	`Type of service [x]:`
	`Set DF bit in IP header? [xx]:` **`n`**
	`Validate reply data? [xx]:` **`n`**
	`Data pattern [xxxxxx]:`
	`Loose, Strict, Record, Timestamp, Verbose [none]:`
Enter sweep range of sizes information	`Sweep range of sizes [x]:`**`y`**
	`Sweep min size [x]:`
	`Sweep max size [xxxx]:`
	`Sweep interval [x]:`

The interactive `ping` command takes on a life of its own depending on the options that you choose; the above description is just an example of the options that may be available to you on your network router.

Trace — The `trace` command can be run from User Exec mode, or if you are using extended trace, you will need to be in Privileged Exec mode. `Trace` will help you to verify the route that the packets are taking to cross your network. The options that are needed with this command include the protocol that you are using as well as the destination address.

Debug — As the name indicates, `debug` is a command that will allow you to troubleshoot a variety of router anomalies and internetworking troubles. There are numerous options that you can use with the `debug` command from Privileged Exec mode. Here are a few `debug` options that can be used to troubleshoot your network problems:

- all — Enables all diagnostic information to be displayed
- broadcast — Displays information about MAC broadcasts
- ip routing — Displays information on RIP table updates
- ip security — Displays information for IP security options

Caution

The debug commands should be used with caution, due to the fact that when used improperly they can consume a lot of router resources. Don't use the "all" option unless you are willing to contribute excessive load to your network.

Test — The `test` command has several options to assist in troubleshooting your router problems. Some options can be used in User Exec mode, others in Privileged Exec mode. Most of the `test` command options are not useful in troubleshooting a live network environment. Be careful when using this command.

Caution

The test command is mostly used by personnel performing router configuration testing prior to shipment. Be cautious when using this command; don't use this in a live network environment!

Rebooting a Router Although the task of rebooting your network router is simple, there are a few things to consider before doing it, especially during peak user hours. If you are having network problems that require a power-off reboot of your router, be sure that your router's configuration register is set to boot from the proper image. This is especially important with routers that are at remote locations. Although this shouldn't be a problem, it's important to know how the configuration register works and how you can change it should the need arise. Sometimes, routers will remain up for a long period of time; it's only when the router is rebooted that problems surface. The 16-bit configuration register is located in Non Volatile RAM (NVRAM) and sets the boot location for each router. To verify the configuration register setting, you will need to get into Privileged Exec mode/Configuration mode on your router and then issue the *config*-register command in Privileged Exec mode with the appropriate register settings. The least significant four bits make up the boot field register. Here are the boot field register settings and the system image load location associated with each setting:

- 0x0 — Router will boot to ROM monitor mode.
- 0x1 — Router will boot from ROM image.
- 0x2 through 0xF — Router will boot normally and then look for system image in NVRAM.

 Tip

To verify the boot location for the router, check the status of the configuration register with the show version command. The boot location is listed in the last line of the command.

There is an option to perform a router reload on off-peak hours. In Privileged Exec mode, enter the reload in command that will allow you to specify an hour and minute time period before the router will reboot. Or, you can enter the reload at command where the option is to reload the router at a specified time.

Interface Configuration

There are many interface configuration commands. As we discussed previously, the Interface Configuration mode is a sub-area of the Global Configuration mode. There are a wide variety of configuration commands that allow you to implement detailed configurations for your specific protocols and networking environment. Another feature that adds flexibility to your interface configurations is the sub-interface configurations. A sub-interface is the method to allow one physical channel to be multiplexed into several logical channels. Most network implementations use some type of sub-interface method. As an example, T1s can be broken down to specific sub-interfaces to allow network applications to use only a specific amount of bandwidth.

The syntax and options of all the interface configuration commands are beyond the scope of this book. Consult your router documentation to get a clearer picture of all the available configurations that you can use in your network, or better yet, use the context-sensitive help to get you started on your router configurations.

Listed here are a few configuration commands that you can use to get started with some of the protocols and technologies that we have discussed thus far in the *Cisco Network Design Handbook*. Commands in bold type are entered as shown. Italicized commands are parameters that are unique to your network.

AppleTalk To enable AppleTalk routing:

Appletalk routing *router-number*

(router-number is a unique number in your AppleTalk network.)
To assign an AppleTalk address to a router interface:

appletalk address *network.node*

To assign a domain number to a router interface:

appletalk domain-group *domain-number*

(domain-number is a predefined AppleTalk domain number.)
To assign an AppleTalk access-list to a router interface:

appletalk access-group *access-list-number*

To assign a routing protocol to use on an AppleTalk interface:

appletalk protocol *routing protocol*

(routing protocol is the routing protocol to use.)

ATM To assign an encapsulation method to a serial interface:

encapsulation atm-dxi

(All keywords are required for this command.)

To map a protocol to a specific VPI and VCI:

dxi map *protocol protocol-address vpi vci*

(protocol can be any number of protocol keywords including ip, appletalk, bridging, decnet, etc. *protocol-address* is a predefined AppleTalk domain number. *vpi* is a Virtual Path Identifier. *vci* is a Virtual Channel Identifier.)
  To show protocol addresses map to a serial interface:

show dxi map

(All keywords are required for this command.)
  To show ATM traffic:

show atm traffic

(All keywords are required for this command.)
  To enable ATM AAL3/4 on a router interface:

atm aal aal3/4

(All keywords are required for this command.)

BGP To start configuration of BGP on a router interface:

router bgp *autonomous-system*

(autonomous-system is the autonomous system number that will announce BGP router to other BGP routers.)
  To specify a BGP confederation:

bgp confederation identifier *autonomous-system*

(autonomous-system is the autonomous system number.)
  To reset a BGP connection:

clear ip bgp *address*

(address is the BGP neighbor address.)
  To show BGP paths:

show ip bgp paths

(All keywords are required for this command.)

Cisco Gateway Discovery Protocol To enable GDP discovery process on a router:

`ip gdp gdp`

(All keywords are required for this command.)
    To enable GDP discovery process by using the IGRP routing protocol:

`ip gdp igrp`

(All keywords are required for this command.)

Cisco Discovery Protocol To enable CDP on a router interface:

`cdp enable`

(All keywords are required for this command.)
    To assign a domain number to a router interface:

`cdp holdtime` *seconds*

(*seconds* is the number of seconds that a device should hold the cdp information packet before releasing.)

Cisco Data Link Switching Plus To enable and disable DLSW+:

`dlsw disable`

(All keywords are required for this command.)
    To display reachability information for DLSW:

`show dlsw reachability`

(All keywords are required for this command.)
    To display DLSW peer information:

`show dlsw peers` *type number ip-address*

(*type* is the interface type; *number* is the interface number; *ip-address* is the peer IP address.)

DECnet To enable DECnet routing:

`decnet` *network-number* `routing` *area number.node number* (*network-number* is the network number (between 0 and 3); *area number* is the DECnet area number; *node number* is the DECnet node number.)

To create a DECnet access group:

decnet access-group *access-list number*

(*access-list number* is a number between 300 and 399 for extended access list.)

To show DECnet interface and configuration status:

show decnet interface *type number*

(*type* is the interface type; *number* is the interface number.)

EIGRP To start EIGRP routing:

router eigrp *process-id*

(*process-id* is the autonomous system or process number that identifies routes to other EIGRP routers.)

To show EIGRP topology table:

show ip eigrp topology *as-number ip-address*

(*as-number* is the autonomous system number; *ip-address* is the IP address.)

To enable split-horizon on an EIGRP interface:

ip split-horizon eigrp *as-number*

(*as-number* is the autonomous system number.)

To show EIGRP traffic statistics:

show ip eigrp traffic *as-number*

(*as-number* is the autonomous system number.)

To show EIGRP neighbors:

show ip eigrp neighbors *type number*

(*type* is the interface type; *number* is the interface number.)

To clear an EIGRP neighbor from the neighbor table:

clear ip eigrp neighbors *ip-address*

(*ip-address* is the IP address of the neighbor to be removed.)

Ethernet To begin the configuration process of an Ethernet interface on your router:

`interface ethernet` *interface*

(*interface* is the number of the interface that you are configuring.)
    To show Ethernet interface information:

`show interfaces ethernet` *port*

(*port* is the port number for interface.)

FDDI To begin the configuration process of an FDDI interface on your router:

`interface fddi` *interface*

(*interface* is the number of the interface that you are configuring.)
    To show information about an FDDI interface:

`show interfaces fddi` *number*

(*number* is the port number or port/slot number of the FDDI interface.)

Frame Relay To enable Frame Relay on a router interface:

`encapsulation frame-relay` *cisco*/*ietf*

(*cisco* uses Cisco encapsulation method; *ietf* uses IETF encapsulation method.)
    To assign mapping from network addresses to Frame Relay DLCI:

`frame-relay map` *protocol protocol-address dlci*

(*protocol* is the protocol that is being supported on the interface; *protocol-address* is the destination address; *dlci* is the DLCI number.)
    To specify a static route for PVC switching:

`frame-relay route` *in-dlci out-interface out-dlci*

(*in-dlci* is the specific DLCI where packets are received; *out-interface* is the router interface to use; *out-dlci* is the specific DLCI where packets are transmitted.)

To display information about the DLCI interface:

show interfaces serial *number*

(*number* is the interface number.)

IBM SNA To set the encapsulation method for SDLC:

encapsulation sdlc

(All keywords are required for this command.)

To assign a router interface as either a primary or secondary SDLC station:

sdlc role *none/primary/secondary*

(*none* assigns as a primary or secondary station depending on the end station configuration; *primary* assigns as a primary station; *secondary* assigns as a secondary station.)

To enable APPN routing:

appn routing

(All keywords are required for this command.)

IGRP To start IGRP on a router:

router igrp *process-id*

(*process-id* is the autonomous system or process number that identifies routes to other IGRP routers.)

IP To enable IP routing:

ip routing

(All keywords are required for this command.)

To create a standard IP access list:

access-list access-list-number *deny/permit source wildcard*

(*deny/permit* denies or permits conditions; *source* is where data is coming from; *wildcard* represents wildcard bits applied to the source address.)

To allow network packets with no default routes to be routed efficiently:

ip classless

(All keywords are required for this command.)

To set an IP address for an interface:

ip address *ip-address mask*

(*ip-address* is the specified IP address for the interface; *mask* is the IP address mask.)

To enable forwarding of UDP broadcasts through an interface:

ip helper-address *address*

(*address* is the address to be used when performing UDP broadcast forwarding.)

To clear an IP address from the routing table:

clear ip route *network mask*

(*network mask* is the network address and subnet mask to be removed.)

To assign default domain names for IP addresses:

ip domain name *name*

(*name* is used to complete unqualified domain names.)

ISDN To configure an ISDN BRI interface:

isdn bri *number.subinterface-number multipoint/point-to-point*

(*number* is the port number that is factory-assigned to the router interface; *sub-interface-number* is the sub-interface number for the assigned port; *multipoint/point-to-point* is an optional parameter that specifies the sub-interface type.)

To show information about ISDN BRI:

show controllers bri *number*

(*number* is the interface number.)

To configure an ISDN switch type:

isdn switch-type *switch-type*

(*switch-type* is the switch type provided by the network provider.)
To show information about ISDN PRI services:

show isdn services

(All keywords are required for this command.)

IS-IS To enable IS-IS routing:

router is-is *tag*

(*tag* is used to name a routing process; this option is not necessary, but if used must be a unique process name on the configured router.)
To configure a router for an IS-IS level:

is-type *level-1/level-2/level-2 only*

(*level-1* configures the router as a Level 1 station router; *level-2* configures the router as a Level 2 station and area router; *level-2 only* configures the router as a Level 2 area router only.)
To configure the password for a specified IS-IS router interface:

is-password *password level-1/level-2*

(*password* is the assigned password; *level-1* configures the password for Level 1; *level-2* configures the password for Level 2.)

NLSP To enable NLSP on a router interface:

ipx nlsp *tag* **enable**

(*tag* is the optional NLSP process name.)

Novell IPX To start IPX routing on a router interface:

ipx network *network* **encapsulation** *encapsulation-type*

(*network* is the IPX network number; *encapsulation-type* is the type of encapsulation for the interface — snap, sap, novell-ether, novell-fddi.)

To shut down an IPX network, resulting in *administratively down* status:

ipx down *network*

(*network* is the IPX network number.)
To show the contents of the IPX routing table for a particular network:

show ipx route *network*

(*network* is the network number.)
To show IPX traffic information:

show ipx traffic

(All keywords are required for this command.)
OSPF To enable OSPF on a router:

router ospf *process-id*

(*process-id* is the identification for the OSPF process assigned to the local router.)
To display OSPF processes routing information:

show ip ospf *process-id*

(*process-id* is used to show specific process information; it can be excluded for a full listing of processes.)
To display OSPF interface routing information:

show ip ospf interface *type number*

(*type* is the interface type; *number* is the interface number.)
To configure OSPF network type:

ip ospf network *broadcast/non-broadcast/point-to-multipoint*

(*broadcast* sets network type to broadcast; *non-broadcast* sets network type to nonbroadcast; *point-to-multipoint* sets network type to point-to-multipoint.)
To set the hello packet interval:

ip ospf hello-interval *seconds*

(*seconds* is the hello interval time in seconds.)

PPP To enable PPP encapsulation on a router interface:

encapsulation ppp

(All keywords are required for this command.)
   To enable PPP callback:

ppp callback *accept/initiate*

(*accept* accepts callback requests; *initiate* initiates a callback.)

RIP To configure RIP on a router:

router rip

(All keywords are required for this command.)
   To specify the RIP version to receive on an interface:

ip rip receive version *1/2*

(*1* receives only RIPv1 packets on the interface; *2* receives only RIPv2 packets on the interface.)
   To specify the RIP version to send on an interface:

ip rip send version *1/2*

(*1* receives only RIPv1 packets on the interface; *2* receives only RIPv2 packets on the interface.)

SMDS To enable SMDS service on a router interface:

encapsulation smds

(All keywords are required for this command.)
   To assign a specific SMDS address for an interface:

smds address *smds-address*

(*smds-address* is the unique SMDS address.)
   To show SMDS packet statistics:

show smds traffic

(All keywords are required for this command.)

Source Route Bridging To configure a router interface for Source Route Bridging:

`source-bridge` *local-ring bridge-number target-ring*

(*local-ring* identifies a ring within the Token Ring network; *bridge-number* identifies a bridge between local and target rings; *target-ring* identifies a destination ring number.)

Token Ring To begin the configuration of a Token Ring interface on your router:

`interface tokenring` *number*

(*number* identifies the interface number to be configured.)

Miscellaneous Router Management Commands To shut down an interface:

`shutdown` *interface*

(*interface* is the interface to shut down.)
 To display the debugging capabilities of your router:

`show debugging`

(All keywords are required for this command.)
 To show the status of SNMP:

`show snmp`

(All keywords are required for this command.)
 This command allows you to set certain memory size specifications and create a dump of core memory when the limits have been reached. To trap memory size problems:

`exception memory` *fragment size minimum size*

(*fragment size* represents the contiguous blocks of free pool memory; *minimum size* is the minimum size of free pool memory.)

To create a syslog host to log router messages:

logging *host*

(*host* is the address of the host to be used as the syslog server.)

To display the physical statistics for your router such as power, temperature, etc.:

show environment

(All keywords are required for this command.)

Feature Sets

Feature Sets are software image packages that are developed for the purpose of expediting the release of the Cisco IOS software and enabling end-users to have the correct options and features that their unique network infrastructures demand.

Each Cisco hardware platform has a basic feature set. Also, the user can select the plus feature set that includes additional functionality. Don't confuse a feature set with a feature pack. A feature *set* is the actual software image that has the features that you need for your network. A feature *pack* is the physical bundle or pack that you receive with your hardware. The feature pack includes a CD-ROM with the software feature set, a Remote Software Loader (RSL), software licensing agreements, and Cisco documentation. It's important to take a look at each feature set and the capabilities of each one. These are a few feature sets that Cisco offers, listed alphabetically:

- CFRAD (Frame Relay Access Products)
- Desktop(IP/IPX/AppleTalk/DEC)
- Enterprise
- IP Routing
- IP/IPX/IBM/APPN
- ISDN
- LAN FRAD (LAN Frame Relay Access Device)
- OSPF LANFRAD (OSPF LAN Frame Relay Access Device)
- Remote Access Server

Within each feature set there is a basic option feature set and a plus option feature set. There are also other specialty feature sets available for special configurations.

Network Optimization Methods – Quality of Service

This section covers network optimization methods that you will encounter in your network design process. Each method is a description of a feature of Cisco network software, or a definition of a network technology that is used in Cisco networks that will help you to optimize your network design.

Quality of Service (QoS) is basically a measurement system for an infrastructure that is based on a variety of components. Within a Cisco network, QoS is a feature that is available on certain switches. The entire concept of QoS refers to the network's ability to provide enhanced services. QoS technologies focus on the ability to provide bandwidth guarantees with increased throughput. QoS means a lot of things to different people in the networking industry. Of course, we all have unique vantage pointsto maintain our own understanding of what QoS means today and will mean in the future. For this book, we refer to QoS as a set of software features available within the Cisco IOS to enhance network functionality and provide quality network services within an Enterprise network.

We discuss a few of the QoS features, including detection methods, commonly referred to as congestion management techniques, queuing, traffic shaping, and committed access rates.

Detection Methods

Detection methods enable networks to anticipate and avoid congestion. Network bottleneck areas can be monitored to provide proactive congestion avoidance. Congestion-avoidance techniques use a packet-dropping method referred to as tail-drop. Random Early Detection (RED) is a detection method that is used primarily in high-speed networks. RED drops packets in a random fashion, thereby reducing the chance that entire networks will slow due to synchronization across the network.

Cisco has a RED implementation called Weighted Random Early Detection (WRED) that allows packet-dropping parameters to be configured by the network administrator. The network administrator enables WRED on a router interface and can configure the packet drop rate.

Random Early Detection

RED is actually a very simple concept. RED addresses network congestion by dropping packets when network congestion is imminent. RED works well on networks where the protocol is aware and sensitive to packet dropping. If the protocol slows down network traffic when packets are dropped, that's great. Protocols such as TCP/IP do respond to packet loss and slow network traffic.

 Caution

Most RED implementations are based on the premise that when packets are dropped, the traffic loss will temporarily slow down the network. Although this works with TCP/IP networks, it is not as effective with AppleTalk or Novell network implementations.

RED's implementation on a TCP/IP network works with the TCP queuing mechanism. RED will attempt to reduce the queue size of the source host by dropping packets and therefore notifying the source that the transmission rate of the packets should decrease. Hopefully, this process slows down network traffic and avoids congestion.

RED will selectively drop packets early prior to network congestion. If a RED implementation is not used, network congestion will fill output buffers. Full output buffers will cause a condition called tail drop, which will drop all additional packets in the transmission stream. Tail drop in turn causes TCP traffic to slow down throughout the entire network. Once the congestion clears, the traffic flow will increase until the next network congestion. RED overcomes the tail drop scenario by selectively dropping packets when a router interface reports congestion. This selective packet dropping will prevent the entire network from slowing down and will keep the traffic flowing at a less reduced rate. RED can also drop more packets from a higher transmission path than a lower transmission path. Weighted Random Early Detection (WRED) is a feature in Cisco IOS software that allows packet types to be dropped based on priority settings.

Weighted Random Early Detection

Weighted Random Early Detection (WRED) can be configured by a network administrator to determine the packet drop rate. The `random-detect` command is used to start the router interface configuration.

WRED uses average queue length to decide when to drop packets and allows the network administrator to configure packet dropping based on IP precedence. By default, WRED won't drop IP traffic packets prior to other traffic. It's important to configure WRED based on your unique network. The whole concept behind WRED is based on priorities, but be careful that any non-IP traffic is not taking the brunt of the WRED packet-dropping method. Of course, maybe non-IP traffic is not a priority, which is okay, but be sure you are aware of protocol traffic and consequences of using any RED implementation on your network.

Committed Access Rate

The Committed Access Rate (CAR) is a configurable parameter. To enable CAR on a router interface, use the `rate-limit` command. CAR allows the network administrator to set traffic classifications for each specific interface. Based on the policies set for particular interfaces, CAR will determine when the network packet will be processed, dropped, or rerouted.

Traffic Shaping

Traffic shaping can be used to limit the amount of traffic that a particular router interface processes. The purpose of traffic shaping is to reach the QoS goals for that particular interface. Traffic shaping can be used as a congestion management technique also. Traffic shaping avoids network congestion by reducing outbound traffic on a particular interface. The bit rate is configured with the `traffic-shape rate` command.

To enable traffic shaping on an interface:

`traffic-shape rate` *bit-rate*

(*bit-rate* is the configured bit rate for outbound interface.)

To display the traffic shaping configuration:

`show traffic-shape` *interface*

(*interface* is the interface configured for traffic shaping.)

Queuing

Queuing is a congestion management method that is part of the entire Quality of Service (QoS) implementations on Cisco network components. We discuss four main queuing types: Weighted Fair Queuing, Priority Queuing, Custom Queuing, and First In First Out Queuing. Here are two show commands that will help you to identify queuing strategies currently in place in your routing environment:

To show the queuing statistics for a router interface:

show queue `interface-type interface-number`

(*interface-type* is the interface name; *interface-number* is the interface number.)

To display queuing strategies currently in use:

show queuing `custom/fair/priority/red`

(*custom* shows the status of the custom queuing configuration; *fair* shows the status of the fair queuing configuration; *priority* shows the status of the priority queuing configuration; *red* shows the status of the WRED configuration.)

Weighted Fair Queuing

Weighted Fair Queuing (WFQ) allows all network traffic to have adequate bandwidth for their processes. WFQ processes traffic by weights and identifies network traffic as conversations. Each conversation is weighted and given adequate bandwidth. The interesting part of WFQ is that it has the ability to move interactive-type traffic to the front of the traffic queue to reduce response times. WFQ also is able to adapt to changing network conditions.

Priority Queuing

Priority Queuing is properly named. Priority Queuing sets priorities for network traffic. High-priority traffic gets serviced before lower-priority traffic. There are basically four types of priorities: high, medium, normal, and low. Filters are available to configure so you can set the priorities based on the packets that are transmitted.

You are responsible to set the criteria for the filters. As simple as it is, Priority Queuing will give priority to high-priority traffic. If you don't have a priority assigned, the packet will default to normal priority. The great thing about Priority Queuing is that if you have mission-critical applications that far and above are the priority for your network, then set your filters to assure that the mission-critical applications get high priority. Be aware that due to the fact that Priority Queuing works strictly on priorities, certain traffic may not get the needed bandwidth if high-priority, mission-critical applications are constantly using bandwidth resources.

Custom Queuing

Custom Queuing allows you to set the byte count for each router interface and to determine how much data should be transmitted from the queue at any one time. This process allows you to share network resources with other applications that have minimum bandwidth requirements to adequately process data.

One of the best things about Custom Queuing is you are able to configure the queue size so that all network applications get some type of bandwidth.

First In First Out Queuing

First In First Out Queuing (FIFO) has no mechanism to prioritize data traffic. Because there are no filters and no priority mechanisms, FIFO Queuing is the fastest queuing method. FIFO Queuing works best on fast high-speed links that don't experience much network congestion. One problem with FIFO Queuing is that if you have a network application that is low priority using a lot of bandwidth, FIFO won't make any distinctions and will let the application consume the bandwidth. FIFO requires no configuration at the router.

Cisco Software Product Offerings

Cisco Systems has developed quite a few software product offerings to help you in your network design and management. Here are just a few Cisco products that will help you in your network design and management. There are a variety of excellent products that other network vendors have developed, but they are beyond the scope of this book.

Security Software Products

Two Cisco security products, Cisco Security Manager and Cisco PIX Firewall, can provide your network with the needed security enhancements to prevent unauthorized access to your important data.

Cisco Security Manager

Cisco Security Manager is a graphical-user application that can run on an Intel Windows platform. With Cisco Security Manager, you can manage and set policies for the Cisco PIX Firewall.

Cisco Security Manager can provide network monitoring functions as well as reporting features. The network administrator can configure Cisco Security Manager to report system status messages that either pass threshold levels or are of extreme importance in a variety of ways. In the most important circumstances, the application should be configured to page the network administrator or responsible personnel. Lesser problems can be reported via e-mail or a graphical report. Cisco Security Manager comes in two types: stand-alone and distributed, as discussed in the next sections.

Stand-alone Cisco Security Manager

The Stand-alone Cisco Security Manager is a single workstation setup that has all the applications and features of the Cisco Security Manager installed. Unlike the Distributed Cisco Security Manager, every function is carried out from one central location. Small networks will benefit from the stand-alone version of Cisco Security Manager.

Distributed Cisco Security Manager

The Distributed Cisco Security Manager has all the feature sets and applications that the stand-alone version does; it's just that with the distributed version, you can install each feature on a separate workstation or system. Larger networks with more traffic will benefit in having the workstations distributed throughout the network. By implementing the distributed version, reporting information and status traffic for Cisco Security Manager is not causing traffic delays or degradation. Both the stand-alone and distributed versions of Cisco Security Manager have four main feature sets. The feature sets are Policy Manager, Primary Policy Database, Policy Distribution Point, and Policy Monitor Point.

- Policy Manager is installed with any of the feature sets described.

- Primary Policy Database provides report scheduling and a centralized database repository for storing configuration data. The Primary Policy Database workstation is referred to as the Primary Server. Secondary Servers are workstations that are configured with other Cisco Security Manager feature sets. PIX Firewalls can be managed from a Primary Server.

- Policy Distribution Point translates data into a PIX Firewall-compatible format to enable PIX Firewall management.

- Policy Monitor Point reports network anomalies through alerts and event notification reports. The network administrator can set the threshold levels for alerts and events.

Cisco PIX Firewall

The Cisco PIX Firewall is a security mechanism that helps to prevent (or prevents) crackers, wannabe crackers, and other malcontents from damaging your network environment. Is it the thrill of the chase or boredom that puts people in places where they should not be?

The Cisco PIX Firewall works to prevent unauthorized access between network segments or network servers. Cisco PIX Firewall has security features that allow you to set the level of access that certain users have to your important business data. Protecting business knowledge has been one of the key management initiatives in the past years. How do you retain knowledge? One of the ways to retain it is to retain valued employees that have the knowledge. Another way is to retain the knowledge that the valued worker has. Knowledge databases are important to consulting firms and many industries. This trend makes security that much more important.

Cisco PIX Firewall takes the traffic from an outside source, analyzes it, filters it, and processes it before it reaches the protective layer of corporate networks. The Cisco PIX Firewall can also be used to configure internal security settings within an intranet environment.

Management Software Products: CiscoWorks 2000

Cisco has a variety of software solutions to assist you in managing your Cisco-centric network. Each software product has features that will provide needed assistance in network management solutions.

CiscoWorks 2000 is the new product family of applications designed to help you manage your network. Some of the applications are Web-based; some are console-based. There are three main applications: Resource Manager, CiscoWorks for Switched Internetworks (CWSI), and Internetwork Performance Monitor (IPM).

Resource Manager is a suite of network management tools that allows network administrators to monitor and track network devices. Resource Manager is a Web-based tool that needs a server and client to run. A network server will run the application, and clients throughout the network can access the Web interface to manage the network environment. This application is more of an intranet-based application that multiple departments can use to manage the network. There are also components within Resource Manager that enable upgrade capabilities for Cisco devices.

CiscoWorks for Switched Internetworks (CWSI) allows network personnel to configure and monitor a switched network through a group of network management tools. There are several applications within CWSI: Network Map, VlanDirector, UserTracking, CiscoView, TrafficDirector, and ATMDirector.

- *Network Map* shows router, switch, and link configurations on your network. Network Map also displays VLAN configurations. Reporting status of network applications is also available.

- *VlanDirector* allows network administrators to configure VLANs with mouse clicks and drag-and-drop technology. Be sure that you understand what's behind the graphical interface before configuring VLANs on your network. VlanDirector is able to report the network with various graphical views. When the VlanDirector application is opened for the first time, a network discovery is performed and a current report of VLAN configuration is available.

- *UserTracking* reads network devices to report information about the status and functions of end-user workstations. UserTracking can track information such as IP addresses and hardware addresses on VLAN, Ethernet, and Token Ring networks.

- *CiscoView* is the central component for most of the Cisco management tools discussed in this chapter. CiscoView gives network personnel a graphical tool to display report information, configure certain devices, and monitor network device status and statistics.

- *TrafficDirector* is basically an SNMP-compatible application that allows network administrators to monitor network traffic. Certain other functions such as trend analysis and fault isolation are available. TrafficDirector uses SNMP agents to alert network personnel of threshold limit network conditions. These alerts can be configured for each individual network need. TrafficDirector is also a graphical user interface that interprets traffic data and reports data in a graphical format for ease of use and interpretation.

- *ATMDirector* uses the CiscoView application to monitor network performance on an ATM network. ATMDirector performs a network discovery and provides a network topology map. Other features include configuration of VLANs, problem identification and isolation, and network monitoring.

Internetwork Performance Monitor (IPM) provides management support for multi-protocol network environments. IPM has three components: the IPM server, the IPM client, and the Response Time Reporter (RTR). Basically, IPM performs router response time analysis between network components. Router-to-router and router-to-mainframe analysis is done to check latency issues, SNMP alert conditions, and statistic gathering.

IPM performs network analysis by accessing the administrator-configurable parameters that are stored in the application. Display of real-time data is also available.

Key Points

The Cisco IOS operating system allows you to configure and manage a variety of network components. This chapter covered the Cisco IOS and some of the ways to use this powerful tool to manage your unique internetworking environment. We covered specific commands to use for different routing protocols, as well as router management tools. Network Optimization methods allow you to change and tune your environment to get the best out of your infrastructure investment. Finally, we covered some Cisco software applications that allow you to configure, test, and manage your Cisco-centric network.

Part IV

Managing Your Network Design

Chapter

Chapter 8

Network Addressing
and Security

Network addressing is the way that hierarchical networks communicate in an orderly fashion. There are a variety of ways to get your network optimized through addressing mechanisms and design. Security is becoming increasingly important with sophisticated and knowledgeable network hackers attempting to compromise Web site security and other important data repositories. This chapter covers some of the techniques to provide network addressing, as well as important considerations you should take into account when designing a security policy for your network.

Network Addressing

Addressing is the fundamental way that two computers or systems communicate over a network connection. This section covers IP addressing and some of the types of IP addressing that are in use today, including IP addressing, Variable Length Subnet Masking, Network Address Translation, IP Multicast, Cisco Group Management Protocol, and Classless Interdomain Routing.

IP Addressing

IP addresses are network layer addresses that are required for each unique host and network that uses TCP/IP to communicate to other hosts and networks. There are currently five classes of IP addresses that are in use today. Each IP address consists of a network number and host number.

IP Classes

There are currently five classes of IP addresses in use on the Internet. Each class has a different use and purpose and is described as follows:

Class A Addressing Class A addresses are identified by the high-order bit being set to zero. Class A addresses range from 1.0.0.0 through 126.0.0.0. The address 127.0.0.0 has been reserved as a loopback address and cannot be used as a valid Internet address.

Class B Addressing Class B addresses are identified by the two high-order bits set to one zero, as 1 0. Class B addresses range from 128.0.0.0 through 191.255.0.0.

Class C Addressing Class C addresses are identified by the three high-order bits being set to one one zero, as 1 1 0. Class C addresses range from 192.0.0.0 through 223.255.255.0.

Class D Addressing Class D addresses are reserved for multicast addressing. Class D addresses are identified by the first four high-order bits being set to one one one zero, as 1 1 1 0.

Class E Addressing Class E addresses are used for experimental work. Class E addresses are identified by the first four high-order bits being set to one one one one, as 1 1 1 1.

Classless

Classless routing works by sending a prefix along with the IP address of the host, which enables more efficient use of IP addresses. If you are using a classful routing algorithm, you can implement subnet changes and the way that your IP addresses are being validated with the `ip classless` command. If a router receives data packets that do not have a default gateway configured, the `ip classless` command will allow the packets to be routed through the best subnetted network:

```
ip classless
```

(All keywords are required for this command.)

Classful

Classful IP addressing has a network address along with a host address. Classful addressing was originally created with three types of address classes: A, B, and C. There are now five types of IP address classes.

Variable Length Subnet Masking

You can vary the size of a subnet by using Variable Length Subnet Masking (VLSM). VLSM is used with classless routing protocols, and it works by sending a prefix with the IP address to delineate the subnets accordingly.

Network Address Translation

Network Address Translation (NAT) is a technology that allows companies to conserve global IP addresses and still connect to the Internet with valid IP addresses. The incredible growth of the Internet and the subsequent depletion of legal IP addresses have prompted network vendors to come up with new addressing solutions such as NAT.

NAT has the ability to translate an internal IP address to a valid Internet IP address for use on the Internet. This way, a company needs only a few valid IP addresses for Internet access, instead of a valid IP address for each workstation or host. Another feature of NAT is the ability to provide load balancing through the NAT gateway, across a group of network servers running the same type of application.

NAT works by connecting an inside network with an outside network. The inside network has the addresses that need translation into valid Internet addresses, and the outside network has valid Internet addresses that need no translation. You can configure just one router on the network as the NAT gateway. If you do configure more than one router with NAT, the NAT tables must be synchronized.

 Caution

Although the IP addresses on your workstations or hosts may be valid Internet addresses, if they are not registered to you, they will be in conflict with the registered global Internet addresses.

Routers that are configured with NAT store the addressing information in a NAT table. The NAT table contains five unique fields that contain information such as inside addresses, outside addresses, and protocol type. Some of the NAT terminology:

- Inside network — Network that has addresses that need to be translated.

- Inside IP address — The randomly assigned IP address on a host within an inside network.

- Outside network — Network communicating with the inside network. As defined, outside network addresses have valid Internet addresses and do not need translation.

To enable NAT on an interface:

ip nat *inside outside*

(*inside/outside* is the type of network interface.)
To show translations that are active:

show ip nat translations

To show translation statistics:

show ip nat statistics

Translation types

There are a few types of address translation; discussed here are static and dynamic address translation.

Static Address Translation Static Address Translation is the process of establishing a connection between an inside network local address and valid global Internet address.

Dynamic Source Address Translation With Dynamic Source Address Translation, you can take a group of inside network local addresses and associate them with a group of valid global Internet addresses. Any inside local address can be translated to any of the valid global Internet addresses.

IP Multicast

IP Multicast is an alternative transmission method for packets on an internetwork. Before multicasting, packets were sent either by broadcasting or by unicasting. IP Multicasting works by allowing transmission to a group of member hosts, rather than just one host (unicasting) or all hosts (broadcasting). IP Multicasting permits a single stream of data to be sent to stations requesting the data stream, saving network resources and providing a more optimized network environment. Some of the applications that IP multicasting works well with are distance learning, online training, and business video communication.

When operating in a multicast environment, all multicast group members send and receive packets through a single multicast group address. Any host can send to the multicast group, but only multicast group members are able to receive packets from the multicast group.

Joining and leaving a multicast group is a dynamic process; hosts can leave and join at any time by sending Internet Group Management Protocol (IGMP) messages. Group membership is also not exclusive. That is, a host can join and remain a member of one multicast group, and then join another multicast group. The host will then receive multicast traffic from both multicast group addresses, and will also be able to send to both multicast group addresses. IP Multicast addresses are valid Internet class D addresses in the range of 224.0.0.0 to 239.255.255.255. Each host that joins a specific multicast group sends and receives data through the unique multicast IP address.

To enable IP multicast routing on your Cisco router, enter:

```
ip multicast-routing
```

There are three main components to IP Multicast routing as it pertains to Cisco hardware. IGMP tracks membership information between routers. Protocol-Independent Multicast (PIM) works between routers to keep membership and forwarding tables. Cisco Group Management Protocol (CGMP) is used to track membership information between Cisco routers and Cisco Catalyst switches. Multicast routing protocols allow routers to determine which network segments are supposed to receive multicast traffic

There are at least three ways to support IP multicast: flooding of User Datagram Protocol (UDP) packets, broadcasting to specific subnets, and using IGMP.

UDP Flooding

UDP packets are flooded out to the interfaces that are in the forwarded state. The forwarded state is created by the spanning tree algorithm.

Subnet Broadcast

During subnet broadcasting, packets are sent out to all subnets of a certain network only.

The Internet Group Management Protocol

IGMP is used by IP host devices to join and leave IP multicast groups. Then the IGMP routers multicast their group membership information to other multicast routers by sending out queries during a specified time period. Any host that remains a member of multicast group will respond to the queries in order to remain included in the group. Routers build multicast groups by listening to IGMP messages, sending and receiving queries to determine which multicast groups are available and where they are located. There are at least three ways that routers communicate with each other to determine this information: Distance Vector Multicast Routing Protocol (DVMRP), Multicast Open Shortest Path First (MOSPF), and Protocol-Independent Multicast (PIM).

Distance Vector Multicast Routing Protocol DVRMP uses reverse path flooding to communicate with other routers and determine multicast group memberships. Reverse path flooding works by sending packets out to all of the paths except for the source path.

Multicast Open Shortest Path First MOSPF works by including information about multicast groups within Open Shortest Path First (OSPF) link-state messages. MOSPF is available only on OSPF network and calculates the routes for each multicast group once the router receives traffic information for that group.

Protocol-Independent Multicast PIM works between routers to keep membership and forwarding tables. There are two modes that PIM operates: dense mode and sparse mode, referring to the amount of members in the multicast group. In dense mode, a large audience of recipients receives the multicast group traffic.

- **Dense-Mode Protocol-Independent Multicast**—Dense-mode PIM computes the shortest path between a source and all multicast group members. Dense-mode PIM does not require the computation of routing tables. Dense mode refers to traffic that will be sent for almost all attached networks.

- **Sparse-Mode Protocol-Independent Multicast**—Sparse-mode PIM provides a registration service for a multicast group by using the IGMP protocol. IGMP allows a host to join or leave a multicast group by sending an appropriate membership message. Sparse-mode refers to traffic that is sent out to few networks.

Cisco Group Management Protocol

Cisco Group Management Protocol is used to allow Cisco Catalyst switches to understand IGMP messages and thereby determine group membership information. CGMP works by managing or limiting the amount of IP multicast traffic that is sent to specific Cisco Catalyst switch ports on an internetwork. When implementing CGMP into your internetwork, you will need to ensure that you have a connected router that is running both CGMP and the Internet Group Membership Protocol (IGMP). IGMP is used to establish a network host's membership in IP multicast groups. IGMP communicates between hosts and multicast routers on a single network. Cisco Catalyst switches require CGMP because they are unable to distinguish between IGMP messages and IP multicast data.

Classless Interdomain Routing

Classless Interdomain Routing (CIDR) enables routers to group and summarize routes together in order to reduce the amount of routing information sent across the internetwork. CIDR uses route aggregation to reduce the routing table size and to achieve higher performance across Internet backbone routers. Route aggregation combines IP networks by describing a network path by a shared prefix route. Routes outside the shared CIDR route treat the prefix route networks as a single network or entity and thereby reduce the amount of route information required to maintain connectivity to all the individual networks and routes.

Security

When people talk about security and maintaining a secure network environment, there is a tendency to go a bit overboard on the technology side while neglecting the human side of security. Let's face it, unless people were sometimes prone to be where they shouldn't be, much of the security would be less pervasive than it is today. Then again, clients want to be assured that their data is safe, and they look for ways to control access to the lifeblood of their businesses: their data.

I'm sure that everyone has a tale to tell about security lapses, breaches, and less-than-secure environments. Here are a few examples of why things other than technology mean a lot in the world of security.

A client was implementing a large financial system and was interested in the security features of the new network. They would be spending millions of dollars and wanted to be assured that their network and data would be safe. Only thing is, they forgot to lock the door. An assessment team came in and compromised their network within the first minute. They forgot to lock the door that houses all the network routers and the ATM switches. The assessment team had walked off the street, into a side door and into the equipment room. This room was accessible to *anyone* who was able to open the side door.

A corporation was deciding on a location for its data center. The data center would house critical client data and would feature locked doors, access keys, guards, exterior lighting, password policies, and no visitors in the building. Only thing is, the data center would have been located within 20 feet of a frequently used railroad line and on the "bad weather" path for a local airport. It's not known whether the corporation chose the data center location, but the chance for a security problem as far as building integrity was high.

A lot of times, programmers like to leave a "backdoor" entryway into their applications in the case of system failure or other application anomaly. Backdoors can be a very high threat to security. Although electronic "backdoors" are left open by some programmers, leaving a back-door open to a data center can compromise data without programming knowledge or intricate hacking abilities, as explained in the following true story: A client had a secured data center with massive mainframe systems running highly sensitive personal data. No one could access the mainframe floor, except a select group of personnel that had been screened and trained appropriately. A group of contract employees came to work there for a specific project and happened to be housed in the room next to the mainframe systems. The contractors were not security specialists, but they had the mainframe systems compromised within a few days of arriving. They just opened the backdoor that was left open for them.

In all of these situations, no damage was done. Yet. But the potential was there. It's important to test situations, to take a look at your environment from an outsider's view. If you know nothing about the network, how would you get in? When you begin to think the way of the intruder, you may find some good security solutions, without compromising your budget.

In this section, we cover the areas of security policies and security technologies.

Security Policies

Security policies are essential to providing business users access to network services within the boundaries of secure data and network transmissions. Policies and standards allow network users the freedom to use network services and to perform the company's business in a secure environment.

Remote access has become an increasingly important issue for many businesses. Although there are exceptions, most security policies must allow access to sensitive data at any time and from any place.

Software features such as data encryption and authentication are impor-tant, as well as hardware solutions such as firewalls. It is also important to remember physical security when implementing secure networks.

The process for setting up a good security policy is outlined in this section. There are certainly other concerns that may come up depending on your unique network situation. The main process for setting up a security policy is listed here:

- Set goals
- Analyze the risk and your environment

- Define the Security Policy
- Get agreement within your organization
- Communicate the Security Policy
- Implement the Security Policy
- Evaluate the Security Policy

Set Goals

The first step is to set your goals for your environment. You may decide that you want to secure everything that would be threatened, but you do need specific goals so that when you choose your procedures, policies, and tools, they will be able to meet your goals. Some of the goals for securing your network should be related to:

- Keeping the business running
- Securing your assets
- Cost versus benefit analysis

Keeping the Business Running   You'll want to be sure that your overall security policy allows for IT services that are designed to enhance business processes to be used effectively. An effective model for IT services includes the idea that the network and related components are in place to help rather than hinder the business that it serves. The same should be true with any security process that is put in place. Keeping the goal of effective delivery of IT services to end-users in mind is important when implementing any new technology, especially security policies. If you decide to limit user access to between 7 a.m. and 6 p.m., and then roll out 100 laptops for remote users to access the system, you will need to change the access restrictions. People will want to access the system before 7 a.m. and after 6 p.m., especially when they are traveling.

Securing Your Assets   Of course, keeping your data secure is an important part of the goals of your security policy. Does this mean that you are keeping it secure from outsiders or insiders? Certain information should be kept from employees, such as personnel records and salary and benefit information. This is one of the reasons that a security officer from the company should be involved at a detailed level with some of the security functions. You'll also want to consider in a more overall security policy the securing of hardware components and software licenses, as well as proprietary information.

Cost Versus Benefit Analysis What are some of the goals as far as what it will cost? Does it make sense to spend thousands of dollars on a software security system that looks like it can do the job, but which no one can configure or understand? You will need to take a look at what the goals are for the security policy as they pertain to cost versus benefits. Here you can look at the possibility of risk versus the cost of the solution. You can categorize risks as high, medium, and low. You can also decide what is high cost, medium cost, and low cost. Next, decide which implementations will meet your financial budget for the security policy. By matching up the cost versus the solution, you may decide that you want to only implement high-risk categories first. Then, you can look at medium-risk, low-cost categories, or all medium-risk categories. By categorizing risk levels and cost levels, matching them up, and then prioritizing them, you can begin to see where your goals for a cost-effective and efficient security solution might be.

Analyze the Risk and Your Environment

Once you have set the goals for your security policy, you can then analyze the risk that you are facing when implementing the security policy. You will also need to take a look at your environment and assess what it is that you are attempting to protect.

Identify Your Assets What are the assets that you are protecting? In certain situations, you may also be looking at assets such as security information that someone has memorized or secured. Here is a short list of possible asset areas as it relates to IT security:

- **Hardware**
    - Transmission media
    - Hubs
    - Switches
    - Routers
    - Workstations

- Spare equipment
- Printers
- Scanners
- Assorted peripherals
- Laptops
- Proprietary systems
- Phone systems

■ **Software**
- Source code
- Application programs
- Licenses
- Utilities
- Operating systems
- Proprietary systems

■ **Other**
- Documentation
- Project data
- Stored media
- Security logs
- Patent information

Identify the Risk   Identify the risk in your environment. If you have a corporate Web site and your Web site is your main revenue generator, the risk of hackers hitting your site and corrupting it is high. You may feel that you have a greater risk from internal sources such as employees, contractors, visitors, or vendors. There are at least three areas of risk that you will want to take a look at: information denial, unauthorized access of information, and the likelihood of an attack.

- **Information denial.** The risk of information denial is a big one. If your business cannot continue to operate due to the inability to access critical information, you are losing money, productivity, and the ability to compete. In the case of a corporate Web site, if users cannot access the information that they need in a timely manner, this can lead to public relations problems as your company is seen as incompetent or technically inept.

- **Unauthorized access of information.** What is the risk of having someone access information when they are not authorized to access the information? It can have the widespread effect of demoralizing the company if management bonuses, raises, or other perks are found out and published company-wide. Since information is the lifeblood and competitive edge for corporations worldwide, be sure that you understand the likelihood and ramifications of someone accessing information that they are not authorized to access.

- **Identify the likelihood of attack or threat.** Is the likelihood of an attack imminent? This can change from day to day. Are there certain times of the year that an attack or security breach would be expected or likely? There can be levels of security that are put in place on certain occasions.

Define the Security Policy

Defining a security policy is the process of figuring out just what is needed to get your security policy in working order. This section describes some of the things that you need to think about when defining your security policy.

AAA Cisco has incorporated commands into its security mechanisms that are ordered around the Accountability, Authentication, and Availability (AAA) parameters. The AAA methodology is an important part of any security policy or implementation.

- **Accountability** — Who is responsible, end-user as well as computer systems

- **Authentication** — Password policy, user identification

- **Availability** — Data recovery, system availability

What To Do During Security Threat or Incident What you do during a security threat or incident should be well documented and rehearsed. All of the emotion and turmoil can easily be put aside if each one on the security team understands his or her roles and responsibilities. With that said, it's important that there is a security team that knows its roles and responsibilities. You should have procedures in place so that everyone has his or her roles strictly defined and rehearsed. It's also important to have secondary personnel who understand that they may be called upon to take responsibilities if an event occurs. If you are in a high-profile business, you will need to also understand how to deal with the media. It may be a good idea to leak specific information to the media in a controlled fashion. Also, part of your security policy should be that employees and personnel should not talk to or take calls from the media during a specific event.

In certain situations, or corporations, it may be wise to set up a security level system. Security Level 3 (S3) would be normal day-to-day operations where all normal security policies are in place. Security Level 2 (S2) would be implemented during an event such as a client visit to a data center, a company picnic, or any other situation that differs from the norm. Security Level 1 (S1) would be a potential threat situation, such as corporate Web sites getting hit by hackers. If everyone else is being hit and you are operating a high-profile site, you may be next. Security Level 0 (S0) comes about during a security breach incident.

Within each of the security levels, S3 through S0, security personnel should know and understand what roles and responsibilities that they have. The overall security policy can change according to the current security level of the business. Here's a simple example of user access during the different security levels.

- Security Level 3 — Normal restricted access for authorized users.
- Security Level 2 — Normal restricted access for authorized users, track failed logins closely, and follow up on any abnormal access attempts.
- Security Level 1 — Access during normal business hours only. Prohibit any changes to Web sites or corporate knowledge databases from any user without prior authorization.
- Security Level 0 — Access to limited users. Security personnel have logged, higher-level access to determine and correct problems.

■ You can create a leveled security policy that will allow you to tighten or loosen the security settings and implementations as potential, or real, risks become apparent or strike your infrastructure.

Must Be Enforceable The easiest security policy that you can put in place is the one where no one can access anything and everything is secure. Of course, this won't go over very well. You will need to come up with a security policy that is enforceable. Depending on the assets that you are attempting to secure, you will want to take a look at just how you can enforce your security policy. If changing passwords is a policy that you are ready to implement, will it cause users to write the passwords down on pieces of paper and stick them to their monitors just because they're too much to remember with all the changes? To be enforceable, the security policy needs to be seamless, at least as much as possible. Be creative. You might try to enforce a policy that only certain people can access an equipment room. If you find that the door is left propped open with a book on a regular basis because of the amount of traffic, then rethink your policy. Take the lock off the main door and secure the equipment itself in a more manageable fashion.

Must Be Able to Be Implemented Along with the fact that the security policy must be enforceable, it must be able to be implemented. Don't waste time on policies, procedures, hardware, and software that would put good security measures in place, but that aren't in the budget. Be realistic. Maybe you can implement security one step at a time within the budget constraints and the culture of your company.

Get Agreement within the Organization

Getting agreement and signoff at the highest levels of the corporation go a long way in getting your security policy implemented. Depending on your organization, it may be profitable to have certain departments work with you to get this agreement.

In fact, because the security policy will affect the organization as a whole, it may be a good idea to get key contributors involved in the high-level overview of the policy. You certainly want to be sure that people understand that their business needs will still be met, and that they'll still be able to do their jobs.

Communicate the Security Policy

Communicate your security policy to those that will be affected by its implementation. It's important how this is done. There are several ways to accomplish this, and all can work together to communicate to employees at various times and levels throughout the organization.

First-time Employees During the orientation process for new employees, there can be an overview of the organization's security policy. It doesn't have to be extensive; just some conversation to let them know that there is a security policy in place. You may also want them to sign an agreement that they understand the security policy and all that it entails. However, depending on the company, culture, and business, this may not be appropriate.

During System Usage Certainly at logon, you can include a message that warns users that their keystrokes can be monitored, or something to the effect that only authorized users are allowed access to the system. Never put out a logon banner such as "Welcome." There may be legal implications if you put a welcome message out and then try to prosecute illegal access.

Security Policy Postings Post the security policy in open areas, bulletin boards, or electronic newsletters. It's important that the information be visible to all personnel, whether they have access to a computer or not.

Seminars/Meetings If the security policy is new and is making major changes to the environment, depending on the business culture, you may want to have an informative seminar or some smaller meetings to discuss the new policy and the impact that it will have on the workforce.

Visitors Visitors to the building, campus environment, or system should be well aware of your policy for security. Of course, you don't want to tell too much about it, but you may want visitors to sign a disclaimer before they enter the building if they will have access to sensitive materials or systems.

Vendors/Third Party More than likely at some time or another, third-party entities such as trading partners, e-commerce entities, or vendors may have access to certain types of data or a look inside at your technology infrastructure. Be sure that your security policy is communicated to them, at the level that is appropriate, but don't give away the store.

Implement the Security Policy

Implementing the security policy can take a variety of forms. There are several layers for security policies that will span hardware, software, processes, and procedures.

Before you do any implementation, be sure that corporate officers and key management personnel are aware of the security policies and the effect that it will have on any business process or productivity.

On the hardware side, firewalls are a common implementation for network security. Cisco has hardware and software firewall solutions.

It's important to implement security policies for network components as well as for mainframe systems, network servers, and workstations. Identify the risk to the business versus the cost of the implementation.

Evaluate the Security Policy

Part of your security policy should be a regular evaluation. If you can't evaluate or you don't have the tools to verify that your security policy is in place, then it would be better to not have one and save the money. You will need to secure your network with policies, procedures, software, common sense, and user compliance. All of these things work together to secure the IT environment. There are a few other things that you can do to work toward keeping a secure environment.

When your policies and procedures have been agreed upon, and are in place within your environment, it's important to do regular audits. It will usually be the responsibility of a security officer to complete regular audits due to the possibility that proprietary data may be compromised. Also, keeping abreast of the latest security threats and viruses is important to keep your network secure and reliable.

Security Technologies

There are several key security technologies that you can use to configure, enhance, and deliver a secure network. This section covers security methods and Cisco tools.

Security Methods

There are a few key security methods that are used to enhance security on your network. This section covers RADIUS, AAA, TACACS+, Kerberos, and the IPSec protocol.

RADIUS Remote Authentication Dial-In User Service (RADIUS) technology works to authenticate users from a specific RADIUS server. The RADIUS client software runs on the Cisco router and sends requests for user authentication to the RADIUS server. There is a movement within the ISP companies to provide RADIUS authentication proxy services for roaming subscribers. Authentication remains the responsibility of the local ISP, with the remote ISP forwarding the authentication requests for network services.

Following are several Cisco IOS commands that are used to configure RADIUS on your network.

To specify a RADIUS server host on your network:

`radius-server host` *hostname ip-address port-number* `port-number`

(*hostname* is the RADIUS server host DNS name; *ip-address* is the RADIUS server host IP address; *port-number* is the authentication requests port number; *port-number* is the accounting requests port number.)

Use the following command to specify that a RADIUS server on your network is using a proprietary system. Cisco will support non-standard implementations as long as you enter this command when configuring RADIUS:

`radius-server host` *hostname ip-address* `non-standard`

(*hostname* is the RADIUS server host DNS name; *ip-address* is the RADIUS server host IP address.)

To set the encryption key for communication between a RADIUS server and a Cisco router:

`radius-server key` *string*

(*string* is the Encryption key used on the Cisco router and the RADIUS server. The keys must match.)

The default time for a router timeout while waiting for a reply from a RADIUS host is five seconds. If you want to change the default time:

radius-server timeout *seconds*

(*seconds* is the timeout interval waiting for RADIUS server reply.)

To change the default of three times and set the number of times that a router looks for a specific RADIUS server or RADIUS service, you can set the retransmit option:

radius-server retransmit *retries*

(*retries* is the number of retransmission attempts.)

AAA Authentication, Authorization, and Accounting (AAA) is a mechanism or process that encompasses the verification of the user identity, user access, and user tracking on a remote access network.

Here are several authentication Cisco IOS commands that are used to configure AAA on your network.

To enable AAA authentication at login:

aaa authentication login default *list-name method*

(*list-name* is the string that lists the available authentication methods; *method* is the keyword used to describe the authentication method.) The authentication methods are:

- enable: uses enable password
- krb5: uses Kerberos 5
- line: uses line password
- local: uses local username database
- none: doesn't use authentication
- radius: uses RADIUS authentication
- tacacs+: uses TACACS+

Enter the following code to provide an authentication banner that is displayed on your network when users log in for authentication. This is important for legal reasons and should not in any way be an invitation to use the services. The banner should be written to warn against any unauthorized access. It may be good to note on the banner that accesses are being logged.

aaa authentication banner *xstringx*

(*x* is the character at the beginning and end of the *string* that is the delimiting character, and cannot be used within the *string; string* is the character string used as the banner, and cannot include the delimiting character; *x* is the character at the beginning and end of the *string* that is the delimiting character, and cannot be used within the *string*.)

If a user authentication fails during login, you may want to display a message after the failed login. Use this command to display a banner after a failed login:

aaa authentication fail-message *xstringx*

(*x* is the character at the beginning and end of the *string* that is the delimiting character, and cannot be used within the *string; string* is the character string used as the banner, and cannot include the delimiting character; *x* is the character at the beginning and end of the *string* that is the delimiting character, and cannot be used within the *string*.)

AAA authorization provides a way to limit a user's access to network resources. A user profile is stored in an authentication database for retrieval when the user logs in.

To enable user-specific parameters for network access:

aaa authorization *network/exec/commands level/*
list-name/method

(*network* is the authorization for network-related service requests; *exec* is the authorization to see if a user can access EXEC command mode; *commands* is the authorization for commands; *level* is the command level that is authorized (from 0-15); *list-name* is the name of the list with the authentication methods that are used,)

method authorization methods are:

- tacacs+: gets authentication from a TACACS+ server
- if-authenticated: access allowed if authentication succeeds
- none: authorization not performed
- local: use local user database for authentication
- radius: use RADIUS for user authentication

AAA accounting is disabled by default. If you need to track user services and the resources that they are using, you may want to enable AAA accounting. AAA accounting works with a security implementation such as RADIUS or TACACS+.

To enable AAA accounting:

aaa accounting *system/network/exec/connection/*
commands level/list-name none/method

(*system* is the accounting for system events; *network* is the accounting for network-related service requests; *exec* is the accounting for EXEC command mode sessions; *connection* is the outbound connection information; *commands* is the accounting for all commands; *level* is the command level that is authorized (from 0-15); *list-name* is the name of the list with the accounting methods that are used; *none* means that no accounting is being used.)

method authorization methods as listed:

- tacacs+: uses TACACS+ for accounting
- radius: uses RADIUS for accounting

Note: There are other options to the **aaa accounting** command that are not described here.

TACACS+ Terminal Access Controller Access Control System (TACACS+) is a more recent implementation of TACACS and is compatible with the Cisco IOS. TACACS+ is basically a database server that provides authentication, authorization, and accounting functions for a Cisco router network group of users and services. TACACS provides a security management system for your Cisco network.

First, you will need to set up your router to run TACACS+. You will need to enable AAA on your router. The following steps will prepare your router for TACACS+:

- Enable AAA on your router.
- Specify the IP address for TACACS+ use.
- Specify an encryption key.
- Define a method list.
- Apply method lists to an interface.

Next, you will configure your router for TACACS+ with the following commands.

Create an entry for a TACACS+ host:

tacacs-server host *name* **single-connection port** *integer*
timeout *integer* **key** *string*

(*name* is the name of the TACACS+ host; *integer* is the TCP port number for connection to the TACACS+ host; *integer* is the timeout value for response from the TACACS+ host; *string* specifies the encryption key string.)

Next, you will need to set up the key that TACACS+ uses for authentication and encryption:

tacacs-server key *key*

(*key* is the encryption and authentication key.)

To complete the TACACS+ configuration, you will need to specify TACACS+ authentication, authorization, and accounting.

Kerberos   Kerberos is a security mechanism that authenticates network resource requests. Kerberos is an encryption key-based system, which means that it uses a third-party entity to verify users and user credentials. A Kerberos server has certain users, hosts, and services that are registered to it and which comprise a Kerberos *realm*.

Here are some Kerberos commands that are unique to the Cisco IOS environment:

To enable the Cisco IOS software to specify a Kerberos server:

kerberos server *kerberos-realm hostname ip-address*
port-number

(*kerberos-realm* is the name of the Kerberos realm, case-sensitive, uppercase only; *hostname* is the Kerberos host server name; *ip-address* is the Kerberos host IP address; *port-number* is the Kerberos host monitor port.)

If you want to map a specific host name or DNS domain to a specific Kerberos realm:

kerberos realm *dns-domain/host/kerberos-realm*

(*dns-domains* is the DNS domain name; *host* is the DNS host name; *kerberos-realm* is the Kerberos realm that is being mapped to.)

Kerberos authenticates users and then issues credentials that are stored in a cache system for later authentication purposes. To show the current credential cache:

```
show kerberos creds
```

(All keywords are required for this command.)

Kerberos authenticates users and then issues credentials that are stored in a cache system for later authentication purposes. To clear the contents of the credentials cache:

```
clear kerberos creds
```

(All keywords are required for this command.)

IPSec IPSec is a standards-based security protocol implementation that provides security protection on Cisco networks. IPSec is a standard that will allow secure data transmission across IP networks such as the Internet. There are two main functions to IPSec that allow data to be sent across a network in a secure fashion: data encryption and data integrity. IPSec allows the data to be sent with only the sender and receiver understanding the security key that is needed for the message or transmission.

Cisco Tools

Cisco Tools for network security are available as software packages or products, hardware products, and the Cisco IOS features.

Cisco Software Products Two Cisco Security products, Cisco Security Manager and Cisco PIX Firewall, can provide your network with the needed security enhancements to prevent unauthorized access to your important data.

Cisco Security Manager is a graphical user application that can run on an Intel Windows platform. With Cisco Security Manager, you can manage and set policies for the PIX Firewall.

Cisco Security Manager can provide network monitoring functions as well as reporting features. The network administrator can configure Cisco Security Manager to report system status messages that either pass threshold levels or are of extreme importance in a variety of ways. In the most important circumstances, the application should be configured to page the network administrator or responsible personnel. Lesser problems can be reported via e-mail or a graphical report. Cisco Security Manager comes in two types: stand-alone and distributed, as discussed in the next paragraphs.

The stand-alone *Cisco Security Manager* is a single workstation setup that has all the applications and features of the Cisco Security Manager installed. Unlike the Distributed Security Manager, every function is carried out from one central location. Small networks will benefit from the stand-alone version of Cisco Security Manager.

The *Distributed Cisco Security Manager* has all the feature sets and applications that the stand-alone version does; it's just that with the distributed version, you can install each feature on a separate workstation or system. Larger networks with more traffic will benefit in having the workstations distributed throughout the network. This way, reporting information and status traffic for Cisco Security Manager are not causing traffic delays or degradation. Both the stand-alone and distributed versions of Cisco Security Manager have four main feature sets. The feature sets are Policy Manager, Primary Policy Database, Policy Distribution Point, and Policy Monitor Point.

Policy Manager manages the Cisco Security Manager interface and is installed with any of the feature sets described.

Primary Policy Database provides report scheduling and a centralized database repository for storing configuration data. The Primary Policy Database workstation is referred to as the Primary Server. Secondary Servers are workstations that are configured with other Cisco Security Manager feature sets. PIX Firewalls can be managed from a Primary Server.

Policy Distribution Point translates data into a PIX Firewall-compatible format to enable PIX Firewall management.

Policy Monitor Point reports network anomalies through alerts and event notification reports. The network administrator can set the threshold levels for alerts and events.

Cisco Hardware Products   Cisco's main hardware implementation for security is the Cisco PIX Firewall system.

The *Cisco PIX Firewall* is a security mechanism that helps to prevent (or prevents) hackers, wannabe hackers, and other malcontents from damaging your network environment.

The Cisco PIX Firewall works to prevent unauthorized access between network segments or network servers. Cisco PIX Firewall has security features that allow you to set the level of access that certain users have to your important business data.

Cisco PIX Firewall takes the traffic from an outside "untrusted" source, analyzes it, filters it, and processes it before it reaches the protective layer of corporate networks. The Cisco PIX Firewall can also be used to configure internal security settings within an intranet environment.

Software/Cisco IOS There are several software methods to enable security functions on your internetwork. Access lists, null interface, passwords, and Lock and Key security are discussed in this section.

Access lists are part of a security policy but are not the only part. Be sure that you use access lists with caution, and not to secure your network. Access lists are used to filter network traffic based on the criteria that you create. If you have three different protocols running through your router, and you are using access lists to control access, you will need a separate access list for each protocol. When you create an access list, you will need to identify the list by either a unique name or number, depending on the network protocol that you are using. The last step is to assign the access list to an interface. Here are some common protocol types and their associated access list numbers:

IP	1–99, 1300–1999
Extended IP	100–199, 2000–2699
DECnet	300–399
AppleTalk	600–699
IPX	800–899
IPX Extended	900–999

To create n standard IP access list:

access-list *number permit/deny source-address mask*

(*number* is the access list number, an integer between 1–99 and 1300–1999; *permit/deny* permits or denies data; *source-address* is the source address of the data; *mask* is the subnet mask.)

To apply an IP access list to an interface:

ip access-group *number in/out*

(*number* is the number of the access list; *in* is the packet checking from outside the router in; *out* is the packet checking from inside the router out.)
To display access list information for the router:

show access-lists

(All keywords are required for this command.)
The *null interface* on a router is an interface that cannot receive traffic; neither can it forward traffic. If you are looking for an alternative to access lists and the overhead involved, you can use the null interface specification to redirect network traffic to an unusable interface.
To create a null interface:

interface null 0

Router *passwords* are obviously a way to keep intruders from accessing your network and to log access to your network routers. Passwords restrict access to your network, and privilege levels allow access to specific network resources depending on the privilege level of the user. This section discusses specific Cisco IOS password and privilege commands.
To enable and specify a password for a router:

password *password*

(*password* is the case-sensitive character string that is the router password.)
To set passwords for specific privilege levels for the router:

enable password level *password*

(*password* is the case-sensitive character string that is the router password.)
To log into a privileged mode:

enable *level*

(*level* is the privilege level that is accessed.)
To show your current privilege level:

show privilege

(All keywords are required for this command.)

Lock and Key Security filters IP traffic. Lock and Key is configured at the router and can provide a specific user access to an interface even if the router is configured for no access. The Lock and Key Security feature allows an interface to be reconfigured so that a user can be routed through a locked interface by using dynamic access lists. Once the user has been routed and has reached his or her destination, the interface is reconfigured and locked down for no further access. Users access the interface through Telnet and get authenticated at the router.

Lock and Key Security can be compared to access list security. Although access lists are in themselves not security mechanisms, they do allow traffic restrictions and block certain types of traffic.

You can use Lock and Key Security to allow a specific user or group of users limited access to a host on your network. You can configure Lock and Key Security to only allow access for a limited time and for a limited number of users or user.

The process for Lock and Key Security on a Cisco router starts by a user initiating a Telnet session to a router on the outside of a network. The user will be prompted for a password, and once the password is entered, the router goes through an authentication process. Once the authentication process is complete, the user's access information is added to a dynamic access list. The user accesses the host or data that is required and then completes the session. The Lock and Key Security feature can allow a user a specific period of session time or allow access to only certain hosts or networks. Once the user completes the session, the dynamic access list is reconfigured and the session is ended.

To enable Lock and Key Security on a router, you can use the **access-enable** Cisco IOS command.

The **access enable** command will create an entry in a dynamic access list:

access-enable *host timeout minutes*

(*host* is the optional parameter and allows specific access from the host Telnet session only; *timeout* is an optional parameter and sets a timeout for the access list entry; *minutes* is an optional parameter and specifies the number of minutes for access list entry timeout.)

Key Points

In this chapter, we covered two very important topics: network addressing and security. Certain IP addressing mechanisms such as VLSM and NAT can give you the tools to configure your network and to provide IP addressing and routing capabilities that would be hard to come by with straight classful IP addressing.

Network security is fast becoming a major concern as more and more businesses move their corporate data and communication systems to infrastructures that they can't always control. There are many tools which can provide a secure and functioning network environment. Although coming up with an overall security policy is not an easy task, it's well worth the effort.

Chapter 9

Proposal, Testing, and Management

This chapter covers the proposal, testing, and management of your network design. I cover how to provide information and documentation about your network design during the proposal stage, prior to the design, during the design, and after implementation is complete. The network design proposal can be the most important part, for a simple reason — if you don't get your client to sign a contract, or if you can't get the project sponsor to sign off on the design, there won't be a project. Testing is an ongoing process that starts prior to the network design and continues after implementation is complete. Finally, I cover network management and all that goes with it. In the network management section, I cover infrastructure management and maintenance, network processes, and personnel.

Network Proposal

The network proposal is the most important part of the design process because if you don't get the proposal right, you won't get the contract. Or if you're working within your organization, you'll need to sell it to the project sponsors. If you do use a network proposal template, please be sure it is generic. Be sure that if you use Microsoft Word that you change the properties of the network proposal document to reflect the individual client. With the document closed, right-click the icon and check the properties. It's just not professional to see a network proposal with other company information on it.

If you're having problems writing the report, just have fun with it. Create a first version in which you put whatever you can think of into the report. Include emotions, feelings, biases — get it out of your system. From there, you can edit it, make changes, and, eventually, take out the emotions and stick to the facts. Ultimately, your report should be a professional document, but it may take a little brainstorming to get there.

Your network design proposal should include a title page, executive summary, overview, solution, costs, and benefits.

Title Page

The title page is simply the name of the proposal, your company or department name, the date, and logos of the companies involved if appropriate. After the title page, you may want to include a table of contents if the document is longer than 10 pages.

Executive Summary

In the executive summary, you will be writing to individuals who want to know very quickly what the problem is and how you will fix it. You do not necessarily have to put costs here. You may want to discuss the costs and not include them in the proposal document. If costs and pricing are to be included, you can refer to the page in the document where they are outlined. This way, the explanations and reasons for the costs are also detailed along with the costs. With the executive summary only running about a page in length, you don't want to show the overall cost of the project without additional information to show exactly how you arrived at the projected costs.

Overview

The overview may be a few pages describing who you are, why you're writing the proposal, and what the problem is. You may want to include some recent history about the network if you know it or about recent projects that will influence this project or that created a need for it. Be careful. You're writing a document that will be read by many people. Stay to the facts and report. There is no need to editorialize. Also be careful about appearing too biased about a particular technology or vendor.

Who You Are

It's not important to get real wordy here. Just a paragraph telling about your organization or department as a whole. There is no need to include promotional items such as how many clients you have serviced or anything like that.

Why You Are Writing the Proposal

Here you can say something about why specifically you, your company, or your department is presenting the proposal. If it was at the request of the CIO or other company executive, include that here.

Describe the Problem

In clear terms, define the problem. This should be a very unbiased account of what the problem is. Write this as if you're writing a news story. Make this section a factual account of what your analysis of the network produced.

Solution

The solutions section of the network design proposal is where you get into the details about your proposed design. You might want to discuss some common solutions to the problem and then fully describe your solution.

List Some Common Solutions

This is a tricky part of the proposal, and in some cases it is better left out. Here you might describe some of the solutions of your competition or other solutions that you've looked at and found to be ineffective for this proposal. If you do list a common solution, be sure that you fully discount it and be sure that you have good information to back it up. Otherwise, a client or project sponsor may think that the common solution is better than your proposed solution.

Describe Your Solution

In this section, you will describe your solution in detail. Starting with why this is the best solution for the network, you will discuss the existing network and the proposed network, along with all the technical details of your new design. There may be a consideration to include multiple solutions to your client. Maybe in some cases this is a good idea, if they have asked for it. But if you begin to present multiple solutions, things will get cloudy, the client will have too many choices to make, and nothing will get done. It's best to research your solution and come up with the best one that will fit the client's business needs.

Why This Is the Best Solution Why is this the best solution? Don't make this a generic statement. Why is this the best solution for the client or the project sponsor? Tell them in detail why this solution will work for their unique network. You'll need to do some homework to understand why your design is the best solution. Each client wants to know that you have his or her unique interests in mind, and that you aren't offering a cookie-cutter solution.

Diagram of the Existing Network Provide as much detail as you can about the state of the existing network. This should be a factual report, not an editorial about different technologies and products in place. Present a graphical image of the existing network or the part of the network that you're proposing a design for.

Diagram of the Proposed Network The diagram of the proposed network goes in this section. Be sure that it is accurate. These, along with the costs of the project, are the pages that people will look at over and over again. Most management personnel like to see a graphical representation of information. If they can look at one page and get an overview of the project, you will be making it easier for them to make a clear decision. Make the graphical format of the proposed network consistent with the diagram of the existing network. Put some color in the areas of change, and it will help highlight the changes. Don't go overboard with colors, one or two at the most.

Training It may be appropriate to add something here about training. No one wants a project to be rolled out without the means to support the environment. If you offer training services, include the specifics in this section. You may only want to state that "knowledge transfer" will occur as the project progresses. Sometimes this is the best method. Getting the support personnel involved in the project from the beginning is one of the best methods to assure a knowledge transfer.

Technical Specifications The technical specification section should include many things. Here you want to assure the client that you have thought of everything that is needed for the technical end of the project. The following list has suggestions for what will be included in this section of the design proposal:

- Topology — Explain the topology of the network. Is it hierarchical, flat, routed, switched, or a combination of them all.

- Technologies — What technologies will you use in the network? Include WAN and LAN technologies along with how the technology will be used in the design.

- Routing protocols — Which routing protocols are you using and why. If you're restructuring the entire network, describe why you have decided to use a specific routing protocol.

- Routed protocols — Discuss routed protocols that will be in use in your design. Explain the operation of any new protocols that are not currently in use but will be included in your design.

- Hardware — The hardware section may get a little tricky. If you propose Cisco network components and you're a Cisco reseller, of course the client will want to know why Cisco is better than another vendor. Then again, they will know you're a reseller before they ask you to come in. But, be prepared to discuss this here if it is appropriate.

- Software — What software applications are needed to complete your network design? If you need additional software packages, describe them in detail and discuss their merits.

- Addressing — How will the new design be addressed and named? Will it fit in with the current addressing structure of the network, or will changes be needed?

- Security — What security functions will need to be put in place with the new design? If the design is related to Internet access, be sure that any concerns about data security are addressed here.

- Maintenance — What will be needed to maintain the new network? Will additional staff be needed, or will the current staff be okay? If specific hardware is to be installed and there are unique maintenance processes to be put in place, briefly describe them in this section.

- Management — When it's all completed, how will the new network be managed? Are the current tools or processes enough, or will additional management tools, processes, or staff be needed to operate the network in a productive way?

Costs

This section of the proposal will be looked at over and over by the decision makers. Be sure that your numbers add up properly. It doesn't take a financial person much time to calculate and check your figures. Don't think they won't. It's inbred. You should have costs broken down clearly. You may want to include soft costs when you're detailing what it is costing the corporation to not do the project.

What Is It Costing the Corporation Now?

If the current network design is clearly costing the corporation a lot of money and you know how much that cost is, you may include those costs here.

Soft Costs What are the soft costs of the network as it is today? Include the amount of hours that it takes to isolate or troubleshoot problems, network downtime costs, costs to the image of the company, and other soft costs.

Hard Costs These are costs such as loss of revenue, equipment leases, and additional employees to support the network or application.

What Is the Cost of the Project?

Management personnel and decision makers will zero into this area of the design proposal. All of the other information that you present might be glossed over, but this is the page that they will stare at. Depending on the network design, you may have a graduated scale of costs, depending on the options that you're offering. There are at least three areas of costs that you will want to include in this section: personnel, hardware, and software.

Personnel What are the consulting fees? Here you will include the cost of consulting services and the details of what types of consultants and skill sets will be needed to complete the project. Be sure to be specific. If you say that you will need two Cisco Engineers, and the client has two on staff, they may assume that they can use those two Cisco Engineers for the project. Give enough detail to show that the consultants must be full-time (as in number of hours in a year) and dedicated to the project.

Hardware What will the hardware cost? List each area of the network design such as hubs, switches, routers, servers, access devices, and other internetworking equipment that will be needed to complete your design.

Software Software costs can include just about everything else. If necessary, include Cisco IOS feature sets here, software upgrade costs, application costs, license fees, and the cost of other associated software costs. Management tools can be included here.

What Will It Cost If the Project Is Not Done?

This area may or may not be included at your discretion. If you do include it, be sure that your facts are correct. It's important to be factual. Although some emotion does play into the sales process, you're dealing with people who look at the bottom line and what is best for the business. Don't include fear tactics or other possibly insulting types of editorial comments here. Just stick to the facts. Make it encouraging and thought-provoking. When the client reads this, they may think: "What if we *don't* do it?" Maybe something like: "With the enhanced network design and added multimedia services support, Silly String will become a leader in the value-added network services arena for the string business in North America." Basically, you're telling them what they can expect from the network design. This ties into the benefits section of the network design proposal.

Benefits

How will this network design, and specifically *your* proposed design, benefit the client's business?

What Are the Immediate Benefits of the Project?

The immediate benefits of the project should somehow tie into the section of the proposal where you detail what it is costing the client. You can include some of the same things that you did in the soft and hard costs of the client's previous network design. Include areas such as reduced time to isolate and troubleshoot problems, increased network availability, and better company image due to increased service levels.

What Are the Long-term Benefits of the Project?

When you talk about long-term benefits, you will need to include some information about how this network design will contribute to the financial success of the client's company. Here you can talk about Return on Investment (ROI). The company sees this network design as an investment in the business, and you need to show them just how quickly they will get a return on their investment. Include soft-cost returns as well as hard-cost returns here. You should be able to calculate the real dollar value of soft costs and include this in your ROI assessment. Most vendors supply this type of information with their products.

Proposal Summary

You may want to include an overall summary of the proposal on the last page. It's not necessary, however, and may be best not to be included. But if you decide that a summary is a good way to bring the document to a need closure, just summarize each of the sections in your proposal in a one-page format.

Cisco Network Design Proposal Tool

Cisco has a Network Design Proposal tool that can help you in developing a network proposal specifically for Cisco products. Included is generic marketing information about each of the Cisco product lines. It is helpful because it will also help you select hardware based on the type of network design that you're doing. The information is at a high level and is consistent with the audience that a proposal will be presented to. The tool is a graphical interface that allows you to enter information based on your network design. The result is a Microsoft Word template document where you can fill in more specific information about the project or proposal.

Should the Proposal Be Free?

There are two schools of thought on whether the assessment and/or the proposal should be free. One says yes; one says no. Depending on the situation, a client may not have even decided on who they want to do the work. In this case, I would not waste my time offering an assessment or proposal for no charge. You're giving away important information that will allow the client to make an informed decision, which might possibly not include you. You could spend all your time giving away free work. I think that this is one of the things that the client does not understand. If a consultant constantly gave away free assessments or proposals, he or she would have no income and therefore not be able to provide any services.

Once the sales presentations have been done, and the pre-sales meetings are concluded, the client should have decided which consulting company that they want to do the work. Then an assessment will be done. But it still should not be free. The assessment should cover the costs of the assessment, without too much mark-up. It should be priced low enough that the client is getting a very good deal, and even if they decide to walk away from the table then, they have information that they can use, and you're not left spending your time and money for nothing.

Let's say that you're bringing in three consultants to complete a network assessment. You're checking traffic patterns, network anomalies, protocols in use, etc. You charge the client a low rate and assess the network for a week. Get an assessment out to the client the next week and charge them $15,000. If the client balks at this, then maybe you can reduce the contract amount by the assessment amount. Given that the client signs a contract worth $300,000 or more, you will reduce the contract fee by $15,000, thereby giving the client the assessment for free without doing work for nothing.

Other folks will say that giving away free work is a way to build partnerships with clients. I agree. But a partnership involves two parties. If the client is also willing to contribute to the partnership in some way, say by providing lab equipment for testing or some other tangible service, then by all means it is a partnership. Certainly, there is no reason not to provide services as appropriate.

The other part of free services is if you're a very large firm, you can afford to give away services as part of your business and sales process. Smaller consulting firms of 1 to 20 people should be careful about providing free assessments in exchange for the possibility of the contract.

When dealing with government agencies, realize that the process is very slow and can be very political. Based on what the government agency bias is at the point in time of the contract, you may not get the business even if you're the best provider. If you're in the select group of business partners, from there you compete with others for lowest cost. Either way, be sure that when dealing with government entities that you have an experienced staff that knows and understands how government entities work.

Testing

Testing should be done in all stages of network design. I will cover some common methods of testing prior to implementation, during implementation, and after implementation. Testing and baselining should be performed on a weekly basis. There is nothing wrong with constantly testing and evaluating your network. Exception conditions should always be reported with a diagnostic tool for quick response and problem resolution. Weekly testing can be an automated process that provides detailed reports through exception-reporting software.

Tools

Network tools are varied but basically are an automated way to get data from your network for baselining, troubleshooting, trend analysis, and reporting. In this section, I talk about Cisco NetSys Baseliner, an application that will allow you to view your network by querying router configuration files. I also discuss the Network Associates Sniffer, a non-Cisco product that will be used as an example of what a good network analyzer tool can do for you. And, of course, there are the Cisco IOS commands, when you're doing a more basic baseline. You can save the information from the Cisco IOS commands and reissue them to compare results.

Cisco NetSys Baseliner

Cisco NetSys Baseliner is a Microsoft Windows-based application that requires Windows NT Workstation or Server to operate, as well as a Web browser such as Netscape Navigator or Internet Explorer. This is an important tool to use when testing your network design. A well-defined baseline can save you a lot of needless work. If you define your baseline prior to the design work, you can see how many problems already exist and what can be done to solve them in your new design. If you don't do a baseline, you may be setting yourself up for trouble. Latent problems within a network can and will surface unexpectedly and will be seen as a result of your design, testing, or implementation. Although time-consuming, a baseline will also give details in black-and-white about the changes that you have made with your design.

You may have a client who tells you that they are not willing to pay for the baseline or any kind of assessment because they already know what the problems are, they just need you to fix it. That's fine; some pro bono work won't hurt too badly, as long as you do get a signed contract or a buy-in from the project sponsors.

With Cisco NetSys Baseliner, you can see a graphical view of your network that is based on actual router configuration files. If there are errors in the router configuration files, Cisco NetSys Baseliner will identify the errors with a report. The reports can be published on a Web server in HTML format. This way, you can easily get out the information about your report to the interested participants. You can talk about the problems on the network all you like, but it is hard to argue with a visual representation of the data. People are generally more likely to get more information from a visual image that they can refer to from time to time rather than from a lot of statistics or conversation. Of course, you may need to interpret the results of the NetSys report, but the results are available for later review. Cisco NetSys will report on all the data and routing protocols in your network along with a health report checklist. You can use the software to provide specific network information through queries and menus on the application interface. Another neat feature is the ability to search the NetSys database that is created when the baseline is developed. This way, you can search for a specific device and find detailed information about the device. You can also run the application offline, when you're not connected to the network. You can make the changes that you think are necessary and have NetSys identify any potential problems. Of course, any modeling software like this is helpful, but it cannot possibly re-create an actual network environment with all the specifics and unique situations in your network.

Network Associates Sniffer

Any type of network analyzer would be a good tool to use during the testing of your network design. One of the more commonly used and popular software tools is the Network Associates Sniffer. There are a variety of network analyzers on the market with a variety of features and costs, some even free. The network analyzer that you have is only important if you can justify the cost. If you're doing consulting work, using a free or shareware tool is not a good way to do business. This section describes in a little more detail how you can use the Network Associates Sniffer to aid you in baselining your network.

Here is a basic outline of what features are available and how you can use the Network Associates Sniffer to gain information about your network:

Monitoring Network Activity The features listed below will help you to monitor network activity with the Network Associates Sniffer:

- The Dashboard displays number of packets per second, network utilization, and errors per second.
- You can monitor the packet size and network utilization distribution to allow you to see a global view of network activity. This will also allow you to isolate large packet loads.
- You can capture network activity data and export the data into an Excel spreadsheet for analysis.
- The host table option allows you to view the busiest nodes within a specific routing protocol.
- The Protocol Distribution feature reports real-time network usage based on common network routed protocols, such as IPX/SPX, TCP/IP, NetBIOS, AppleTalk, DECnet, and SNA.

Capturing Packets You can capture packets on your network based on a unique protocol or certain data patterns. You can also capture and filter different types of errored packets such as CRC errors, runts, and jabber.

Filtering You can use the predefined filters that come with the Sniffer product or create your own based on what type of traffic you're looking for, or filtering out.

Generating Traffic You can generate your own network traffic with the packet generator. You can also edit packets and create network traffic suitable for the specific network design that you're testing.

Cisco IOS Commands

One of the best ways to get a baseline for your network is to go right to the source. If you're in a time crunch or just are not able to get a baseline done in the proper manner, you can at least get some statistical data from your routers. As mentioned in Chapter 7, there is a command, show tech-support, that will provide a wealth of information for each router. There probably is nothing wrong with having this information available at anytime, whether or not you're looking for a specific baseline during a design project. The following output shows the *partial* results of the show tech-support command on a non-production router for example purposes:

```
router#sh tech-support
----------------- show version ------------------
```

show version command will display information such as system hardware, software version, configuration file information, and boot images, as shown:

```
Cisco Internetwork Operating System Software
IOS (tm) 2500 Software (C2500-J-L), Version 11.2(18),
RELEASE SOFTWARE (fc1)
Copyright (c) 1986-1999 by cisco Systems, Inc.
Compiled Mon 05-Apr-99 20:17 by
Image text-base: 0x0303F240, data-base: 0x00001000
ROM: System Bootstrap, Version 11.0(10c), SOFTWARE
BOOTFLASH: 3000 Bootstrap Software (IGS-BOOT-R), Version
11.0(10c), RELEASE SOFTWARE (fc1)
uptime is 6 minutes
System restarted by power-on
```

System image file is "flash:c2500-j-l_112-18", booted via flash

------------------ **show running-config** ------------------

show running-config command will display the current configuration that is running on the router at the present time, as shown:

```
Current configuration:
!version 11.2
service config
no service password-encryption
service udp-small-servers
service tcp-small-servers
!interface Ethernet0
 ip address 199.xx.xx.x 255.255.255.0
interface Serial0
 no ip address
 shutdown
```

------------------ **show controllers** ------------------

show controllers command will display controller information. This command can be entered for specific interfaces as well.

```
LANCE unit 0, idb 0xAFEB4, ds 0xB1998, regaddr = 0x2130000, reset_mask 0x2
IB at 0x206DAC: mode=0x0000, mcfilter 0001/0000/0108/0000
station address 0010.7b39.fcb3  default station address 0010.7b39.fcb3
buffer size 1524
RX ring with 16 entries at 0x206DF0
Rxhead = 0x206DF0 (0), Rxp = 0xB19B4 (0)
00 pak=0x0B4618 ds=0x210A2E status=0x80 max_size=1524 pak_size=0
01 pak=0x0B4448 ds=0x210376 status=0x80 max_size=1524 pak_size=0
02 pak=0x0B4278 ds=0x20FCBE status=0x80 max_size=1524 pak_size=0
03 pak=0x0B40A8 ds=0x20F606 status=0x80 max_size=1524 pak_size=0
04 pak=0x0B3ED8 ds=0x20EF4E status=0x80 max_size=1524 pak_size=0
05 pak=0x0B3D08 ds=0x20E896 status=0x80 max_size=1524 pak_size=0
```

```
06 pak=0x0B3B38 ds=0x20E1DE status=0x80 max_size=1524 pak_size=0
07 pak=0x0B3968 ds=0x20DB26 status=0x80 max_size=1524 pak_size=0
```

------------------ **show stacks** ------------------

show stacks command will display stack information for processes that are on the router. This command will also display the reason for the last reboot of the router (not shown here).

```
Minimum process stacks:
    Free/Size   Name
    1812/2000   Autoinstall
    1728/2000   Setup
    3604/4000   BootP Resolver
    2728/4000   Init
```

------------------ **show interfaces** ------------------

show interfaces command will display information for all configured interfaces on the router, as shown:

```
Async1 is down, line protocol is down
  Hardware is Async Serial
  Interface is unnumbered.  Using address of Ethernet0 (199.xx.xx.x)
  MTU 1500 bytes, BW 9 Kbit, DLY 100000 usec, rely 255/255, load 1/255
  Encapsulation SLIP, loopback not set
  DTR is pulsed for 5 seconds on reset
  Last input never, output never, output hang never
  Last clearing of "show interface" counters never
  Input queue: 0/75/0 (size/max/drops); Total output drops: 0
  Queueing strategy: weighted fair
```

------------------ **show process memory** ------------------

show process memory command will display memory utilization statistics, as shown:

```
Total: 3774796, Used: 1742500, Free: 2032296
  PID TTY  Allocated   Freed   Holding  Getbufs  Retbufs Process
```

```
0    0    81556      1244      1629696    0         0    *Init*

0    0    316        14880     316        0         0    *Sched*

0    0    2053808    498404    0          458340    0    *Dead*
```

------------------- **show process cpu** -------------------

show process cpu command will display information about the active processes running on the router, as shown:

```
CPU utilization for five seconds: 12%/10%; one minute: 14%; five minutes: 14%

PID  Runtime(ms)  Invoked  uSecs   5Sec    1Min    5Min    TTY  Process

 1       0          120     0       0.00%   0.00%   0.00%   0    Load Meter

 2       3428       729     4702    0.00%   1.28%   3.68%   0    Exec

 3       1436       34      42235   0.00%   0.21%   0.15%   0    Check heaps
```

------------------- **show buffers** -------------------

show buffers command will display information about buffer pools available, as shown:

```
Buffer elements:
    500 in free list (500 max allowed)
    262 hits, 0 misses, 0 created
Public buffer pools:
Small buffers, 104 bytes (total 50, permanent 50):
    50 in free list (20 min, 150 max allowed)
    716 hits, 0 misses, 0 trims, 0 created
    0 failures (0 no memory)
Middle buffers, 600 bytes (total 25, permanent 25)
```

Prior to Design

There are a variety of ways to test your network prior to the implementation or design of the network. Some of the tools available to create a baseline were discussed in the previous section. In this section, I discuss using alternative methods to test or provide information about your network components and design.

Success Stories

Success stories are solutions that you have previously completed at another client site. It may be a good idea to check with the client that you worked with previously to assure that it's okay to talk about your work with them. Of course, be careful to not discuss any proprietary information or anything that would compromise your integrity, the relationship, or the contract that you have with the previous client.

When you talk about your success stories, tell your current client the problems that were faced, how they were addressed, and the overall outcome. If you can get testimonials from previous clients, that would be great. Just use this information and success story information with caution. Use it like salt. A little is better than a lot.

Vendor Success Stories

Vendor success stories have a little less impact than your own. They are pre-written marketing materials that talk about the technology or hardware that is involved in your design. If these are used, it's best that it come from the vendor itself. If you're interested in bringing in Cisco hardware and solutions for your network design, having a Cisco representative there to discuss some success stories with the client may be appropriate.

Component Testing from Lab

Component testing may have value if the network existed in a vacuum. You will get some results that prove that a specific software or hardware component can operate at a specific level of service. But in reality, that will do nothing for the client. Use these component tests for your own information. Telling the client about them may hurt you more than help you.

Pilot

A pilot is a small test environment that is used for smaller-scale implementations. You will perform a pilot test just as you would your prototype testing, but on a smaller scale.

Prototype

To get information about how the new network design scenario will work, you can implement a network prototype, which is a functional network that has certain features available that provide testing and functionality data for your new design.

A prototype network can be built in a separate lab, but if you're going through the network design process, it makes sense to go through the online commercial network. Now, this is where a baseline comes in handy. With the baseline data, you can make certain changes to the network by adding the prototype design. Then test the same parameters as you did with the baseline. Document your results. Of course, hopefully you won't make any *detrimental* changes, but you're integrating into the commercial network, and just by doing that, you've made changes.

Make sure that your prototype is well documented and that you have some of the client team members involved in the testing of the prototype, at least in the beginning.

You can use the initial prototype to firm up your testing script and the tests that will run. Be realistic about the prototype. If you have it running in a lab, not affecting network users, then it's not very much of a help to you. At some time, you will need to gauge how much of the network design that you will need to implement before the testing is validated. If you're measuring response times from engineering workstations in another building, you will need to implement at least that much to verify that the response times are valid.

It's better to spend the time up-front to get your prototype, testing scripts, and procedures in place. It will take a while to determine how to run the tests and what tests to run. Given that each situation is unique and that each network designer will come up with a slight variation in design, you will change your testing script accordingly.

During Design

You will need to do a lot of testing during the network design process. Based on your project timeline and testing methods, you will create a baseline, test a function, implement a change, test again, and move to the next step in the project.

After Implementation of Design

Ongoing testing should be done at an exception level for every network. Basically, this is what SNMP network management tools do. They test for conditions and parameters, and report exceptions.

Management

Managing your network can be one of the most challenging aspects of the project, or job responsibilities. With the network hardware and software in place and functioning, you need to be sure that everything runs smoothly. I will discuss some software tools that can be used to properly maintain your infrastructure. Included in this section are the processes that need to be in place to effectively run a network. And, of course, you need the people to run it. What is more important and more misunderstood is the process and placement of qualified individuals to run a corporate network IT department. You may not have to manage technical professionals, but you will have to deal with the politics, humanness, and differences that you will find with your network staff or client. I discuss some of these issues, and throughout this section, I present an approach to deal with personnel issues in the technical workplace.

Infrastructure

When managing your network infrastructure, it is important to automate as much as possible. This section covers some Cisco tools that are available to assist you in managing your network hardware and network software. Maintaining a network environment in many cases has been described as "fire-fighting." Network staff is constantly rushing to fight fires out of the fear of being seen as "they don't care" or "they can't do anything right." We covered some network management software tools in Chapter 7. This section covers some infrastructure management tools that have not yet been covered.

Netsys Tools

Cisco has developed a tool that will help you manage your networks. With Cisco Netsys Service-Level Management Suite (Cisco NSM), you can define and assess network connectivity information, performance issues, problem isolation, and resolution. The product suite is a policy-based solution with four main components: Connectivity Service Manager, Performance Service Manager, LAN Service Manager, and WAN Service Manager.

Connectivity Service Manager The NetSys Connectivity Service Manager is a tool that allows you to monitor your network configuration as well as verify that resources are available for your network users. You can establish service-level policies for specific areas of your network including reliability, connectivity, and security.

Performance Service Manager NetSys Performance Service Manager is a tool that enables you to optimize your network as well as analyze trends and traffic flows. You can optimize network services as well as plan network changes. Performance tuning along with problem diagnosis are also capabilities built in to the Performance Service Manager.

LAN Service Manager Netsys LAN Service Manager works with the other Netsys suite tools and adds the capability to view and diagnose LAN switching topologies. You can also verify that your LAN domains are configured properly and functioning as they should.

WAN Service Manager Netsys WAN Service Manager provides a way to analyze WAN switching configurations and troubleshooting capabilities. You can also create a model for network impairment and see how the network would react based on a failure condition. Also, you can test configuration changes prior to actual implementation. WAN Service Manager allows you to see your changes and the effect that they have on network traffic before you make the changes on your live network.

Cisco IOS

There are more Cisco IOS commands than there is space to discuss them. Here are just a few Cisco IOS commands that will help you manage your routers and network in the areas of network monitoring, optimization, and troubleshooting.

Network Monitoring Here are a few network monitoring commands that will enable you to monitor your network and routers:

To monitor your network performance by using response time reporter (rtr) statistics:

rtr `probe`

(*probe* is the number of rtr probe instances you're starting.)

To show RMON agent status on the router:

show rmon `table`

(*table* is the type of table to be displayed. Certain table types are only available on specific router platforms.)

To show the status of SNMP communications on the router:

show snmp

Optimization To make adjustments to the default buffer pool sizes on a router:

buffer `size type number`

(*size* is the buffer size: it can be small, middle, big, very big, large, or huge; *type* is the interface type and number of the interface buffer pool; *number* is the number of buffers to be allocated.)

To change the time of load statistics data usage:

load-interval

(*seconds* is the length of time, in seconds, that data is used to compute load statistics on the router; the default is 300, or 5 minutes.)

To set random detect on an interface:

random-detect `weighting`

(*weighting* is an optional parameter that defines packet drop rate.)

To show the status of queuing operations on the router:

show queuing `type interface`

(*type* is the type of queuing; *interface* is the router interface number.)

Troubleshooting To set up logging on the router to send messages somewhere else besides the router console:

```
logging on
```

To clear messages in the log buffer:

```
clear logging
```

To set the logging message severity level on your router console:

```
logging console level
```

(*level* — there are eight levels, 0–7, that can be configured with this command. If you use this command, any level number that you enter, the appropriate level messages will be displayed along with any lower-level messages. For instance, if you configure the logging on your router to be level 4, you will also receive messages for levels 0–4.) The levels for console logging are:

0. emergency messages only

1. immediate action required

2. critical situation exists

3. error condition is present

4. warning condition reported

5. significant condition is present, needs attention

6. informational message

7. debug messages

To set up a core dump for your router:

```
exception dump ip-address
```

(*ip-address* is the network address of the host or server where the core dump will be sent if the router crashes.)

To set a trace for a particular user:

```
trace protocol destination
```

(*protocol* is an optional parameter for the protocol that is used; *destination* is the destination address.)

Processes

Processes can be a variety of things. In this section, I cover some processes that need to be addressed to keep your network running smoothly. I cover clients (defined as your end-user community), baselines, automation, cost of your services, and marketing your department.

Change Management

There should be a process to review and document changes to your network. An internetworking environment can quickly become unmanageable when changes are made without review or notice. Because there will be a variety of changes in areas such as software application patches, network upgrades, client requests, and other areas, it may be advisable to have a company-wide change management team. This will be especially important in a service provider company. Because outside clients are being billed and expect a certain level of service, you might consider doing everything possible to assure that the agreed-upon service level agreement is being met.

Clients

End-users, or clients, are probably one of the most important aspects of maintaining your network. After all, what else is the network for? The network exists to support applications that provide network services to your clients. If you want to know how your network is really running, you might ask the network engineers. But if you want to know how it's *perceived* to be running, you should ask your clients.

It may be possible to have a feedback mechanism by a survey, a Web page feedback form, or e-mail to find out what people think about the service that you're providing. It's a good idea to survey the organization and document the attitudes, etc., when they come in. Then make changes as you feel is necessary. After a few months, send out the survey again and watch the results. What you did really may have an impact on the users' perspective of your network services. And maybe you did very little! Maybe the perception of better service was a result of you asking them for their feedback!

The Importance of a Baseline

Creating a baseline for your network is not only the best practice techni-cally, but will also allow you to have a documented analysis of your net-work. When new problems arise, you will have a baseline to work from. When you create your baseline, do it over several days and be sure that you've captured the normal business activity baseline. If you have one or several days where the network usage is always unusually high due to billing processing or other resource-intensive activity, it might be a good idea to have a baseline for the billing period. This way, when anxious users complain that the network is slow, you can point to the baseline and com-municate that this is normal for this time of the month. Although you can do this anyway without a baseline, a baseline for unique situations will pos-sibly help to alleviate further problems down the line.

Automating Low-level Tasks

It is extremely important to begin to automate low-level tasks that exist in your IT department. Identify what processes and procedures are manual and time-consuming. If possible, automate the lower-level tasks and allow the employees who are performing the lower-level tasks to learn newer higher-level tasks. This way, you have a semi-automated workplace, with a higher-level technical employee. It's sort of on the same lines as taking an entry-level class. Although entry-level classes are important, it may be bet-ter to learn the entry-level material on your own, and then if you're really interested or show potential, go and pay for the higher-level classes. You've spent the same amount of money for one class, and you're further ahead.

If you find that an employee does not want to learn new tasks, or for some reason cannot learn the new tasks, it would make sense to sit down and dis-cuss alternatives with the employee. Certainly, each employee has value to the organization; otherwise, they would not be there. It's important to look at the individual abilities and decide how you would fit this employee into your department or another department within your organization.

The 90/10 Problem

The 90/10 problem is the situation when 90 percent of your time or your staff's time is taken up by 10 percent of your clients, or end-users. Part of the maintenance of your network is to determine who and what is taking up your support time. Of course, a lot of the way to market your department is to be sure that your end-user clients are satisfied. Marketing will help present a positive image to the corporation as a whole. However, you may have a department in your company that has very specific needs, has a bone to pick with you, or otherwise takes up a great deal of your resources. Pleasing this type of client is time-consuming and frustrating. If you know the cost of your services, as discussed in the next section, and you feel that your services cannot be gotten at a cheaper price or better service level anywhere else, somehow make it known to that client. Sure, work with them to help them be productive, but don't let your entire IT staff be consumed by one specific client or department.

The Cost of Your Services

It's important to know what the costs of your services are to your client or your company. Financial folks can very easily find out what the costs of a network outage are, and will let you know it. You don't have to promote these costs, or only do it at an appropriate time or level of the business. You should know, however, how much your network group services are worth. If the work can be done cheaper when outsourced, it would be better that you know about it before anyone else. Then you will have the information that you need to make changes in either your service levels, costs, or department personnel. You don't have to know exact specifics, but when the network is running well, you're in the background. It's only when there is a problem that everyone hears about the IT department. Knowing the costs of your services is an important way to keep a balance in the minds of the folks running the company business.

Human Errors

There, I said it. People do make mistakes. And in an IT environment, those mistakes can be costly. It is an art to create an environment where people feel empowered to do their jobs, yet are cautious enough to be careful about mistakes. No matter what you do, people will still choose the wrong thing to do, and a mistake will occur. More important at the time of the mistake is not who did it, but why it was done. You might have an employee who makes a mistake write up a procedure that will ensure that it never happens again. It could be as simple as labeling the routers on the front instead of the back, or covering all the on/off switches with a plastic cover so they cannot be bumped and powered off.

Resist the witch-hunt. Witch-hunts make people nervous, frozen, and very unhappy. In a service environment, you will need to have qualified professionals performing the work. But haranguing them and making them walk on eggshells for fear of their jobs is not an effective way to manage.

Another thought about human errors is to track when they were done, not just what was done. Do more errors occur at specific times of the day, days of the week, or months of the year? Look at it a little more closely. Could it be that on Mondays errors occur most, or maybe Friday afternoon? Tracking the times may help you understand why they are occurring. In an environment where there is 24x7 coverage, taking the time to understand the human side of operation will go a long way in providing excellent service to your clients.

If you have a staff of professionals who work odd shifts, such as 10 days in a row then 4 days off, are they more susceptible to mistakes on their first day back to work? If you find this to be a trend, then let everyone know it. On the first day back, they should be more careful about mistakes. It may not be that the level of concentration isn't there; it could just be that they aren't aware of the changes that were made when they were off for the long weekend.

Marketing the IT Department

As the IT department becomes the critical link in information flow to business users, it is vitally important that the IT department have a marketing plan to its clients or internal end-users. Most of the headaches and politics are a result of the perceived power of the IT department and the unintentionally projected "I don't care" image of the technical staff. This doesn't mean to say that your technical staff doesn't care about the end-user. That may be far from the truth. But it will take more than the IT Director or Manager to be standing up in meetings and defending IT actions to make people believe that the IT department is there to serve the company's best interests.

Creating an Image Creating an image is another important way to market your IT department. A specific logo may not be appropriate, but there is nothing wrong with outfitting your group with a specific colored shirt that they can wear to signify their team affiliation. You may have them wear a colored polo shirt with an embroidered text that says something like "General Manufacturing" or "Network Services Group." You may want to coordinate your team colors with an Intranet presence. You're attempting to create an image that people will remember and feel comfortable with. You will then use this image of your department each time that you communicate to your end-users. You can customize your e-mail so that it has your department mission statement or colors incorporated into your communication. Depending on the corporate culture, this approach may not work or may not be encouraged. You can certainly think of other creative ways to market your IT staff as being a team of highly skilled technical professionals who are valuable to the organization.

Also, there would be nothing wrong with creating some premiums, such as mugs, keychains, pens, and other items, to give out as promotional items to further market your image to your company as a whole. This may seem like a juvenile approach in a highly technical and professional corporation. But the company as a whole does market their products and services to promote and produce revenues. You might also take that approach within your own department.

Intranet Presence Marketing the IT department can be as easy as an intranet presence. Set up a Web server and create a Web site. It's not that easy, you say. You're right. There has to be a reason for company personnel to visit your site. It may be advantageous to have some graphics personnel and marketing personnel help you with this. Graphics will make the site pleasing to the eye, and marketing will get people to the site to hear and see your message. This can be a free value-added service for the departments in your company. Offer to give them space on your Web server for their Web site in exchange for something like a pizza party. That may sound childish, but it just might work.

If you do decide to set up an Intranet presence, take the time to plan it well. This doesn't have to be the default site for everyone's Web browser, but it certainly wouldn't hurt to get it in their "favorites." Make the site a tool that will market your team. The front page of your department's Web site should be quick to load. Don't put a lot of graphics on the front page. Maybe a department graphic, mission statement, and a message from the IT director. You might want to set this up as a newspaper, with columns that have headings and then the full story on another page. Put thumbnail photos of your staff on a page that lists all of your team. When the thumbnail image is clicked, you can have an additional page with photos of the individuals at work, showing what they do in a normal day. Then you can add some background information about the person as well as his or her credentials. You may want to add a section about some of the feedback that you've gotten about this individual. Also include how this individual has contributed to the department as well as to the company as a whole. Be sure that you make all the pages similar in style, just changing the photos, background information, and credentials as appropriate.

Don't Underestimate the Power of Food There is more to food than the physical effect that is has to sustain life. Food is a very nice way to socialize, encourage, and nourish relationships. I don't want to make this more than it is. Just remember that the coldest and harshest days can be turned around, if only for a moment, with a donut or a piece of pizza. And don't forget the coffee.

In one situation, a project leader decided that Friday should be bagel day. As a consultant at a world-renowned hospital, he thought that the consistency of bagel day on casual business Fridays would be a good idea. His project team was in a small room somewhat set apart from the management and staff that he needed to interface with on a daily basis. He ran a six-month project with a team of up to six other consultants. Each Friday, he would show up with the bagels. Within an hour, two to three of the hospital management staff would show up with smiles on their faces, looking at the bagel box. They stood around and chatted, laughed and talked for a few minutes. Then they thanked the entire team for the bagels. Everyone invited them back for next week and even asked if there was a certain bagel type that they wanted. Each week, the same hospital staff managers would come back looking for their specific bagels. These bagels did not make the project. The hospital staff still was looking for excellent results from the Project Manager. And they got them. But this Project Manager knew the softer side of the project and did an excellent job in this area. He understood people as people and took the time to get to know them. He completed the project on time, under budget, and with excellent results. Long after the project was completed, the hospital management staff still remembers this Project Manager and his approach to getting things done.

Seen as Problem Solvers Years ago, there was a lot of talk about how people who didn't keep up with technology would end up working at a fast-food joint flipping burgers. The phrase "You want fries with that?" was an attempt to encourage (or push) fellow workers to keep up and learn the latest technology and to let them know that they might be slipping just a bit. But when you go to McDonalds, you will be taken care of. They are there to serve the client, you. There is actually a Service Level Agreement also. If you're not happy, they fix it. However, McDonald's also makes a lot of money. All that service is not without cost for you, the client. What about IT departments? Is it that much different? There is nothing wrong with serving others, but commonly the IT department is seen as the jerks who took the network down. That needs to change. Not for the sake of your ego, but with a better image within the company that you work for, the easier (at times) your job will be.

Some of us might remember the days of President Nixon and the Nixon administration. One of the chief counsels on the White House staff, John Dean, was new at the White House. He decided that he would only be influential if he would be able to promote his staff and services from within the White House. He decided he and his staff would be seen as the "problem solvers." His influence and impact grew within the White House as he provided legal services to the White House staff as well as needed advice on a casual basis. The point is that even as a White House attorney, John Dean understood the value of marketing his services to the people that he worked for.

Working with Clients One of easiest things that you and your staff can do is to realize that you have end-users as clients. Once you realize that you and your staff are providing a service, almost as a separate entity within your organization, you will see how the relationship should be. Although some of these suggestions may not be appropriate, they may just work to provide services to your end-users and allow you to be seen as an efficient, functioning, purposeful team.

When working with clients during a project, the fear and uncertainty that they express should be taken with great consideration. Many people are afraid of change and will work against you and your team's efforts. During the initial phases of a project, it is especially important that you communicate with your end-user base that will be affected. You don't need to tell the entire company if they are not affected. But if you're installing switches and servers to support a new financial package, it's important that the end-users who will be affected are aware of what is going on that will directly affect them. People will assume the worst, if given the chance.

Service Level Agreements Service Level Agreements (SLA) come in all forms and variations. Cisco's NetSys Service-Level Management Suite is a full-featured system for larger service provider networks to implement SLA agreements based on specific service goals and parameters. If your company is a service provider, you will already have detailed and legally correct service level agreements with your outside customers. But even in a smaller IT department, a service level agreement that states what services you will provide, how they will be delivered, and the level of service that your client (the end-user population) can expect can work to your advantage. At least this way, your clients realize that you're serious about the business of providing a service. The SLA doesn't have to be 20 pages of legal verbiage. It can be as simple as the following sample SLA:

Service Level Agreement (Sample)

Network Service Group — Little Cup Computer Systems

Date mm/dd/yy through mm/dd/yy

Overview: The Network Service Group (NSG) of Little Cup Computer Systems (LCCS) provides network services such as e-mail, Internet access, database functions, end-user support, remote access, Web server administration, router configuration management, and support.

Services: NSG agrees to provide the services detailed below within the specified time limits and by doing so, will achieve its goal of providing excellent network services to LCCS.

End User Support: NSG will respond to any and all help desk calls within 2 hours. Each help desk call will be tracked with a client ticket. Any client ticket that has not been resolved within 4 hours will be escalated to the NSG Supervisor for resolution.

Database & Server Maintenance: NSG will provide application support as it pertains to Novell NetWare and Microsoft NT Server operating system configuration and system backups. The NSG staff will maintain and configure the NSG network servers to provide network access during normal business hours of 7 a.m. – 7 p.m. local time.

Network Management: NSG will manage and support all associate network components including bridges, switches, routers, and internetworking devices to allow LCCS employees to be productive and to complete business during normal business hours.

There is a lot more to an SLA than is described here. But the point of this is that you can make up your own SLA depending on how you have defined your IT department. One of the best parts of the SLA for you is that you also define to your clients how the problems will be solved. In the SLA agreement example, it doesn't say anything about how problems will be solved if they go to someone's voice mail. A well-worded and thought-out SLA can help communicate your IT department's services and how clients can get the best service possible.

The other advantage to the SLA is that once you have the SLA signed by the client, or end-user community, you can track your progress. If you do achieve the goals for network availability and services as outlined in your SLA, you're also letting the corporation know that you do in fact provide excellent network services to the company.

In the SLA, you define what excellence is. Of course, an SLA agreement will be reviewed and changed by the client, but this way you have the agreement in black-and-white, and if you do achieve your goals, you have also achieved the excellence that goes along with that.

Success Stories There are plenty of success stories that you have in your IT department. You don't have to look far to get some positive feedback from your end-user clients. If you get an e-mail expressing thanks for a job well done, get permission from the person who sent the e-mail and post it on your internal Web server or bulletin board. Each project that you complete should be a success story. You don't have to keep people apprised of each detail as you go about the project. Maybe it could just be an announcement that a project has begun and then an announcement when the project is complete, along with details about how this will help the business.

Along with success stories, you can put a client comments page on your intranet page. There it is, in black-and-white, the good comments and feedback that sometimes get hidden in the flurry of activity at a typical IT department.

Revenue for the IT Department What about revenue for the IT department? Are there ways to develop a software product, service, or other feature that you can "sell" to your company, in regards to network services? Maybe you don't get cash for it, but you may get intangible revenue such as "good mind share" or "good image."

Big 5 consulting firms work on the premise that if you bring in revenue for the business, that is, if you develop, market, and sell a product, you may very well be on your way to a partnership. Even smaller consulting firms look for ways that a consultant can bring in business without the sales and marketing background. Each department has skills that they can bring to the market and sell services. If it is possible to do within your organization, look for ways to create revenue either for the business or for your department.

Marketing Within the IT Department You may have tried a lot of different ways to market the IT department, some with success, some without. You may also want to consider how to market the IT department within itself. It doesn't have to be a sales pitch. But the personnel in the department need to understand that they are important, have value, and are appreciated. Possibly, the IT department can develop a program of some sort to encourage people to excell. If morale is very low, look to join the group together by having them focus their attention to some outside entity, such as sponsoring a food drive or something charitable.

Personnel

Without the people, the network is not needed. After all, the network was installed by people, is managed by people, is changed by people, and serves people at their daily tasks and responsibilities. So your network personnel, or IT personnel, are a very valuable asset. This section covers how to organize an IT department or network group, how to keep your employees, and what to do before they leave.

How Should an IT Department Be Organized?

Business management has changed over the years and goes from one extreme to the other. First, it was a militaristic hierarchy that discouraged communication and new ideas. Then, it went to a flattened workplace where everyone did everything and no one still knew what was going on.

The answer in my opinion is not how the IT department should be organized, but that it is organized. It should be organized at a visionary level, operational level, and technical level.

The questions to ask to form this department at a visionary level are:

- What are your responsibilities?
- Who do you report to?
- How far out is your vision for this business?

The questions to ask to form this department at an operational level are:

- Do you focus on the vision for the business, how the business processes are run, or the daily operation of the business?
- What do you do during the day?
- Who relies on you for answers?

The questions to ask to form this department at a technical level are:

- What are the problems that you encounter on a daily basis?

   Based on the answers to these questions, each employee, whether at the executive, management, or technical level, should have clearly defined roles at each of the levels: visionary, operational, and technical.

Executive The executive level of the IT department is the IT Director, Vice President, or CIO, depending on the organization. The executive level should primarily function at the visionary level. This person should have a clear vision of where the department is heading, the technical goals of the organization, and how the IT department will serve the changing business needs over the coming years. The executive should have a vision for the department as far out as 3-5 years.

   The executive's secondary function should be at an operational level, which includes employee programs, processes, and procedures that affect the business as a whole. The operational level should be known as far as 1-3 years in advance. The executive will be sponsoring processes, programs, and major projects. At a technical level, the executive should be involved at the 1-3 month timeframe at the most. It's not important that the executive know about daily support issues and troubles. But it is important that major issues that are unresolved be escalated as soon as possible.

Management The management level could be an IT Manager or IT Director, depending on how the business is organized. The manager should spend most of his or her time at the operational level, developing processes, plans, and operational aspects of the specific department that he or she is managing. The manager should have a vision for the department as far out as 2-3 years. This vision will coincide with the executive-level vision. At an operational level, the manager will be involved at the 6-month to 2-year timeframe. This involves being aware of operational issues that will affect the IT department within the upcoming 2 years. At a technical level, the manager should be current with the latest technologies at least to the point of knowing what technologies are being developed and how they will affect the business. Managers will need to know of any support issues or vendor issues that cannot be resolved by the technical team.

Technical The technical level of the business is generally everyone else in the IT department, including supervisors, senior personnel, and support personnel. The technical employees will focus their attention at the technical, or task, level. Their responsibilities include the day-to-day operation of the business, technical projects, support calls, and other functions that are started and finished within a week's timeframe. Other technical issues involve projects that are less than 6 months in length. At an operational or process level, the technical employee may be asked to contribute to the creation of processes depending on the culture of the business. At the visionary level, it's important for the technical employee to be aware of the business goals. It is a unique position for the technical employee that he or she should be as aware as possible of newer technologies that are being developed that can help the business be more productive and grow competitively. The technical employee can also be used as a resource to test and verify vendor claims about the new technologies that are being presented to the executive and management staff.

How Do You Keep Them?

Keeping good employees is a tough business. No easy answers. The easiest way to answer that is by answering the question yourself. Why do you stay? Or why do you want to leave? It is politics, time on the job, boredom, etc. There are so many reasons. Here are a few suggestions that might work. They are not solutions for every situation, but they are based on experience.

Each employee is motivated in his or her own way. Some want the challenge, some want to be heard, some want their own way all the time, and some want to do nothing. Of course, that's the way it is everywhere. Described here are some real folks that I've encountered over the years. Their names are changed for obvious reasons. Two of them have stayed at their technical employer for many years. These case studies may give you a look inside at the real reasons people stay and how to make it work for your situation.

- **Case 1: Roberta:** Roberta is a very intelligent middle-aged woman who chose the technology field a few years out of high school. She started with Little Cup Computer Systems in 1982. Since then, she has progressively increased her technical knowledge at the same company, same building. She bought a home and wants to live there until she retires.

- **Case 2: Paul:** Paul also started at Little Cup Computer Systems in 1982. He bought a home close to Little Cup Computer Systems and has raised his large family there. He also has lived in the same house for several years and will probably retire there.

- **Case 3: Ben:** Ben started at Little Cup Computer Systems in 1983. He kept pushing for promotions and challenges and eventually got frustrated at the lack of movement at Little Cup and quit. He is now working as a contract consultant, moving from job to job and loving it.

What keeps Roberta and Paul at Little Cup Computer Systems? What made Ben leave?

Is it that Roberta and Paul are just not with it and Ben is the guru? Not at all. Ben left because of his personality type. He was just not patient enough for a larger company environment and felt that he would make a difference on his own. Roberta and Paul are still at Little Cup and making great progress. Since we last checked in with them, both of them had received major management awards with cash bonuses and recognition.

So, if you're looking to keep people at your workplace, all the incentives and programs in the world won't work.

Keeping employees should no longer be the focus of IT management. The suggestions in this chapter are presented as a possible solution for IT departments. It won't work with every IT department. This is not to say that employees should be discouraged from staying. This is a proposed way to manage employees and their expectations in the workplace. It is meant to be a winning solution for both employee and employer.

Phase 1: Planning Planning is probably the most important phase. When properly planned, these methods can move along accordingly. It is not especially important that there be targeted timelines, but rather targeted goal lines. Once a specific goal has been reached, then you can move on to the next phase.

- Step 1: Decide how you want to progress through the phases presented here. Set goal lines and benefits to the organization.
- Step 2: Make changes to this process as necessary.
- Step 3: Fully commit in your mind that the changes will be an improvement.
- Step 4: Present your ideas to senior management for approval.
- Step 5: Once approved, set up a schedule for assessments.

Phase 2: Assess These are not typical IT employee assessments. This is more of a career-mentoring program. You can develop your own approach based on the culture of the company, the employee who you're talking to, and the overall history of the organization and business. Your goal is to find out what employees want to do with their careers. It is important that you understand this for each employee. Some want to stay forever; some may think about leaving. If you cannot get an honest response to this question, you'll have to take a look at the past history of the employees and get a feel for where each person is at in his or her career. You're simply looking to find out if employees are willing to stay or are looking to go. Let's look at an example.

You have 10 positions in your organization. One slot is open and has been for six months. You've interviewed but can't find the right person for the job.

Figure 9-1 shows the current organizational reporting structure after phase 2, the assessment phase.

Current Organizational Reporting Structure

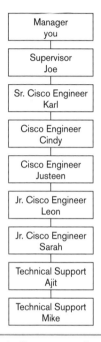

Figure 9-1 *Current organizational reporting structure*

Here is your current staff and the assessments that you have made concerning whether people are going to stay with the company or are looking for other opportunities:

- Position #1 — Joe, Supervisor: Joe is interested in staying and has shown potential to be able to assume responsibilities as a manager.

- Position #2 — Karl, Sr. Cisco Engineer: Karl has stated that he does not feel challenged by the network environment. He is taking classes on his own and frequently calls in sick to work. He is an excellent technical resource. The company relies on him for a great deal, and he is instrumental in working with clients. You also have information that he has been interviewing with other companies over the past several months.

- Position #3 — Cindy, Cisco Engineer: Cindy is also not content with her environment. She feels that she should be at the Sr. Engineer level and complains that she knows as much as Karl and is more responsible at the job. And she's right. She is an excellent technical resource, and, regardless of her discontent, she does not let it affect the team. She is seen as a leader and a mentor by the rest of the technical staff.

- Position #5 — Justeen, Cisco Engineer: Justeen has about three-years experience in her career. She is thrilled with the possibility of being in a corporation like this and just bought a home near the office so she can be here in the event of a disaster or other support issue. She has tremendous potential and was brought in at the Engineer level instead of Jr. Engineer due to her ability to learn and to provide her a competitive salary.

- Position #6 — Leon, Jr. Cisco Engineer: Leon has taken a lot of programming self-study courses and has recently graduated from Cisco Academy. He spends a lot of time on the Internet. He is not sure what technical direction he wants to take in his career.

- Position #7 — Sarah, Jr. Cisco Engineer: Sarah is here because she has to be. She is pregnant and is not sure that she will return after her baby is born. Although technically sound, she lacks the inter-personal skills necessary to be effective at her job.

- Position #8 — Ajit, Technical Support: Ajit was hired about one year ago and shows promise in the area of Cisco technologies. He has proven himself as a valued member of the team.

- Position #9 — Mike, Technical Support: Mike was just hired about six months ago and is working out well. He likes the environment and is a competent employee.

- Position #10 — Open: This position can be at any level since most of the employees work on a variety of tasks. This position was vacated when a Sr. Cisco Engineer quit after getting his CCIE cer-tification.

Phase 3: Realign Your next phase is to realign the department so that you can maximize your investments in your employees. This is a difficult thing to do. People do not like changes that they cannot control. This realignment process should be explained thoroughly and clearly. Explain why you're making changes and when. Explain to each person that he or she is valuable and that you appreciate his or her contributions. Explain that each person is being placed within a certain part of the organization due to the business needs. Assure them that their positions are not threatened in any way. But if you do assure them of this, be certain of it.

When you realign, you're setting up your organization to reflect what the business needs. Hopefully, this realignment will contribute to a more positive work environment and more productive employees. It is possibly, and highly likely, that some people will quit during this realignment. Expect it.

The realignment phase may take many months to implement due to current responsibilities and projects. It can also be complicated with budget constraints and other business deadlines and politics.

Phase 4: Implement New Organization Structure Figure 9-2 shows the new organizational reporting structure after phase 3, the realignment phase.

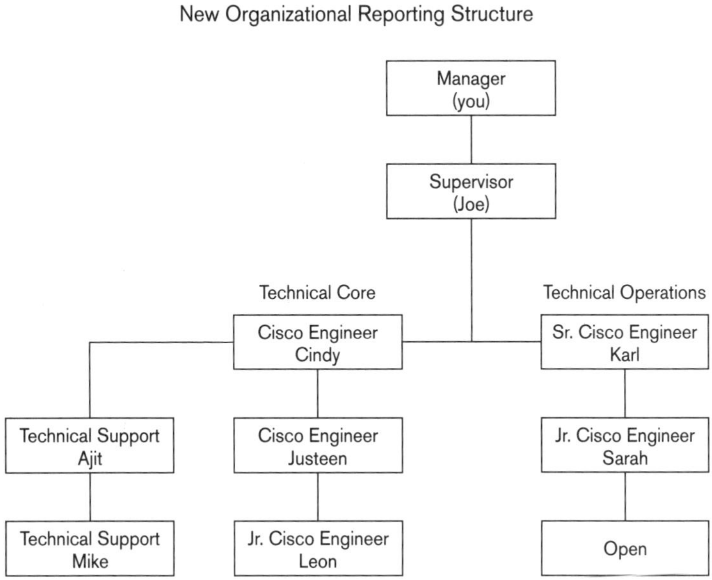

New Organizational Reporting Structure

Figure 9-2 *New organizational reporting structure*

The *Management Staff,* responsible for the management and vision of the IT department, consists of:

- Manager (you): As Manager, you will need to delegate as much as possible of the daily tasks and projects to your Supervisor, Joe. You should not be receiving or responding to any more help calls to your voice mail. Your focus should be in the area of marketing the IT department, working with other departments within the organization, and overall planning.

- Supervisor (Joe): Joe will have overall responsibility for all the projects in the department. He will be responsible for daily personnel issues and performance reviews.

The *Technical Core Staff* is headed up by Cindy, who has proven herself in the role of Cisco Engineer. She has the ability to lead, but more importantly, she has the desire to lead and the tendency to stay with the team.

- Cindy, Sr. Cisco Engineer *(promoted to Sr. Engineer level with salary action)* — Cindy has proven herself as a leader and will move into more of a supervisory position with this change. She will stay abreast of Karl's projects in the event that he leaves the company or calls in sick.

- Justeen, Cisco Engineer — Justeen will be given additional responsibilities that will allow her to gain exposure throughout the organization. She will be given some of the more visible projects within your department.

- Leon, Jr. Cisco Engineer — Leon is capable in his position and should remain in the role that he is performing. Exposure to the core group tasks should help him decide on a career direction.

- Ajit, Sr. Technical Support *(promoted to Sr. Technical Support with salary action)* — Ajit is promoted to Sr. Technical Support and is being positioned to lead the Technical Support team as it continues to grow and becomes as large as the Technical Core Staff.

- Mike, Technical Support — Mike continues to perform at a satisfactory level. He performs well in his position and can be counted on to contribute at higher levels as the team grows.

The *Technical Operations Staff* is project-oriented. But there's more to it. You'll notice that both of these employees expressed certain dissatisfaction with the status quo. This is a chance for them to prove themselves. It is also an opportunity for you to take them out of the daily operation and rejuvenate the core staff. The Technical Operations Staff is not an elite group. They work with the Core Technology group in the implementation phases of projects. The projects will start from Joe, the Supervisor, and will be reviewed by Cindy, the Sr. Cisco Engineer and leader of the Core Technology group. Cindy will assign the project to a Core Technology Engineer who will work with either Karl or Sarah to see that it is implemented.

If either Karl or Sarah do leave the company, the openings in the Technical Operations Staff should be staffed with consultants or people whose job experience shows limited time at each employer. If you need the technical skills of someone, but do not expect them to stay, put them in this group. This way, you can use their skills in important projects, but not allow them to adversely impact the daily operation of the network.

- Karl, Sr. Cisco Operations Engineer *(lateral move to Sr. Cisco Operations Engineer)* — Karl was moved into this position for two reasons. First, he cannot remain in a leadership position with his lack of motivation and tendency to call in sick. The rest of the team will be affected adversely. Second, Karl is not pleased with his position and seems to be looking to leave. You're positioning Karl to be an effective employee and a valued contributor as a Sr. Cisco Operations Engineer. However, if he does leave, your daily operation won't be affected.

- Sarah, Jr. Cisco Operations Engineer — It's obvious that Sarah is ready to go. She is being positioned to be out of the core daily operation of the business. Her responsibilities can be picked up quickly by a replacement.

- Open Position — You may want to fill this open position with a consultant. You will be paying for someone to come in and pick up on projects and stay abreast of Karl's projects should he decide to leave.

Phase 5: Evaluate Changes The final phase, which will probably be ongoing, is the assessment of all these changes. When staffing changes happen, usually you will see some people leave and others come. It will take about a year for the department to function well as you have designed it.

Knowledge Retention Versus Staff Retention

There has been quite a bit of discussion about knowledge retention, knowledge databases, warehouses, or whatever you might call it. The thing that you really want to do is to retain the knowledge that each individual employee has before her or she leaves. This way, when you hire in the staff and retain the knowledge that they have, if they leave, you're less impacted than if all the knowledge is tied up in the one employee who everyone relies on.

There are major applications and initiatives within consulting firms to retain knowledge. Some statistics in the area of employee retention for consulting firms point to the reason why firms want to retain knowledge. It's not really important how you decide to retain the knowledge. There are quite a few ways to do this, but it's more important that it is done, rather than how it is done. You won't be able to have consultants come in, have them design and configure a network, and then ask them to transfer all their knowledge to your staff. (Of course, they are expected to document the design and possibly train the key staff personnel, if that is even necessary.) But you can be sure that your staff's daily functions are documented, and documented well. Make it a "developmental area" in their annual reviews that they work toward documenting the processes and procedures that they work with daily. You will get some pushback on this. People feel that they are less valued if the knowledge that they have is out in the open for all to see and learn. But the likelihood that the documentation and processes will remain static is remote. It's important that documentation remain "green" and usable.

It may be worthwhile to have a documentation specialist get the processes and procedures online and get them into HTML format. This will help to get the information out to many people in an efficient manner and ensure that processes are documented.

Key Points

This chapter covered information about network design proposals, testing tools, and network management.

In the network proposal section, we discussed some of the ways to create a network proposal and what should be included in each section. The sections of a network design proposal should include an executive summary, an overview, the proposed solution, costs, benefits, and, finally, a summary page.

The testing section covered tools to use to gather networking information about your design. The first section covered tools such as Cisco NetSys Baseliner, Network Associates Sniffer, and Cisco IOS commands. There are other ways to gather information about your network design such as vendor success stories, component testing, pilots and prototypes, and your own success stories with other clients.

The final section covered network management and addressed some of the challenges that network personnel face after the network is designed and the management is performed. Network infrastructure management, network processes, and network personnel were covered in this section.

Appendix

Network Design Checklist

As a network administrator, you can use the following hierarchical network design checklist to help evaluate and understand an existing network, or to plan expansion of that network. It will allow you to "walk through" the material covered in this book and compare it to the actual structure of an existing network.

Network Topologies

❏ Flat
❏ Hierarchical
❏ Mesh
    ❏ Full Mesh
    ❏ Partial Mesh
❏ Redundant
❏ Campus/LAN
    ❏ Traditional LANs
        ❏ Ring
        ❏ Bus
        ❏ Star
    ❏ Switched LANs
    ❏ VLANs
❏ Enterprise/WAN
❏ Secure

Network Technologies

- ❏ ATM
- ❏ DSL
- ❏ Ethernet / 802.3
- ❏ FDDI
- ❏ Frame Relay
- ❏ Gigabit Ethernet
- ❏ ISDN
- ❏ PPP
- ❏ SMDS
- ❏ Token Ring/802.5

Network Routing Protocols

- ❏ BGP
- ❏ EIGRP
- ❏ IGRP
- ❏ IS-IS
- ❏ NLSP
- ❏ OSPF
- ❏ RIP v1
- ❏ RIP v2

Network Protocol Suites

- ❏ AppleTalk
- ❏ DECnet
- ❏ IBM SNA
- ❏ Novell IPX
- ❏ TCP/IP

Cisco Specific Protocols and Others

❏ Cisco Group Management Protocol (CGMP)

❏ Cisco Hot Standby Routing Protocol (HSRP)

❏ Cisco Discovery Protocol (CDP)

❏ Cisco Data Link Switching Plus (DLSw+)

❏ Cisco Gateway Discovery Protocol (GDP)

❏ Reliable SAP Update Protocol (RSUP)

❏ Resource Reservation Protocol (RSVP)

❏ Source Route Bridging (SRB)

❏ Source Route Transparent Bridging (SRT)

❏ Virtual Trunk Protocol (VTP)

Network Hardware

❏ Transmission Media

    ❏ Cabling

    ❏ Data Circuits

    ❏ Satellite

❏ Hubs

❏ Bridges

❏ Switches

❏ Routers

❏ Miscellaneous

Network Software

- ❑ Cisco IOS
  - ❑ Router configuration
    - ❑ Maintenance
    - ❑ Interface Configuration
  - ❑ Feature Sets
- ❑ Network Optimization
  - ❑ QoS
    - ❑ Detection
    - ❑ Committed Access Rate
    - ❑ Queuing
    - ❑ Traffic Shaping
- ❑ Cisco Product Offerings
  - ❑ Security Products
  - ❑ Management Products

Network Addressing and Security

- ❑ Network Addressing
  - ❑ IP Addressing scheme
  - ❑ VLSM
  - ❑ NAT
- ❑ Security
  - ❑ Policies
  - ❑ Technologies

Network Management

- ❑ Proposal
- ❑ Testing
- ❑ Management

Index

Numbers

90/10 problem, network management, 290–291

A

AAA (Accountability, Authentication,
   Availability) security policy, 251, 257–259
   accounting command, 259
   authentication banner command, 258
   authentication fail-message command, 258
   authentication login default command, 257
   authorization command, 258
AARP (AppleTalk Address Resolution Protocol),
   98
ABR (Area Border Router), 87–88
access layer
   hierarchical network topology, 7–9
   routers, 192
access-enable command, 198, 200, 265
access-list command, 204, 220, 263
access -list-number command, 220
access lists, 263–264
access-template command, 200
Accountability, Authentication, Availability
   (AAA) security policy, 251, 257–259
Adaption Layers ATM (Asynchronous Transfer
   Mode), 35
Address Resolution Protocol (ARP), 112
addresses, Class A, B, C, D, E, 240
addressing
   IP, 239–241
   SMDS (Switched Multimegabit Data
      Service), 59
ADSL (Asymmetric Digital Subscriber Line),
   37–38
Advanced Peer-to-Peer Networking (APPN),
   105–107
algorithms, DUAL (diffusing-update algorithm),
   73, 75
alias command, 204
analyzing risk, 249–251

anycast addressing, IPv6 (Internet Protocol version 6), 133
apn routing command, 220
apollo command, 204
Apple, Inc., 98
appletalk
   address command, 215
   command, 204
   domain-group command, 215
   protocol command, 215
AppleTalk, 97
   Address Resolution Protocol (AARP), 98
   advantages, 99
   AURP (Update-Based Routing Protocol), 99
   configuration commands, 215
   DDP (Data Delivery Protocol), 99
   disadvantages, 99
   EN (Extended Networks), 98
   network components, 100
   Networks, 98
   NN (Nonextended Networks), 98
   Nodes, 98
   routing command, 215
   RTMP (Routing Table Maintenance
      Protocol), 75, 99
   Sockets, 98
   Update-Based Routing Protocol (AURP), 99
   Zones, 98
Application layer, TCP/IP (Transmission Control
   Protocol/Internet Protocol), 113–114,
   132
APPN (Advanced Peer-to-Peer Networking), 106
   CPs (Control Points), 105
   LEN (Local Entry Networking), 105
   network components, 107
   TGs (Transmission Groups), 105
arap command, 204
architecture, SNA (System Network
   Architecture), 103–108
Area Border Router (ABR), 87–88

Continued

Continued

Continued

my2cents.idgbooks.com

Register This Book — And Win!

Visit **http://my2cents.idgbooks.com** to register this book and we'll automatically enter you in our fantastic monthly prize giveaway. It's also your opportunity to give us feedback: let us know what you thought of this book and how you would like to see other topics covered.

Discover IDG Books Online!

The IDG Books Online Web site is your online resource for tackling technology — at home and at the office. Frequently updated, the IDG Books Online Web site features exclusive software, insider information, online books, and live events!

10 Productive & Career-Enhancing Things You Can Do at www.idgbooks.com

1. Nab source code for your own programming projects.

2. Download software.

3. Read Web exclusives: special articles and book excerpts by IDG Books Worldwide authors.

4. Take advantage of resources to help you advance your career as a Novell or Microsoft professional.

5. Buy IDG Books Worldwide titles or find a convenient bookstore that carries them.

6. Register your book and win a prize.

7. Chat live online with authors.

8. Sign up for regular e-mail updates about our latest books.

9. Suggest a book you'd like to read or write.

10. Give us your 2¢ about our books and about our Web site.

You say you're not on the Web yet? It's easy to get started with IDG Books' *Discover the Internet,* available at local retailers everywhere.